THE ECONOMICS OF PROPERTY RIGHTS

International Studies
in Economics and Econometrics

VOLUME 22

The Economics of Property Rights:

Towards a Theory of Comparative Systems

by

Svetozar Pejovich

*The Center for Education and Research in Free Enterprise,
Texas A&M University, College Station,
Texas, U.S.A.*

KLUWER ACADEMIC PUBLISHERS

DORDRECHT / BOSTON / LONDON

Library of Congress Cataloging-in-Publication Data

ISBN 0-7923-0878-6

Published by Kluwer Academic Publishers,
P.O. Box 17, 3300 AA Dordrecht, The Netherlands.

Kluwer Academic Publishers incorporates
the publishing programmes of
D. Reidel, Martinus Nijhoff, Dr W. Junk and MTP Press.

Sold and distributed in the U.S.A. and Canada
by Kluwer Academic Publishers,
101 Philip Drive, Norwell, MA 02061, U.S.A.

In all other countries, sold and distributed
by Kluwer Academic Publishers Group,
P.O. Box 322, 3300 AH Dordrecht, The Netherlands.

Printed on acid-free paper

To my wife, Susan, and my children

TABLE OF CONTENTS

PREFACE

To understand recent developments in Eastern Europe requires a method of analysis that is capable of internalizing into a theoretical framework (i) the logical premises deduced from the costs of transactions and incentive structures generated by various institutions and (ii) the evidence for refutable implications of those premises. The economics of property rights is such a theory. It expands the scope of the ability of economic analysis to explain a wide range of institutional structures and provides empirical corroboration of its logical implications. The economics of property rights is, then, an effective scholarly instrument that offers more significant understanding of the three current issues in the area of comparative economic studies: (i) evaluating the performance of alternative institutional arrangements, (ii) explaining the failure of socialist institutions in Eastern Europe, and (iii) identifying the costs (political as well as economic) of institutional reforms in that part of the world. In that sense, the book is both timely and relevant.

In the late 1980s East Europeans crossed the threshold of fear and forced their leaders to abandon Marxism. With that theory of history dead and buried, the cost of current sacrifices in the pursuit of socialism has risen relative to the present value of its expected future benefits. Since the rulers in Eastern Europe could not continue to hide their taste for political monopoly behind a façade of words about the inevitability of socialism, they have begun to raise the spectrum of either "humane" socialism or the coexistence of capitalist and socialist institutions. In the process, an institutional vacuum has been created in that part of the world. The book is timely because property rights analysis concentrates on detecting and evaluating differences in the costs of transactions and incentive structures among various (present and potential) institutions.

Research in comparative economics has traditionally relied on neoclassical economic analysis. However, the basic premises from which the logical implications of neoclassical economic analysis are deduced limit that theory's applicability and any reliability to the private-property-type economy. First, neoclassical economic analysis ignores the costs of transactions which are not invariant with respect to the organizational structures. Second, neoclassical economic analysis ignores the incentive effects of alternative institutional arrangements. Thus, the emphasis on property rights analysis makes this book relevant for the study of comparative economic systems in a time when the most important issues are why, how, and at what price institutional reforms. For property rights analysis relates alternative institutions to economic outcome via their effects on the costs of transactions and incentive structures. In the process, it provides the logical premises for various institutions from which refutable implications can be deduced.

I am grateful to the Lynde and Harry Bradley Foundation for the financial support that made this book possible. Over a period of the last ten years, the Earhart Foundation and the Texas Educational Association have supported my research on the economics of socialism upon which parts of this book are based. Armen Alchian, Allan Meltzer, and Steve Wiggins read parts of this manuscript and provided many valuable comments and encouragements. Maureen Creamer and Susan Dederich-Pejovich provided valuable editorial and technical assistance. Susan Mills did an outstanding job in preparing the diagrams for the book. Judy Roessner did her usual perfect job in putting the manuscript together for publication. Finally, I want to thank the Board of Directors of the Center for Free Enterprise at Texas A&M University, in particular Herb Schiff, for their support and encouragement over quite a few years.

Svetozar Pejovich
College Station, Texas
May, 1990

PART ONE

ECONOMIC SYSTEMS, INSTITUTIONS

AND SCARCITY

CHAPTER 1

SCARCITY, INSTITUTIONS AND ECONOMIC BEHAVIOR

No matter how affluent or poor we are as individuals or as a nation, scarcity is always present; that is, what we want exceeds what is available. Nature can be blamed for this state of affairs because it has given us fewer resources than we believe we must have. And other people can be considered culprits because they compete with us for scarce goods. Thus, we all live in a world of scarcity. To get a little bit more of something, a little bit of something else has to be given up.

In addition to being scarce, resources have alternative uses. This means that, in order to survive, all human societies must face and resolve two fundamental issues: who gets what and who does what. The former concerns the distribution of goods that have already been produced. The latter concerns production. Those issues are two sides of the same coin. However, it is useful, for the purpose of analysis, to look at these issues separately. Each time an individual gets a bit of something, that much less is left for others. And every time we assign a resource to produce something, we are giving up a bundle of other things the same resource could have produced.

Scarcity forces all of us to make choices among limited alternatives. Given the inherent instinct for survival, a person makes choices that are purposeful, although not always successful. Human history has been about our search for more utility (which is not necessarily the same thing as more goods). Moreover, we have been consistent in responding to the circumstances that determine the costs of various alternatives. Despite strong pressures from theologians and many philosophers to give up the natural desire for more, human wants are demonstrably boundless. As soon as we get more of something, we want still more of it and of other things. This is a positive statement that is consistent with historical evidence and implies no moral judgment.

The central problem of economics is then one of making choices with respect to the allocation and use of resources. Socioeconomic problems in all societies have the same origin: scarcity. However, solutions to these problems differ from one country to another because the structures of institutions vary across the globe.

As social groups developed, it became clear that social activity involves human interactions at two levels. The first level of social activity is the development, modification and specification of institutions. The second level of social activity is social interaction within the prevailing institutional structure. The former is about the rules of the game, while the latter is about the game itself. And the rules have a great impact on how the game is played. Different institutional arrangements have their own incentive structures, and those incentives have specific and predictable effects on human behavior. Human behavior, in turn, affects both the allocation of resources and the flow

4

of innovation. It follows that economic analysis can provide refutable propositions about the effects of alternative institutional arrangements on the economy. The importance of institutions for the study of different economic systems is thus quite clear.

Institutions develop to govern the interactions among men with respect to problems that have their source in scarcity. Initially, institutions were based on customs which included past experiences, taboos, standards of behavior, and perceptions that individuals had formed about the world around them. In time, religious and other ideologies came to have considerable influence on customs. With the rise of modern states, laws and regulations replaced most customs. The development of institutions can then be deduced from the fact of scarcity and human survival instincts. <u>Institutions are defined as the legal, administrative and customary arrangements for repeated human interactions</u>.

The Sources of Institutional Change

Our improved understanding of how alternative institutions affect the allocation of resources and the flow of innovation is a major contribution of the new institutional theory known as <u>property rights economics</u>. Since changes in institutions must affect the economy's performance, it is important to determine what causes institutions to change, and what determines the direction of change. Historical evidence shows that institutional changes have been both endogenous and exogenous to the system.

ENDOGENOUS CHANGES

The relationship between the rules of the game and the game itself is reciprocal. Rules affect the game in specific and predictable ways and are, in turn, adjusted and modified in response to the development of new opportunities for human interactions. Suppose there is an event that creates opportunities for individuals or groups not deemed profitable before. Such an event could be the opening of new markets, technical progress, or changes in relative prices. Whatever the event, it changes the cost-benefit ratio associated with various social activities and provides incentives for individuals and groups to seek and negotiate new contractual agreements. Professor H. Demsetz has explained the creation of property rights among Indian tribes in North America as follows:

> Before the fur trade became established, hunting was carried on primarily for the purposes of food and the relatively few furs that were required for the hunter's family... Hunting could be practiced freely and was carried on without assessing its impact on other hunters. But these external effects were of such small significance that it did not pay for anyone to take them into account. There did not exist anything resembling private ownership of land....
>
> The advent of the fur trade had two immediate consequences. First, the value of furs to the Indians was increased considerably. Second, and as a

result, the scale of hunting activity rose sharply. Both consequences must have increased considerably the benefits associated with free hunting. The property rights system began to change, and it required to take account of the economic effects made important by the fur trade. The geographical or distributional evidence...indicates an unmistakable correlation between early centers of fur trade and the oldest and most complete development of the private hunting territory. (H. Demsetz, "Toward a Theory of Property Rights," American Economic Journal, 57, 1967, p. 352)

If the prevailing institutional structures are poorly attuned to circumstances and fail to embrace such contracts, utility-seeking individuals will generate spontaneous pressure to modify the rules of the game in order to embrace the novelty. These gradual, evolutionary changes in the prevailing institutional arrangements are adjustments in the rules of the game made in order to adapt the system to changes in the set of social choices. For example, the resumption of population growth in fourteenth-century Europe brought about an increase in the value of land relative to labor. The benefits from the right of ownership in land rose relative to its cost. Slowly, pressures mounted for the right of ownership in land to replace the feudal property-rights structures. In modern times, the expansion of markets and technological developments made mass production of goods relatively cheap and profitable. However, individual entrepreneurs and business firms had to raise large amounts of capital in order to exploit new opportunities and the owner's unlimited liability for debts created a serious problem. Unlimited liability threatened the exploitation of new opportunities because it made contractual agreements for bringing in privately owned resources too costly. A new concept eventually emerged: limited liability. Under this rule each owner's liability would be limited to the value of his investment in the enterprise. Moreover, it shifted the risk to financial institutions, which have a comparative advantage in judging and evaluating investment opportunities. This modification in the rules of the game enhanced the rise of the modern corporation.

EXOGENOUS CHANGES

Institutional changes are also influenced by ideologies, various pressure groups, and bureaucratic judgments about what is best for the public. Instead of adapting the rules of the game to the changing requirements of the game, exogenous changes adapt the game to the rules preferred by a specific interest group. For example, codetermination is a major social experiment in Western Europe (more will be said about codetermination later in this book). Under this system labor representatives participate in the management of business firms. Labor leaders, bureaucrats, and some intellectuals in Western Europe argue that codetermination bestows benefits on labor without any detrimental effects on shareholders. But, if codetermination is beneficial to both shareholders and labor, why must shareholders be forced by law to accept it? Why do they not voluntarily negotiate this institutional restructuring? There is no law in Europe that prohibits the imposition of codetermination. The fact that shareholders must be forced by law to accept codetermination is the best evidence that they are adversely affected by it. Also, the rise of socialism in the East has been clearly brought about by Marxist ideology, imposed by force, and maintained through terror.

The second question is: What determines the direction of institutional change? Why have different countries evolved in radically different directions and at radically different rates? This is a complex issue, the discussion of which runs like a thread throughout this book.

In conclusion, social institutions change in response to forces that are either endogenous or exogenous. The former are changes to the rules of the game that enable individuals to negotiate more effectively the contractual agreements that new economic and social developments have made available. The latter are changes in the rules of the game that are imposed upon the community from without by a "white knight."

SUGGESTED READINGS

Demsetz, H. "Toward a Theory of Property Rights," American Economic Journal, 57, 1967.

North, D. "Institutions, Economic Growth and Freedom," in Freedom, Democracy and Economic Welfare (M. Walker, ed.), Vancouver: The Fraser Institute, 1988.

S. Pejovich, "Toward an Economic Theory of the Creation and Specification of Property Rights," Review of Social Economy, 30, 1972.

CHAPTER 2

THE RISE OF CAPITALISM

In order to compare economic systems we must have some basic understanding of their origins. Do we owe the discovery of alternative institutions to an ingenious human mind? Are capitalism and socialism "predictable" outcomes of the laws of history or "unintended" consequences of the gradual evolution of human knowledge and technology? This chapter will discuss the factors that contributed to the rise of capitalism.

There is a great deal of literature and some disagreement about the genesis of capitalism. It seems best to consider that each and every major factor mentioned in the voluminous literature played some contributing role in the rise of capitalism. The conventional interpretation of the history of Western Europe is that economic and cultural development was interrupted by the fall of the Roman Empire. Then the Middle Ages began and stretched onward nearly a thousand years, from the sixth century to the end of the fifteenth or beginning of the sixteenth. Economic development picked up in the eleventh century but was again interrupted by the Black Death in the fourteenth century.

The Middle Ages

The collapse of the Roman Empire eliminated both Roman law, which was based on private ownership and contracts, and the machinery that enforced it. Initially, barbaric customs and violence replaced Roman law as the means of resolving conflicts of interest among competing individuals and groups. However, the high cost of negotiating, policing, and enforcing one's rights to life and property in post-Roman Europe led to the gradual development of a socioeconomic system that is referred to as the feudal system.

A survival strategy for a weaker man was to turn to a stronger man and give him the nontransferable right of ownership in his land in exchange for protection and an inalienable right of tenancy—the right to hold the land of the lord. The lord-vassal relationship slowly evolved into a basic social institution in medieval Europe. The land held by the vassal was called the feud. A lord could and often did become the vassal of still another man; that is, he became both the lord of a weaker man and the vassal of a stronger man. Eventually, a socioeconomic system developed based on a hierarchy of individuals holding property rights. The king was at the top of this long chain of "contractual" relationships, and the actual tillers of the land (serfs) were at the bottom.

As the Middle Ages progressed the Catholic Church became an increasingly powerful institution. It acquired a substantial monopoly in the field of education. Libraries were located in monasteries and cathedrals, and the vast majority of literate people were monks. The Church thus became the repository of accumulated knowledge. Consequently, it acquired the power to interpret knowledge, to determine its uses, and to influence the direction of its growth. The Catholic Church also was monopolistic in religion, since it had no opposition in matters of faith.

Predictably, the Church played a major role in the development of institutions in the Middle Ages. The church provided the philosophical rationale, the moral justification, and, most importantly, the religious sanction for the socioeconomic system based on a hierarchical method of holding property rights in land. The moral basis for political authority and socioeconomic privileges of medieval nobility was divine right. Kings and lords believed that they governed by the grace of God rather than with the consent of their subjects. This meant that secular rulers in the Middle Ages needed to have the Church—a worldly institution acting as "God's intermediary"—on their side.

The power of the Church explains two important features of community life in the Middle Ages: (i) a strong marriage between theology and philosophy, and (ii) an equal-ly strong marriage between ethics and economics. The laws, customs, and social institutions of the Middle Ages were determined largely by the teaching of theologians. All aspects of social life were prejudged, controlled, and monitored by the Catholic Church. Religious life and everyday social life were indistinguishable in the Middle Ages.

By the end of the ninth century, this synthesis of religion and secular life took the form of a feudal society with a distinct and sharply defined class structure. The mobility between social classes was very low, almost nonexistent. A child born to a peasant was to remain a peasant for the rest of his life. A child born to a nobleman became a member of the nobility. Every man was considered equal in his class and entitled to the means of subsistence suited to his station in life.

Philosophy and science were guided by the call to explain or justify theological tradition. The role of philosophy was to explain and support theological conclusions. Any conflict between the two was considered to be caused by some philosophical error. Thus, philosophy in the Middle Ages was largely a handmaiden to theology. Similarly, economic activities in the Middle Ages were regulated by ethical criteria. The legiti-macy of economic activities was tested by reference to the moral teachings of the Church, not to utility. The medieval Church was thus the final authority in morality, social life, and economic activities.

The attitude of early church fathers toward trade and investment reflected the moral teachings of the Church. The Church recognized the necessity of trade but warned that such economic activity stimulated the acquisitive spirit, which was perilous to the soul. It is then not surprising that trade was dominated by Jews, who lived outside the Christian orbit.

The spirit of acquisition, usury, and the accumulation of wealth were condemned by the Church. The high-water mark of the attack on the spirit of acquisition was reached in the thirteenth century. Thomas Aquinas and his followers, called the Schoolmen, set down explicit rules regarding economic activities in general and the concept of "just" price in particular. According to the Schoolmen, the just price of any good was to be equal to its cost of production plus a margin required to sustain the seller's customary standard of living, and no more than that. It should be noted that the medieval church was also worried that production and exchange could destabilize the feudal order. Thus, its objections to the spirit of acquisition and accumulation were not purely religious. Money was considered a nonproductive medium of exchange, and it was wrong to practice usuary—to charge interest on borrowed funds. The universe was assumed to be static and ordained by God. Each man had a set place in society with obligations and privileges prescribed for his station in life. The only purpose of knowledge was to help people understand God's intentions in creating the universe.

The Great Transformation

The established order was strong and resistant to social change. It is not likely that a single factor or event could have caused its demise. The transformation of the feudal economy of the Middle Ages into capitalism had to be caused by more or less the simultaneous influence of many factors. This section will describe some of those social forces that played a role in the great transition to capitalism.

PHILOSOPHICAL FACTORS

Starting in the fourteenth century, the relationship between philosophy and religion began to be questioned. The process of alienation started with nominalism, an early and primitive attempt to question the dependence of philosophy on theology. The idea of the separation of philosophy from theology gained momentum with the development of the scientific method. Francis Bacon (1561-1626), David Hume (1711-1776), and John Locke (1632-1704), among others, raised the issue of the supremacy of reason and knowledge over the revealed truth. Their objective was to enhance our understanding of the world. Bacon claimed that man's perfection depends on the progress of science and its application to human life. Locke argued that the state should support natural laws and that within this structure the individual should have free rein. Hume defended private property rights.

Descartes (1596-1650), Newton (1642-1727) and Comte (1798-1857), among others, emphasized the importance of mathematics and science. Descartes claimed that mathematics could be extended to all sciences, including philosophy. Newton was concerned with the rules of reasoning in philosophy. Comte argued that actual knowledge depends on testing and experimentation. Immanuel Kant (1724-1804), a leading rationalist in the eighteenth century, insisted on the authority of science.

Those philosophical developments in Western Europe were the result of a desire to improve understanding of the world by emphasizing logical thinking, science and experimentation. In doing so, the thinkers of the time and their theories initiated a radical departure from centuries of medieval tradition.

THE RELIGIOUS REFORMATION

The religious reformation had a profound effect on the relationship between ethics and economics in the Middle Ages. It sanctioned the spirit of acquisition and justified the accumulation of wealth. Moreover, it undermined the Catholic Church monopoly in matters of faith.

Martin Luther (1483-1546) advocated a frugal, hard-working life and provided the spiritual foundation for the work ethic. John Calvin (1509-1564) taught that to prove himself among the chosen, man has to work hard, be frugal, and seek success in his "calling." He gave religious sanction to the accumulation of wealth. The Puritan spirit gave a tremendous impetus to the development of the frugal, hard-working, and accumulating individual. It is interesting to note that capitalism first developed in two countries with Puritan populations: England and Holland.

Philosophical factors and the Reformation emphasized reason, science, knowledge, experimentation, hard work, savings, and the accumulation of wealth. Slowly, the idea that the universe is fixed and ordained by God began to be overtaken by new ideas of human progress and free will. By the second half of the eighteenth century, the world was ready for Adam Smith to turn the age of reason toward a better understanding of economic processes.

NEW FRONTIERS

"New" philosophy gave birth to new ideas. However, tradition in Europe was strong. The old order, with its customs, class privileges, and medieval values, was powerful and resistant to new ideas. Traditional Christianity was too deeply rooted to be so quickly altered. Moreover, Europe was also quite poor and overcrowded to have "room" for the new ideas to be given an empirical test. In short, the new ideas lacked space to be tried out. The exploration and settlement of new frontiers, primarily the Americas, provided an excellent "laboratory."

The most important contribution of new frontiers to the rise of capitalism was in providing a tradition-free space in which to test new ideas. Freedom from religious constraints, from humble origins, and from traditional ethics allowed thousands of people to pursue their individual preferences, to be responsible for their own actions, and to create their own place in a new society. Once those ideas were applied to everyday life and proven successful, they traveled back to Europe and contributed to the transformation of medieval man into modern man.

In addition to providing a tradition-free space for the application of new ideas, the new frontiers made an additional contribution to the rise of capitalism. Of every $100 worth of gold and silver produced in Western Europe and newly-opened territories after

1495, $85 worth was produced by the new frontiers. Taking precious metals and other goods to Europe was risky, but for those who were lucky, a 1000 percent rate of return was not uncommon. An unintended result of this individual risk-taking was to give new ideas a chance to demonstrate their social and economic consequences.

The people who went to America in those early days were often referred to as criminals. Indeed, they were criminals by the prevailing standards of the day, when it was a crime to oppose the established order, reject medieval tradition, complain about the role of the Church in secular affairs, or avoid taxes imposed by monarchs and bishops. Most settlers came to America to escape those feudal restrictions. They had what was considered to be a rebellious desire to live their own lives, make their own choices, and write their own morals. So they escaped to the tradition-free space of the new frontiers.

SOCIOLOGICAL FACTORS

Capitalism requires entrepreneurship, wage labor, and a positive attitude toward work, none of which existed, in an institutional sense, in the Middle Ages.

Medieval nobility could not supply entrepreneurship. Its concerns were wars, politics, and leisure. It was degrading for a nobleman to engage in commercial activities, trade, and crafts. He was born to be a lord, a hunter, a warrior, and a lover. The business class emerged from the ranks of small traders and artisans. Those people were envious of all the status, privileges, and wealth enjoyed by the nobility and wanted to draw a line between themselves and the lower class of peasants. In the quest for status and influence, small traders and artisans turned their attention to the accumulation of wealth. In the process, they laid out the foundation for the emergence of the middle class, a major source of entrepreneurship in capitalism.

The labor force emerged from several sources. The rate of growth of the population in Europe in the aftermath of the Black Death was an important factor. With an increase in the population, the marginal productivity of labor fell relative to the value of land. This change in the economic conditions of life provided incentives for the land-owning aristocracy to replace the feudal system with the nontransferable right of ownership that tied peasants to their land, with private transferable ownership in land. Enclosures of commons, or public grazing lands, and other methods of throwing peasants off the land were an important source of the labor supply. Among the other factors that led to an increase in the labor force were improvements in health care, the gradual disappearance of private armies and guilds, and child labor.

The rise of capitalism also required a positive attitude toward work. In the writings of medieval theologians and philosophers, workers were usually called the "laboring" poor. In the scheme of social values in the Middle Ages, begging and physical labor were considered two traditional methods of survival for the poor. The religious reformation was responsible for a change in this attitude. By giving a strong religious sanction to hard work, the Reformation divorced productive work from welfare. Man's attitude toward work became an important measure of his character and integrity.

CAPITAL FORMATION

On the supply side, two major sources of investable funds are private savings and bank credit. Neither existed in the Middle Ages. Private wealth was spent on the church, palaces, private armies, luxuries, heirs, and many other activities, but not on investment. The Reformation had a strong influence on the supply of private savings. To prove himself among God's elect and avoid temptation, man had to work hard and live frugally. Thus, a religious sanction for the accumulation of wealth opened the door for private savings.

Medieval banks did not give investment credit; their major functions were to safeguard deposits and transfer them from one account to another. This failure of medieval banks to create bank credit is, according to Schumpeter, the late Harvard economist, a major reason that Italian cities, such as Florence, Genoa, and Venice, were not able to sustain their prosperity. The development of the modern banking system began in 1694, when the Bank of England was founded. It gained momentum in 1797, when the British government forbade the Bank to pay its notes in gold, opening the door to a fast increase in the volume of bank credit. When the gold standard was reimposed in 1821, the institution of bank credit, a vital source of capital formation, was already firmly established.

To conclude, the great transformation of medieval man into modern man brought about a new socioeconomic system. Many factors contributed to this transition. Most of those factors were not new. Reason played an important role in Greece; property rights were fully developed in old Rome; and free trade had long been practiced and its benefits savored in the Middle East. But it was when these factors coalesced in Europe that capitalism had its birth. Early writers called the new system laissez-faire and equated it with individualism and industrialization. Adam Smith called it the Natural System of Economic Liberty. He described the system as being self-generating, self-propelling, and self-regulating. It rests on the idea of individual liberty, the freedom of choice, self-determination, and self-responsibility. The term capitalism was used by Marxists with a tone of ethical and social disapproval.

SUGGESTED READINGS

Gilson, E. The Spirit of Medieval Philosophy, New York: Scribner, 1940.
Brinton, C. The Shaping of the Modern Mind, New York: New American Library of World Literature, 1959.
Meckling, W. "Science and Religion: Evidence or Faith," paper presented at the 4th F. Hayek Symposium on Knowledge, Evolution and Competition, Freiburg, 1990.
Webb, W. P. "Ended: 400 Year Boom: Reflection of the Age of the Frontier," Harper Magazine, October, 1951.

Weber, M. The Protestant Ethics and the Spirit of Capitalism, New York: Scribner, 1960.

CHAPTER 3

THE RISE OF SOCIALISM

Catholic theologians and socialists were the most serious critics of early capitalism. They rejected one of the most fundamental premises of capitalism: methodological individualism. Because early socialist critics built their case against capitalism on the moral teachings of the Church, a section of this chapter will deal with the positions of early Catholic philosophers.

Catholic philosophers and socialists believe that each community has a common good; that is, a system of ends representing all absolute social values. Therefore, the prevailing institutional arrangements and rules of the game must channel the behavior of individual members of the community toward the pursuit of the common good. The community is then conceived as an organic whole in which each individual is expected to subordinate his private ends and cooperate with others in pursuing the common good.

The classical liberal (capitalist) community has no common good. It is a voluntary association of individuals who join and leave the community in pursuit of their own private ends. The interaction of utility-seeking individuals in a capitalist community leads to an unintended outcome. The rules of the game in the capitalist community are not developed to serve some preordained common good. The emphasis is on the process of choosing the rules and their acceptance by the community. If the rules of the game are fair, their "unintended" outcomes will also be fair.

Capitalism and Catholic Philosophy

Catholic philosophy has raised the issue of the legitimacy of capitalism as a moral system. The origin of this issue lies in the basic difference between the Catholic and the capitalist concepts of community. The capitalist community is a voluntary association of individuals who, in the pursuit of their own private ends, join and leave the community as they choose. Catholic philosophy considers the community as an organic whole whose members cooperate with each other in the pursuit of a prescribed outcome (common good).

What classical liberals considered as the freeing of man from the constraints of medieval tradition, Catholic philosophers saw as the erosion of morality and rejection of "absolute" values. Catholic philosophy is apprehensive about freedom of choice, not because of any lack of interest in individual liberty, disregard for private rights, or indifference to economic efficiency, but because of a fear that the autonomy of individual choices in the free market does not necessarily generate morally satisfying sets of preferences. Catholic philosophy tends to gloss over the fact that the free market does not generate preferences. It could be said that those who are critical of the freedom of individual choice which the capitalist system allows should direct their criticism toward the institutions—such as schools, churches, households, the streets, the media—that form the preferences, rather than toward the free market in which those preferences are merely revealed. Suppressing the freedom of choice does not change a person's character. It merely deprives the person of a right to make a choice consistent with personal preference and bear the cost (e.g., losing friends) of the action taken.

In fact, the free market has a strong moral content. It promotes the development of individuals, cultivating strength from confronting risk, and places a high value on the keeping of promises. A reputation for honest dealing is a source of wealth. In competitive markets crooks, cheats, and liars do not get repeat business. While the free market does not make people moral, it raises the cost of unethical behavior. Arguing that many moral norms satisfy the requirements of efficiency, Judge Posner writes:

> Honesty, trustworthiness, and love reduce the cost of transactions....Neighborliness...reduces external costs....Charity reduces the demand for costly public welfare programs. Care reduces social waste. (R. Posner, Economic Analysis of Law, Boston: Little, Brown and Co., 1986, pp. 238-9)

Early (Pre-Marx) Socialists

SIR THOMAS MORE (1478-1535)

Thomas More was the first significant critic of capitalism. In his writings he tried to tie what we now call socialism to the moral teachings of the early church fathers.

More opposed the transformation of the traditional society into a money economy. He realized that the world was changing but argued that changes must be made within the bounds of the moral teachings of the Church. On a practical level, More believed in primitive communism. Medieval philosophers and early socialists defined primitive communism as a society in which all resources are held in common and no member of the community is allowed to accumulate private wealth. By establishing common ownership of all resources, More believed, the problems of the emerging industrial society could be resolved or avoided. More also believed that private property rights make a just government impossible. Private property rights, he claimed, lead to social inequalities, which generate behavior that is contrary to divine law.

More's alternative to the emerging capitalist society was Utopia. In Utopia, agriculture is the most important industry. All citizens, including those living in the cities, must spend some time working on collective farms. The supply of goods for all cities is to be calculated in advance, and their citizens have to work on the farms in proportion to their cities' food needs. Every month a member of each family would be required to take the goods produced by the family to the market. In exchange, the family would receive coupons which it would exchange for other goods in the market. Travel would not be unrestricted in Utopia. To travel from one community to another would require permission. And the traveler would have to do a day's work at his destination.

FRENCH SOCIALISTS

In the seventeenth and eighteenth centuries, France was fertile ground for socialist ideas. Unlike Thomas More, who wanted to retreat from capitalism and return to the customs and morality of the old order, French socialists accepted the reality of the rising industrial society and raised a different question: What can be done to eliminate the social and economic inequalities that capitalism had produced?

Comte Henri de Saint-Simon (1760-1825) and Pierre-Joseph Proudhon (1809-1865) were the most prominent French socialists. Saint-Simon participated in the American Revolution and was decorated for bravery during the battle of Yorktown. His primary objective was to find a way to guarantee equal opportunity rather than economic equality, and he believed that the way to achieve this ideal was through collective ownership. As a result of his conclusion, he directed his major criticism of capitalism at private property rights. Long before Marx, Saint-Simon advocated "from each man according to his ability; to each man according to his contribution."

Proudhon opposed all forms of government. He is often regarded as the founding father of anarchism. Like all other socialists, Proudhon opposed private property rights. But, unlike Saint-Simon, he believed in actual economic equality.

AMERICAN SOCIALISTS

Socialists in the United States were few in number and had little influence. George Ripley (1802-1880), a Unitarian minister, bought a two-hundred-acre milk farm in Massachusetts where he planned to replace competition with cooperation. The commune met its demise within a few years. Another commune, the North American Phalanstery at Red Bank in New Jersey did not last long either.

In the late nineteenth century, Eugene V. Debs (1855-1926) organized the Social Democratic Party of America and ran as a socialist for president in all elections from 1900 through 1920. The party and Debs met with little success.

Although socialism per se has never been popular in the United States, welfare legislation such as the New Deal, Social Security, and unemployment insurance has had some public support. In the United States most policies that can be tagged "socialist" have aimed at redistribution of income rather than changes in the institutions of capitalism.

Pre-Marx socialists were by no means in agreement in their views on capitalism and socialism. Yet there was one capitalistic concept which they all condemned: private property rights. Their common line of reasoning behind this condemnation was that nature is good, and thus, the world must be good. It follows that people should be able to live in peace and harmony. To create a "just" society in this inherently good world, the early socialists believed that rulers had merely to use reason, goodwill, and knowledge.

It is precisely on the issue of the role of reason that the most important difference arose between early socialists and Karl Marx.

Marxism

Karl Marx (1818-1883) was born in the Rhineland, Germany. He was one of seven children in a Jewish family that embraced Christianity when he was six years of age. He studied philosophy, history, jurisprudence, and literature in Bonn and Berlin. In 1843, Marx set his goals:

> ...[my task does] not consist in the setting up of utopias, but in the criticism of existing social and political conditions...in interpreting the struggles and aspirations of the age. (H. Laidler, A History of Socialist Thought, New York: T. Y. Crowell Co., 1927, p. 155)

In time, Marx became the most influential critic of capitalism. It is thus important to understand some basic tenets of Marxism.

INFLUENCES ON KARL MARX

Marx was influenced by three contemporary movements: early French socialism, classical German philosophy, and classical British economics.

Early French Socialists. French socialists believed that capitalism was an immoral system. They blamed capitalism for long working hours, child labor, the poverty of working people, unemployment, income inequalities, social injustice and numerous other problems. And they placed the ultimate blame for these problems on private property rights. Thus, they argued that the simplest way to do away with capitalism and the ills to which it seemed linked was to abolish capitalism's fundamental concept: private property rights.

Marx agreed with French socialists that capitalism was not a just system. Although he also agreed that the right of ownership creates most social problems, he considered it naive to think that socialism, once discovered by reason, could conquer the world simply by promising justice and harmony. Marx drew a line between the preference for socialism and the scientific analysis of its place and role in human history. The fallacy of reason, Marx said, is that it ignores the laws of history; even the best idea has to await its moment in history.

Classical German Philosophy. The great thinkers of the Middle Ages conceived of the universe as constant and eternal. Eventually, however, scholars began to realize that human history revealed an endless evolution of social institutions. This discovery that the universe is not immutable generated interest in analyzing social change. The role of reason became one of analyzing history and discovering the truth about the world.

Hegel (1770-1831) was a leading philosopher among those who tried to formulate a theory of social change. His central thesis was that a prevailing set of ideas determines our perceptions about the world in which we live. These common ideas shape our social institutions, the way we interact with each other, and the organization of production and distribution of goods and services. The essence of Hegel's philosophical method was the concept of dialectics: Each idea has its inner contradiction, and within each idea there is a conflict between its positive and negative elements. It is from this internal conflict inherent in all ideas that a new idea eventually emerges. This new idea is not an extension of the old one; it is a qualitatively different concept. The new idea then slowly but surely reshapes all aspects of social life.

Marx accepted Hegel's thesis that human history is shaped by social changes generated from within the social system itself. However, he disagreed with Hegel as to the role of ideas in producing social change, believing instead that the economic conditions of life determine our politics, social institutions, and, most significantly, our philosophy, religion, and ideas. He moved Hegel's concept of progress from the sphere of ideas to the material world. Appropriately then, Marx's method of analysis is called dialectical materialism, which says that (i) all things and phenomena of life are in a constant process of evolution; (ii) all things and phenomena of life are interconnected; (iii) the process of social change occurs through a struggle of opposite tendencies; and (iv) human progress consists of the gradual accumulation of small quantitative changes that lead to a major qualitative change.

In Holy Family, published in 1844, Marx used dialectical materialism to describe the transition from capitalism to socialism. In the struggle between private property, which is the positive element in capitalism, and the rising proletariat, which is the negative element (inner contradiction), the latter will triumph by abolishing both itself and private property rights. Socialism will then have replaced capitalism.

Classical British Economics. Marx was influenced by David Ricardo (1770-1823), from whom he borrowed the labor theory of value. This theory basically said that the value of any commodity is proportional to the average number of labor hours needed for its production. Thus, only labor creates new value; the contribution of capital to the value of a product is equal to its wear and tear. For example, under the labor theory of value, a serving of beer will be worth twice as much as a soft drink if its production requires twice as many labor hours.

Marx modified the labor theory of value to suit his purpose of explaining the returns (profits) to private property. He said that if the value of any good is determined by the average number of hours needed for its production, the value of labor must also be determined by the average number of hours needed for its production. To summarize, each day a worker uses up so much of his energy, which must then be replenished so that he is able to work the next day. He must also be able to support children to eventually replace him in the labor force. The market wage is then the amount of money that is just sufficient to buy the <u>minimum</u> amount of goods needed for the worker's maintenance. Or, put another way, the market wage must be just sufficient to ensure the supply of labor in the long run. The value of this "bundle of goods" is the average number of labor hours needed to produce it.

Suppose the working day is ten hours, but that it takes only five hours to produce the minimum bundle of goods the worker must receive each day. In ten hours, he creates the value that brings the employer (that is, the property owner) the amount of money equal to ten labor-hours. The employer pays the worker the wage that is equal to the value of five labor-hours. The difference between the number of hours the worker labors each day and the number of hours it takes to produce the minimum bundle of goods that he must have each day is the <u>surplus value</u>. The surplus value is returned to the class of property owners as profit. In the Marxist view, however, that return is created by labor.

THE ECONOMIC INTERPRETATION OF HISTORY

Marx believed that economic processes explain the entire history of mankind, a history which he saw as a continuous struggle of inferior man against superior nature. Triggered by man's survival instincts (i.e., desire for more utility), this struggle has as its historical purpose the reversal of the original relationship between man and nature through the process of the production of economic goods.

This historical sequence begins with primitive society. There, man is totally dependent for his economic survival on an alien and hostile environment. All efforts in a primitive society are geared toward the restricted objective of subsistence, that is, toward the appropriation of products in their natural state. Without innovation, primitive society merely reproduces itself through time. However, man's survival instinct leads him to seek ways to produce subsistence more efficiently: the discovery of fire made fish an important source of nourishment, while the bow and arrow increased returns from hunting. As man learned how to use intermediate goods (tools) to increase the supply of food for subsistence, two related developments had to occur.

First, each time man uses a new tool (primitive hammer, arrow, or modern computer), he takes a step toward freeing himself from dependence on nature. The history of mankind is, then, a long journey from man's complete economic subordination to nature to his ultimate mastery over nature. This last stage in man's journey through history Marx called communism. It was not a political or ideological social structure but a definite stage in the relationship between man and nature. In today's jargon, Marx's communism could be called a world without scarcity. At any rate, the economic interpretation of history has, then, a strong pseudo-religious content: salvation will happen in this space and time.

Second, as people learned how to produce and use tools, it became necessary for them to regulate access to those tools in ways that would encourage their production.

To define who has what access to an asset means to define property rights in that asset. In this manner, Marx explained the history and development of property rights.

We can thus say that Marx deduced the <u>historical necessity of property rights</u> from (i) the initial alienation of man to nature, and (ii) his (survival) instinct to reverse that relationship. Property rights did not develop because a few wise men "discovered" their importance. Marx argued that property rights are developed and modified in response to changes in the economic conditions of life. This point defines a very important difference between Marx and early socialists. Marx emphasized the inevitable (necessary) laws of history and played down the role of reason.

While the importance of property rights was recognized by social scientists before Marx, he was the first to have a theory of property rights. Marx's analytical apparatus was primitive and his deterministic views of human history untenable. Yet, he was able <u>to perceive</u> the importance of property rights with regard to the production and distribution of goods, <u>to recognize</u> that property rights are endogenous to the system, and <u>to sense</u> that property relations affect human behavior in specific and predictable ways. Thus, Marx made a contribution toward better understanding of economic processes. In a major attack on classical political economy, Marx wrote:

> Political economy proceeds from the fact of private property, but it does not explain it to us. Political economy expresses in general, abstract formulae the material process through which private property actually passes...it takes for granted what it is supposed to evolve. [Private property] is explained from external circumstances. As to how far these external...circumstances are but the expression of the necessary course of [human] development, political economy teaches us nothing.

THE PROCESS OF SOCIAL CHANGE

To explain the process of social change, Marx used two concepts: (i) relations of production and (ii) productive forces.

In its long journey from complete dependence on nature to mastery over nature, all human society must pass through some definite types of property relations. Marx used the terms relations of production and property rights interchangeably and defined this concept as the relations among men in the process of production, which today, we would call a social system. Through the history of mankind before the final stage is reached, these relations of production are relations among aliens. Private property causes this alienation of man from man. Marx's analysis of the concept of alienated labor, one of his key concepts, can be summarized as follows: (i) Since it does not belong to him, the product of the worker's labor appears to him to be an <u>alien</u> object. (ii) Consequently, the worker considers his work to be imposed labor. Thus, the worker is <u>alienated</u> from his work activity. (iii) What distinguishes man from animals is his conscious life activity. But alienated labor turns man's life activity into a means of existence. It <u>alienates</u> man from his species' life. (iv) The worker is <u>alienated</u> from that other man who takes the product away from him. (v) Those two men who are alienated from each other belong to identifiable social classes. The class struggle is then a major consequence of private property rights.

Economic development changes the relationship between man and nature in the production of goods and services. Marx called this relationship productive forces. The productive forces represent the relation between man and nature in the production of goods and services. In the concept of productive forces Marx included technology, the supply of resources, working habits, and education.

Given the prevailing social system, man's survival instinct brings about improvements in the forces of production. A change in the forces of production means that man becomes a little less dependent on nature. Marx argued, however, that at some level of economic development the prevailing social system will become a fetter to further improvements in the forces of production. Then and only then the prevailing social system will break down, and a new social system will emerge. This new system of property rights will accelerate economic development. But, at some level of economic development, the system that was initially a progressive one will once again become an obstacle to further economic development. The cycle repeats itself until the final stage is reached.

In its journey through history, mankind must pass through definite types of "property relations." Each social system has its historical function to perform. Thus, each system has its birth, life, and death. Marx was firm in saying that a system cannot be born before the old one has performed its historical function, and it will not disappear before its own historical contribution to the progress of mankind has been fully utilized.

> At a certain stage of their development, the forces of production come into conflict with the existing property relations....From forms of development of the forces of production these relations turn into their fetters. Then comes the period of social revolution. With the change of the economic foundation, the entire...superstructure is more or less rapidly transformed. (K. Marx, "A Contribution to the Critique of Political Economy," in Marx and Engels, Basic Writings on Politics and Philosophy (L. Feuer, ed.), Garden City: Doubleday, 1959, pp. 43-4)

According to Marx, the historical function of capitalism was the automation of industry (i.e., high technology).

Profit is a powerful motivating force in a private-property society. It provides property owners with strong incentives to increase productivity in their factories. But higher productivity comes from the development of efficient, cost-effective new machines. Thus, in his search for more profit, a property owner continuously substitutes machines for labor.

Through this process of substitution of more-productive for less-productive machines, the capitalist performs two functions. First, he contributes to economic development, which is a historical function of capitalism. Second, he also contributes to the end of capitalism. How?

While one capitalist is innovating and upgrading, other capitalists do not stand still. They also invest in better machines. However, as the number of workers employed falls relative to the amount of capital used by firms, the surplus value—which comes from human labor only—shrinks relative to the total cost of production. And the average rate of profit falls. A decline in the average rate of profit brings about an increase in the percentage of the labor force out of work. In short, the profit motive pushes the capitalist class to search for and implement more and better technology. The resulting increase in the capital-labor ratio reduces the ratio of surplus value to total investment by capitalism firms. The average rate of profit falls, creating additional pressure for individual capitalists to recapture it by increasing the productivity of their firms relative to that of their competitors. In the process, the industry gets automated, the labor force shrinks, and the rate of profit approaches zero. At that point in time, the capitalist machine would have performed its historical function. The impoverished workers would rise and throw out private property rights to the means of production. And a new system, socialism, would move in.

Historical evidence, economic analysis, and recent developments in Eastern Europe do not support Marx's analysis of the process of social change and its inevitability. In 1987, Hans Albert[1] provided an excellent analysis of the so-called inevitability of socialism.

SUGGESTED READINGS

Feuer, L. (ed.) Marx and Engels, Basic Writings on Politics and Philosophy, Garden City: Doubleday, 1959.

Laidler, H. A History of Socialist Thought, New York: T. Y. Crowell, 1927.

Marx, K. Philosophical and Economic Manuscripts, Moscow: Foreign Languages Publishing House, 1960.

Pejovich, S. (ed.) Socialism: Institutional, Philosophical and Economic Issues, Dordrecht: Kluwer Academic Publishers, 1987.

---

[1]H. Albert, "Is Socialism Inevitable? Historical Prophecy and the Possibilities of Reason," in Socialism: Institutional, Philosophical and Economic Issues (S. Pejovich, ed.), Dordrecht, Kluwer Academic Publishers, 1987, p. 55-88.

PART TWO

THE PRIVATE-PROPERTY

FREE-MARKET ECONOMY

CHAPTER 4

BASIC INSTITUTIONS OF CAPITALISM

The basic institutions of capitalism are: (i) the right of ownership in productive assets, (ii) freedom of contract, and (iii) constitutional (limited) government. Those three institutions set capitalism apart from other social systems. They generate incentives that have specific and predictable effects on the behavior of decision makers, the allocation of resources, and the flow of innovation.

Private Property Rights

THE MEANING OF THE RIGHT OF OWNERSHIP

About the right of ownership, I. Fisher said: "A property right is the liberty or permit to enjoy benefits of wealth while assuming the costs which those benefits entail.... property rights are not physical things or events, but are abstract social relations. A property right is not a thing." (I. Fisher, Elementary Principles of Economics, New York: Macmillan, 1923, p. 27) Instead, property rights are relations among men that arise from the existence of scarce goods and pertain to their use. This definition of property rights is consistent with Roman law, common law, Karl Marx's writings, and the new institutional (property rights) economics.

This definition of property rights makes two important points. The first is that it is wrong to separate human rights from property rights. My right to vote and my right to speak on issues are my property rights because they define the relationship between myself and other people. In other words, the property-rights definition applies to all rights of an individual vis-à-vis other people. The second point derives from the first, in that property rights are relations between individuals. Suppose I own a computer. The right of ownership does not define the relationship between myself and the computer. It defines the relationship between myself and all other people with respect to the right to use the computer. Property rights specify the norms of behavior with respect to economic goods that all persons must observe in their interactions with other people or bear the penalty cost of non-observance.

The right of ownership is a category of the general concept of property rights. Roman law specified several categories of property rights: ownership (the right to use one's property within the limits of law), the right of trespassing (the right to cross another's land), usus fructus (the right to use a thing belonging to someone else or to rent it to others, but not to sell it or change its quality), usus (the right to use a thing belonging to someone else, but not to rent it or sell it or change its quality), and pawn (the right to keep a thing belonging to someone else but not to use it).

The right of ownership contains the following four elements: (i) the right to use an asset (usus), (ii) the right to capture benefits from that asset (usus fructus), (iii) the right to change its form and substance (abusus), and (iv) the right to transfer all or some of the rights specified under (i), (ii), and (iii) to others at a mutually agreed upon price.

The last two elements are the most fundamental components of private property rights. They define the owner's right to bear changes in the value of his asset. Although the right of ownership is not an unrestricted right, it is an exclusive right in the sense that it is limited only by those restrictions that are explicitly stated in the law. Those constraints on the right of ownership may range from substantial ones, such as price controls, to minor restrictions, such as keeping the fence around one's house two feet inside the property line. At this point, it is important to note that legal restrictions on the right of ownership—whether justifiable or not—reduce our set of choices of what to do with the goods we own.

THE RIGHT OF OWNERSHIP AND ECONOMIC BEHAVIOR

The right of ownership affects economic behavior in several important ways.

The exclusivity of ownership means that the owner has the right to choose what to do with his asset (e.g., the right to speak on a social issue), how to use it (e.g., to be opposed to abortion), and who is to be given access to it (e.g., to join an anti-abortion lobby). The owner (or the people he appoints to do it on his behalf) decides what to do with his asset (e.g., he authorizes a real estate agent to sell his home); he captures the benefits of his decision and bears its cost. The exclusivity of ownership creates a strong link between one's right to choose how to use assets and bearing the consequences of that choice.

The right of ownership then creates strong incentives for the owner to seek the highest-valued use for his resources. The world is full of observations that support this proposition. People take better care of homes they own than of those they rent. They are more likely to check and add oil to their own cars than to those they rent. I have two computers. The computer at home is mine while the one in my office belongs to the university. They render absolutely the same flow of services to me, yet I do not treat them equally. I have more rights in the home, the car, and the computer that are mine.

The transferability of ownership means that the owner has the right to transfer his asset to others at mutually agreed upon terms. That is, he can sell his asset or give it away. What are some of the implications of this second component of the right of ownership?

Suppose Ms. Smith is a farmer. She makes about $1,000 per year after direct expenses. Ms. Jones could earn a profit of $1,500 farming the same land. A transfer of the farm from a less-productive farmer to a more-productive farmer would clearly benefit the community. The transferability of ownership provides incentives for resources to seek the most productive owners. Why? Assuming a rate of interest of 10 percent, Ms. Jones is willing to pay up to $15,000 for the farm, while Ms. Smith would have incentives to sell her farm at any price above $10,000.

The constitutional guarantee of ownership divorces economic wealth from political power. As Ivan moves up the Soviet power structure, his economic well-being increases. He gets a better apartment in the city, a bigger weekend home in the country, the right to a more exclusive summer resort, access to special stores, and many other benefits that are directly related to his position in the Soviet hierarchy. If Ivan is kicked out of the Soviet power structure, he loses all economic benefits. Things were not much different in feudalism. Rising or falling in the political power structure had a direct effect on one's economic wealth. However, the right of ownership breaks this link between power and wealth in capitalism. The individual who loses political power does not lose his economic wealth.

Political power is not the exclusive road to economic wealth in socialism, and the separation of power from wealth is far from being perfect in capitalism. But, in general, a major consequence of the absence of private property rights is a marriage of political power and wealth, and a major consequence of the right of ownership is their divorce.

Exclusivity provides incentives for those who own assets to put them into the highest-valued uses; transferability provides incentives for resources to move from less-productive to more-productive owners; and the constitutional guarantee of ownership separates the accumulation of economic wealth from the accumulation of political power.

NEW INSTITUTIONAL ECONOMICS (PROPERTY RIGHTS ECONOMICS)

The standard theory of production and exchange rests on three propositions: (i) private ownership of all resources, (ii) zero transaction costs, and (iii) downward-sloping demand schedules for goods. The first proposition is specific to the capitalist system, the second is an assumption, and the third captures the essence of human behavior in a world of scarcity (i.e., in all societies). Starting with those three propositions, the standard theory of production and exchange has provided important insights into the meaning of the social choice set, the consequences of economic efficiency, the types of market competition, and the properties of market equilibriums.

However, in the standard theory of production and exchange the output is a function of the costs of a set of inputs, given the state of technological knowledge. But this view is misleading because production does not take place in an institutional vacuum. If the output of an economy depended only on the costs of the traditional inputs and some given production function, economic analysis could not explain persistent economic differences between various countries. The fact is that output is a function of the costs of production, which consists of the costs of the traditional inputs and the costs of transacting. Yet, the standard theory of production and exchange makes no allowance for the effects of alternative property rights on transaction costs, income distribution, and incentives to innovate. For example, the production-and-exchange theory has made technical innovation an external phenomenon. It leaves the expansion of the choice set outside the scope of economic analysis and deals with the effects of technical change only <u>after</u> they have been introduced into the economy.

It would be wrong to discard the standard theory of production and exchange. But it is also wrong to use it mechanically across a broad range of issues. The new theory of institutions has expanded the scope of applicability of the standard theory to a wider class of real-world events.

The key concepts underlying the new theory of institutions assert that (i) the concept of the right of ownership is not the only relevant configuration; (ii) alternative property rights affect the allocation of resources and the flow of innovation in specific and predictable ways; and (iii) transaction costs are positive. Transaction costs include the costs of negotiating and monitoring economic behavior, the costs of obtaining information, the agency costs, and the costs of maintaining prevailing institutions.

The Law of Contract

THE MEANING OF CONTRACTS

People enter into contracts because they expect that exchange will make them better off. When I buy a pair of shoes for $50 or read a book, I am in effect saying that I expect my choice of shoes or the book to give me more satisfaction than whatever utility I could have obtained from spending the same amount of resources, including time, on another bundle of goods. Contracts are means by which people seek, identify, and negotiate opportunities for exchange. While the right of ownership creates incentives for people to seek the most productive uses for their assets, the freedom of contract reduces the cost of identifying them. The purpose of exchange is then an aspect of utility. In that sense, the purpose of exchange is independent of the prevailing property rights. However, the <u>extent</u> and <u>terms</u> of exchange are not.

THE LAW OF CONTRACT AND ECONOMIC BEHAVIOR

The law of contract serves three fundamental economic functions. First, it actualizes the relationship between the prevailing property rights and economic value. Second, it encourages exchange that is not simultaneous. Finally, the law of contract reduces the costs of exchange.

The prevailing legal institutions determine the bundles of rights that <u>could</u> be transferred (i.e., any deviation of contractual agreements from the prevailing property rights is not enforceable) by way of contractual agreements. Since the bundle of rights held in various goods affects their market prices, the prevailing property rights constrain the extent of exchange and influence the terms of trade in specific and predictable ways. Being the means by which the bundles of rights are exchanged, the law of contract enhances the relationship between prevailing property rights and economic value.

Market transactions are frequently not simultaneous. Suppose that two individuals, A and B, want to buy my car. A offers to pay $1,000 at the time he takes possession of my car, while B promises to pay $1,500 a year later. If the difference between the two offers were not compensated by the market rate of interest, economic efficiency would require that the car be sold to B. But I will choose a less-efficient alternative and sell my car to A <u>unless</u> the law enforces exchanges which are not simultaneous. The law of contract, by holding people to their promises, encourages the optimal level of economic activity.

Most transactions have consequences that occur <u>after</u> the exchange agreement is concluded. Buying a car, purchasing a home, getting married, signing up for a class in economics, and even eating out are exchange activities that have future consequences. The problem is that future consequences often differ from those that were expected at the time of the agreement. Some risks are foreseeable, some have a low probability of occurring, some losses are difficult to foresee, and some are not foreseeable. But they all increase the cost of contracting. If legal contracts had to be drawn up for each and every possible future contingency of a transaction, the extent of exchange in the community could be reduced. Fortunately, this is not the case. All sorts of standardized contracts, trade customs, warranties, and return privileges reduce the costs of exchange by assigning in advance the losses and gains of the various contingencies.

To summarize, the law of contract enhances the movement of resources from lower- to higher-valued uses by (i) holding people to their promises and (ii) reducing the cost of transacting.

Limited Government

THE GOVERNMENT IN A CAPITALIST SOCIETY

Capitalism emphasizes the right of individuals to make choices according to their own preferences under constraints that include rules. Clearly, the individual choice set depends on laws and regulations imposed by all levels of government. The term limited government means that what the government does is more important than its size.

The primary function of government in a capitalist society is to monitor the game and enforce the rules, rather than to make them as the game is played. Thus, the role of government in a capitalist society is basically a passive one, which could also be described as one of <u>maintaining</u> the environment in which all individuals are free to pursue their self-interests, make their own decisions, and bear the consequences of those decisions. Limited government also means that any changes made in the rules have to be slow, deliberate, and based on the constitution, not on the basis of a majority vote.

A football game can be compared to government. In football the rules of the game are set, and spectators know what to watch for because they know the rules. The players know the rules, and they know how to prepare for the game. The coaches know how to coach within the rules. They have no freedom to change the rules; they have the freedom to choose to play within the rules. Suppose that the blue team is driving down the field and is at the two-yard line. They use the fourth down, and the coach says to the referee, "My players worked so hard, why don't you give them another down?" The referee agrees to do so, and the blue team wins the game. In the short run they have a victory; in the long run, they lost, because next time they will not know how to prepare for the game. Instead of hiring a coach who can prepare them for the game, they will have to hire a coach who can persuade the referee to change the rules. The emphasis will then be on employing people who know how to commit resources to change the rules rather than on employing the most efficient people who know how to play the game within the given rules. That will destroy the game.

The case of Miller et al. vs. Schoene is a good example. For years, Virginians were free to grow apple trees and red cedar trees on their land. Then a fungus appeared that grew on cedar trees but caused no harm to them. However, the fungus was capable of inflicting severe damage on apple trees. The prevailing rules contained no provision forbidding the red cedar owners to grow them. However, the state legislature ruled (and the courts upheld the rulings) that the state biologist had to investigate and, if necessary, condemn and destroy without compensation certain red cedar trees within a two-mile radius of an apple orchard. In effect, the state introduced a new rule that was clearly in favor of the apple growers. The state's reaction to the problem was typical of the standard social welfare approach. However, it was inconsistent with the role of government in a capitalist state. James Buchanan made a very instructive comment on this issue:

...when the parties are allowed freely to bargain and to reach mutually satisfactory agreements, the apple grower's own assessment of probable damage to his crop becomes the measure of his own maximum payment to secure the elimination of the danger. On the other side, the cedar grower's own estimate of the value of his standing trees over and above their value as cut trees becomes the basis of possible willingness to accept or reject proffered compensations. The equity or inequity of compensation is irrelevant; what is relevant is the necessary place of compensation in the trading process between the two parties. Only when transfers are actually made can relative values be measured by those whose interests are directly involved. [In a capitalist society] there is an explicit prejudice in favor of previously existing rules, not because change itself is undesirable, but for the much more elementary reason that only such a prejudice offers incentives for the emergence of voluntary negotiated settlements among the parties themselves. Indirectly, therefore, this prejudice guarantees that resort to the authority of the State is effectively minimized. (J. Buchanan, "Politics, Property and the Law," Journal of Law and Economics, 16, 1972, pp. 439-452)

LIMITED GOVERNMENT AND ECONOMIC BEHAVIOR

From an individual's point of view, rules yield a flow of benefits: the predictability of other people's behavior. Rules are costly, too. The cost borne by an individual is the satisfaction he forgoes by not being able to engage in some specific activities. The flow of benefits from rules depends on their stability. As time goes by people become better and better acquainted with the rules. They learn how to adjust to the system, identify exchange opportunities, and exploit the most beneficial ones. For example, second-year students get more out of the system of rules than freshmen. However, if the schools changed the rules every year, the never-ending process of "learning" the rules would impair the system's ability to enhance the flow of benefits.

The purchase of land, investment in plants and equipment, and many other exchange opportunities have long-run consequences. Since frequent changes or expectations about changes in the rules of the game would increase the risk and uncertainty associated with those decisions, the cost of exchange opportunities that have long-term consequences would increase relative to those transactions that have a shorter time horizon. Thus, for example, Jews in Central Europe before World War II favored investments in jewelry and other short-term, liquid assets. South Americans, seeing unstable political systems around them, prefer lower returns from investments in the United States to the much higher rates of return that are available in their homelands. An investor in Guatemala seeks a much shorter payoff period than one in North Dakota. In general, the flow of benefits from the law is positively related to the period of time over which the prevailing rules of the game are expected to be stable. A stable set of rules reduces the risk and uncertainty about the game itself, provides a measure of certainty about the future, and encourages individuals to exploit the most beneficial exchange opportunities regardless of their time horizons.

The new institutional economics offers a good reason for limiting the role of government. Since decision makers in government do not own the resources they control, they cannot appropriate the full benefits resulting from their actions. Nor do they bear the entire cost. No one has a claim on the capitalized value of public assets. Changes in the value of assets, brought about by decision makers in government, are dispersed throughout the economy. Moreover, pressure groups, including all kinds of advocates, are concerned only about the benefits they expect to receive from government expenditures and transfer payments, but they are rarely concerned about the costs of those projects because the costs are borne by others. It follows that the penalty-reward system associated with public ownership provides public decision makers with weaker incentives to pursue efficient outcomes. Therein lies the source of objection to governmental controls. It has nothing to do with the professionalism, work habits, and integrity of public servants. The issue lies in the weaker incentives they have to seek efficient outcomes.

SUGGESTED READINGS

Alchian, A. "Uncertainty, Evolution and Economic Theory," Journal of Political Economy, 58, 1950.

Alchian, A. Economic Forces at Work, Indianapolis: Liberty Press, 1977, Part II.

Buchanan, J. The Limits of Liberty, Chicago: University of Chicago Press, 1977.

Friedman, M. Capitalism and Freedom, Chicago: University of Chicago Press, 1962.

Furubotn, E. and Pejovich, S. The Economics of Property Rights, Cambridge: Ballinger, 1974, chapters 4-12.

CHAPTER 5

EXCHANGE IN A PRIVATE PROPERTY CAPITALIST ECONOMY

As previously stated in the pages of this book, the allocation of goods is a problem because of the fact of scarcity. Each time a person gets something, that much less is left for others; and each time a source is assigned to produce something, a little bit of something else is not produced. Every society has to face those two fundamental problems, which are fundamentally the questions of <u>who gets what</u> and <u>who does what</u>. And the desire for more utility leads to activity to resolve conflicts of interest; that is, desire for greater utility leads to competition. As long as we live in a world of scarcity we cannot reduce or eliminate competition. However, we can choose between alternative modes of competition. Different societies develop different institutions which, in turn, affect the answers to the questions <u>who gets what</u> and <u>who does what</u>. This and the following chapter discuss the effects of private ownership and contractual freedom on exchange and production, respectively.

Contractual freedom generates knowledge of alternative offers and opportunities for the resources, private ownership provides incentives for the resources to move to their highest-valued uses, and open markets reduce the cost of pursuing the most valuable option because competing parties stand by to offer similar terms. The type of competition generated by private ownership and contractual freedom is called price competition. Price competition means that people are free to seek and negotiate exchange in markets that are open to all and free from supervision by an outside authority.

The legal doctrine of consideration performs two important economic functions in facilitating the movement of resources to wherever they will be put to best use. First, it rejects one-sided contracts, for the promise which is one-sided is not part of the exchange process and cannot be presumed to lead to a more efficient use of resources. Second, by insisting that courts should inquire only as to the existence of consideration for a promise, and not as to the adequacy, the law of contract takes a sound economic position: Only the parties involved know what the goods that are being traded are worth to <u>them</u>. How much satisfaction a person gets from a having a little more of any good is a subjective matter. Moreover, different people value the same good differently.

The Purpose of Exchange

Exchange is one means of seeking more satisfaction. The method of payment by one of the contracting parties could be money or other goods; in exchange for using my lawn mower, a neighbor might drive my children to school. We can say that a person enters into exchange because he expects that his benefits from acquiring a good will exceed his costs. To understand the purpose of exchange, it is important to understand the three terms emphasized here.

The benefit from exchange is the increment in satisfaction a person derives from acquiring the right to use a little more of any good. The important thing to remember from our earlier discussion is that the value of any good to a person depends on the rights that are being transferred. For example, the value of my right to cut trees in a public forest, valuable as it might be, would be higher if I could sell that right to someone else at a mutually agreed-upon price.

The cost of exchange is the satisfaction a person has to give up. When a person spends $50 on shoes, the cost of the shoes is not $50. The real cost of the shoes is the satisfaction he could get from another bundle of goods that $50 could buy. When a boy takes a girl out the evening before an exam is given in school, he gives up the satisfaction of a higher grade that several hours of additional study could have made possible. In general, the cost of exchange is the value of that which is being given up (i.e., opportunity costs).

The act of exchange implies a choice among alternative uses for a person's income, time, and other possessions. His choice is based on some expectations about the future consequences of exchange. However, no person can predict the exact consequences of his choice. A $50 pair of shoes might fall apart within a few days, and a girl might decline future requests for a date. It is the expected benefits that govern our decision to enter into exchange.

People do not carry small computers to calculate the increments in satisfaction they expect to derive from each and every exchange. Sometimes we agonize over our decisions (e.g., choosing a major), sometimes we act on impulse (e.g., hitting a friend), and frequently we act out of habit (e.g., buying the same brand of shoes). However, human behavior is consistent in one significant respect. An increase in the cost of obtaining a specific good (i.e., an increase in the value of that which is being given up) induces people to acquire less of that good. Given relative prices, the bundle of other things that a person is willing to give up in exchange for one unit of a good depends on his preference and income. The importance of income is, however, easy to exaggerate. For example, even though you have $100 to spend, you may choose to forgo a second cup of coffee if its price increases from fifty cents to one dollar. The value of other goods that one dollar could buy, such as beer, is the major factor here. Income is primarily a constraint that defines your set of choices.

We can summarize our discussion in this section of the book as follows: (i) price competition is a method by which people seek to better themselves in an institutional environment that is characterized by private ownership in resources and free exchange; (ii) an inverse relationship exists between the price (cost) of a good and the quantity of that good demanded (i.e., the law of demand); and (iii) the cost of exchange is the value of that which is being given up (i.e., opportunity cost). Money is a convenient, but not the only method for measuring costs.

The Terms and Extent of Exchange

Suppose an important football game is played in your town. The game is a sellout. Bill is the only person in his neighborhood who got a ticket at the regular price of $20. He is quite happy, because he was willing to pay as much as $30 for the ticket. That is, Bill prefers $31 worth of other goods to watching the game. His neighbors belong to the same income class as Bill but have a more intense desire to see the game. Table 5-1 shows the maximum price that each of them is willing to pay for the ticket—that is, the bundle of other things they are willing to sacrifice in order to see the game.

Table 5-1: Who Gets the Ticket

Neighbor 1	$70
Neighbor 2	$60
Neighbor 3	$50
Neighbor 4	$40
Bill (ticket owner)	$30

Here is a case of five people who value the same good differently. They do not know each other's preferences for watching the game. However, as long as private ownership and contractual freedom are not restricted, our five people will, moved by their own desire for more utility, engage in trade. Neighbor 4 will get the ticket from Bill by offering him more than $30. Neighbor 3 will eliminate neighbor 4 from the competition by raising his offer over $40. Neighbor 2 will find it in his self-interest to raise the offer above $50 but will lose out to neighbor 1, who will offer more than $60. The actual price at which neighbor 1 will get the ticket from Bill will be between $61 and $70, say $64.

The important point is that the final allocation of the ticket does not depend on prior knowledge of what each person is willing to pay for the opportunity to watch the game. It depends on the owner's right to sell the ticket (i.e., the right of ownership) and contractual freedom. The actual price will emerge through the process of bidding higher and lower prices. The ticket is ultimately allocated to the highest bidder, and Bill is better off. He exchanged something that he values at as much as $30 for an opportunity to purchase a bundle of goods that is worth more to him. Neighbor 1 is better off because he gave up a bundle of goods worth $64 in exchange for a scarce good that he values at $70. And no one in the community is worse off after the exchange.

The outcome would have been the same if neighbor 4 had been able to purchase the ticket from Bill for, say $36. Neighbor 3 would then bid the ticket away from him for any price in excess of $50, and so on. Neighbor 1 would still get the ticket, and for a similar price, but the gains from the trade would be shared by several people. This outcome is quite possible. Knowledge of others' preferences is not readily available. Thus, the good might change hands several times on its journey to the highest bidder. The allocation of resources would remain the same but the income distribution would not.

Once the good is allocated to the highest bidder, there is no additional exchange that could make some people better off without making some others worse off. Private property rights in resources and contractual freedom provide incentives for individuals to use price competition in order to move resources from lower- to higher-valued uses. In the process, the extent of exchange is maximized, or, as economists would say, the allocation of resources is efficient, given our preferences and incomes.

The freedom of each person to bid higher and lower prices for goods in accordance with his desire for more utility is the essence of price competition. This process of bidding for a good identifies its value in alternative uses. The right of ownership provides incentives to allocate the good to its highest-valued use. Moreover, the government does not have to legislate price competition as a method for the allocation of goods among the competing claimants. Price competition simply happens whenever the right of ownership and contractual freedom are enforced.

Restrictions on Price Competition

Yet, the world is full of observations that cast doubts on the effectiveness of price competition to drive prices to their market-clearing levels; that is, it would appear that price competition tends to leave many exchange opportunities unexploited.

The failure of price competition to explain some events should not overshadow its ability to explain most events. The effective use of price competition requires the right of ownership in resources and contractual freedom. Any restriction or interference with those rights would reduce the extent of exchange, or the efficiency of resource allocation. The factors that most often interfere with the effectiveness of price competition are positive transaction costs, attenuation of private property rights, and nonpecuniary income.

Transaction Costs

Transaction costs are the costs of all the resources required to transfer property rights from one economic agent to another. They include the costs of making an exchange (e.g., discovering exchange opportunities, negotiating exchange, monitoring costs) and the costs of protecting the institutional structure (e.g., maintaining a judiciary system and police force). Let us enumerate some important transaction costs.

INFORMATION

Information about exchange opportunities is not a free good. To produce information about an exchange opportunity takes time, money, and effort. And it might be inefficient to produce some types of information. Suppose that in our football example, neighbor 1 lives across town. He might never learn about the availability of a ticket at a price he is willing to pay. College graduates know that it takes time and money to gather information about employment opportunities, but the search costs might prevent such job hunters from discovering the best alternative for their skills. Shoppers know that by driving around they can find the best food bargains, but it might not be an efficient thing to do given the cost of gasoline and the alternative uses for the time spent shopping around. However, if the price at which a person can obtain information can be reduced, additional exchange opportunities would be exploited. An important issue is then whether institutional arrangements encourage behaviors that tend to reduce transaction costs. The institutions of capitalism qualify.

Neighbor 1 might get his ticket from a scalper (by sharing the gains from exchange with him). The shopper might benefit from reading newspaper ads. The college graduate could produce more information about jobs by going to a "head hunter." There are gains to be captured from additional information, and they are captured by those who produce information, by those who purchase information, and by the community as a whole because of an increase in the extent of exchange (i.e., more efficient allocation of resources).

Predictably, in a private-property, free-market economy, resources are devoted to collecting and selling information about exchange opportunities. Real estate agents, employment agencies, advertisers, marriage services, dating services, and scalpers make a living by selling information about exchange opportunities. Stores incur the cost of holding inventories because it is a low-cost method of economizing on the high cost of information about transient fluctuations in demand. How about those "sticky" prices that do not seem to respond to fluctuations in demand? They are not, as some noneconomists think, a consequence of monopoly power. A seller who responds to transient fluctuations in demand by charging a higher or a lower price is likely to lose some customers. People prefer to patronize stores that sell their products at stable (predictable) prices, and change them only when there is a permanent change in demand.

NEGOTIATING EXCHANGE

The costs of negotiating exchange can be quite substantial. The parties may not know each other. They may not know the product. They also have to negotiate the allocation of risk, losses and benefits, and other future consequences of exchange. Thus, a reduction in the cost of negotiating exchange would increase the extent of trade.

The law of contract serves an important economic function of reducing transaction costs. First, <u>standardized contracts</u> reduce transaction costs by enabling the parties to avoid the cost of negotiating the terms of contract for each and every exchange they make. Second, the law of contract reduces the cost of negotiating exchange by assigning in advance the location of liability for the losses. <u>Warranties, return privileges, and as-is purchases</u> are but a few examples. Third, <u>the law of contract allows the breaching party to choose</u> between performing in accordance with the contract or compensating the other party for sustained damages. For example, some years ago a ship owner ordered a large number of supertankers to be built. Then, the market for oil declined, and the ship owner canceled his contracts. The shipyards sued for the completion of their contracts. However, the court granted them only the right to recover already sustained costs. The completion of the "unneeded" tankers would have used additional resources—a waste from the point of view of the community. Fourth, the law of contract reduces transaction costs by <u>preventing opportunistic behavior</u>. In <u>Alaska Packers' Association vs. Domenico</u>, the defendant hired a group of seamen to fish salmon off the coast of Alaska. The wages to be paid to the seamen were agreed to before the voyage. However, when the ship arrived in Alaskan waters, the seamen refused to work unless they were paid higher wages. Having no access to the labor market, the defendant agreed. But, upon return to San Francisco, he refused to pay his workers the higher wage. The seamen sued and lost. The court held that the defendant's promise to pay the wages over and above the original contract was not supported by fresh consideration. According to Judge Posner, this is the correct economic decision. He wrote: "...as once it is well known that such modifications are unenforceable workers in the position of the seamen in the Domenico case will know that it will do them no good to take advantage of their employers' vulnerability." (R. Posner, <u>Economic Analysis of Law</u>, New York: Brown, 1985, p. 87)

ENFORCING EXCHANGE

The act of exchange can be either simultaneous (e.g., buying fresh produce in a farmers' market) or over a period of time (e.g., I pay for my plane ticket before the airline fulfills its side of the bargain). In either case, but more clearly in the latter, problems with enforcing contractual agreements and of misunderstandings concerning the quality of goods, the bundle of rights being transferred, and delivery dates are to be expected. The absence of a well-defined enforcement mechanism would raise the cost of exchange and reduce the extent of trade. In order to be able to move resources to their highest-valued uses, price competition requires the existence an enforcement mechanism.

The market provides an enforcement mechanism. Individuals who repeatedly fail to perform their side of the bargain lose business to their competitors. A reputable dealer gets more for providing the same service than a fly-by-night operator. Thus, a good reputation is an asset that has monetary value. A new business owner must be willing to sell at a lower price; that is his investment in building his reputation. However, this selection process, important as it is, takes time and is costly. It is costly to many who act in good faith, to those who misunderstood the terms of exchange, and to the community as a whole because real resources have to be used to run credit bureaus, security deposits, and other means of self-protection. By enforcing exchange agreements, the law of contract enhances the market selection process, reduces transaction costs, and performs an important economic function in a private-property society.

Attenuation of Private Property Rights

Exchange exists not only to accomplish the transfer of goods and services but also to permit the exchange of "bundles" of rights in the goods that are traded. This is an important point because it emphasizes the relationship between property rights and economic values. The value of a license to operate a radio station would be greater if the owner had a right to sell that license at a competitive price. It also costs more to play golf at a country club than to use a municipal golf course. Privacy is a valuable good that can be purchased at an additional cost.

Suppose that the government imposes a ceiling on the price of a good, or issues coupons entitling those who get them to a specific amount of the good, or determines that those below a certain age cannot buy the good, or that the good cannot be sold on weekends, or any other type of control. In all those cases the government attenuates (weakens) the right of ownership by interfering with either the owner's right to choose what to do with his asset (i.e., the exclusivity of ownership) or his right to transfer it to another individual at a mutually agreed upon price (i.e., the transferability of ownership). Most restrictions on the exclusivity of ownership (e.g., regulations prohibiting the sale of beer on weekends) reduce the extent of exchange. Most restrictions on the transferability of ownership (e.g., price controls) eliminate price competition as a method for resolving the issue of who gets what. Those restrictions have economic consequences that do not flow from the institutions of capitalism, and therefore they will be discussed in connection with alternative institutional arrangements.

Nonpecuniary Income

We can observe that some goods are sold below their market value even though transaction costs are low. It would be wrong to see in those cases the failure of price competition to move resources to their highest-valued uses.

A person derives satisfaction from a number of specific "goods," such as a pleasant environment, congenial colleagues, friendly neighbors, and clean air. Those are scarce goods, too. Thus, to acquire them something else has to be given up. I might prefer Dallas to New York, humble colleagues in a second-rate academic department to self-centered scholars in a great department, an ethnic neighborhood to a mixed neighborhood, and fresh country air to the air in Los Angeles. Economists call those amenities of life <u>nonpecuniary goods</u>.

The satisfaction we derive from nonpecuniary income can be measured. For example, an additional $5,000 per year would not make me move from Dallas to St. Louis. But $10,000 or $15,000 might, and $50,000 would. Also, I own a house with two apartments. I live in one and rent the other. Suppose that a widow with five children offers to pay $120 per month, while a plumber offers $100. If I want to have a plumber around, I rent the apartment to him. That is, I am willing to exchange a bundle of goods that $20 could buy for a specific good called a friendly plumber. But am I willing to sacrifice $50 or $100 per month in order to have a friendly plumber? There is ultimately a difference in rent income that would make the satisfaction from having a plumber around too costly.

Those simple examples carry an important message. The satisfaction people receive from nonpecuniary goods has its money equivalent. Moreover, the demand for nonpecuniary goods conforms to the law of demand; the higher the cost of purchasing nonpecuniary goods, the less of them is demanded. The fact that the value of nonpecuniary goods can be measured provides economic analysis with a meaningful content and testable implications. They do not interfere with the working of price competition.

To conclude, in a private-property, free-market economy, price competition is a major determinant of who gets what. Both the right of ownership and contractual freedom generate incentives for utility-seeking individuals to identify, negotiate, and execute contractual agreements that tend to maximize the extent of exchange or, in other words, tend to move resources to their highest-valued uses. The end result is the efficient allocation of resources. However, the term <u>tend</u> is quite important here. There is no way to determine whether the allocation of resources <u>is</u> efficient or, for that matter, has ever been efficient. All that economic analysis can tell us is that the institutions of capitalism provide both the freedom and the incentives for individuals to engage in behaviors that move the economy in the direction of efficient allocation of resources. It is in that sense—the direction of its economic activity—that capitalism is an efficient system.

A number of factors interfere with the efficiency of the economic processes in capitalism. Transaction costs are not always easy to reduce, the role of nonpecuniary income is frequently not fully understood, and governments do interfere with the right of ownership and contractual freedom. Economic analysis can help us to appreciate better the role of nonpecuniary goods and to develop techniques for reducing transaction costs. However, inefficiencies arising from the attenuation of property rights and restrictions on contractual freedom are brought about by all levels of government. They affect the behavior of individuals in ways that are not consistent with the efficient allocation of resources.

SUGGESTED READINGS

Alchian, A. "Some Implications of Property Rights Transaction Costs," in <u>Economics and Social Institutions</u> (K. Brunner, ed.), Boston: M. Nijhoff, 1979.

Alchian, A. and Allen, W. <u>University Economics</u>, Belmont: Wadsworth, third edition, 1972, chapter 4-9.

Brunner, K. "The Limits of Economic Policy," in <u>Socialism: Institutional, Philosophical and Economic Issues</u> (S. Pejovich, ed.), Dordrecht: Kluwer Academic Publishers, 1987.

Posner, R. <u>Economic Analysis of Law</u>, New York: Brown, 1986, chapter 2-4.

CHAPTER 6

PRODUCTION IN A PRIVATE PROPERTY CAPITALIST ECONOMY

Property Rights and Production Efficiency

To produce goods we use resources. The supply of resources is finite, however, and resources have alternative uses. Thus, the cost of producing a unit of any good is the value of other goods forgone. Each community has to decide how much of every good to produce and who should produce what. The former issue concerns the "output mix;" the latter is the issue of the efficiency of production. Production is technically efficient when the output of any good cannot be increased without reducing the output of some other good. The concept of efficiency in production requires that each good be produced by the lowest-cost producer of that good and that each additional unit of that good is produced by successively higher-cost producers. As in the case of goods that have been already produced, institutional arrangements affect the outcome.

The purpose of this chapter is to discuss the effects of the institutions of capitalism on the allocation of resources among alternative uses.

Suppose that five firms are producing VCRs. Table 6-1 shows the quantity of VCRs that each firm can produce per unit of time, and their costs in terms of the value of that which is being given up. Thus, the market value of each firm's alternative outputs, whatever they might be, is the most useful measure of their respective costs of producing VCRs.

How does the right of ownership affect the allocation of resources between the production of VCRs and other goods? Given the appropriability of returns, those who own resources have strong incentives to allocate them to their most valuable uses. It means that at any price below $30 none of the five firms in table 6-1 would choose to produce VCRs. They all can make more money by producing something else.

Firm C happens to be the smallest in the group of firms that are assumed to be equipped to produce VCRs. It is also the lowest-cost producer among the five firms. As the price per VCR rises above $30, firm C would switch from whatever it was making to VCRs. In a private-property economy the firm's decision, predicated on its own self-interest, turns out to be beneficial to the community as a whole. For example, at $32 per VCR, the owner(s) makes a profit of $2 per VCR, while the community gives up $30 worth of other goods in exchange for a VCR which it values at $32.

Thirty dollars per VCR is the minimum price at which firm C would be willing to produce VCRs, $50 per VCR is the minimum price for firm E, and so on. The result

TABLE 6-1. Production alternatives for five firms

Firm	Number of VCRs	Market Value of Alternative Output ($)	Cost per VCR ($)
A	250	27,500	110
B	300	27,000	90
C	100	3,000	30
D	200	14,000	70
E	400	20,000	50

of this interaction between the right of ownership and the utility-seeking individuals is an upward-sloping supply schedule. More generally, in a private-property economy the supply schedule of a good slopes upward to the right and shows the minimum price necessary to induce producers to offer each possible quantity for sale.

The upward slope of the supply schedule indicates that production is technically efficient. It says that as a larger output of a good is required, those producers with successively higher costs are drawn into production of that good.

Technical efficiency in production is then an important consequence of private-property rights. Does it mean that a private-property, free-market economy is always or sometimes or ever efficient? Economic analysis cannot tell us that. However, economic analysis does tell us that the right of ownership and contractual freedom provide incentives that affect the behavior of economic agents in ways that enhance efficiency in production. To say that capitalism is an efficient system means that it has incentives that tend to produce efficient outcomes.

Economic analysis provides testable implications for the effects various restrictions have on the allocation of resources among alternative uses. For example, legal restrictions on the freedom of entry (i.e., the freedom of exchange) create inefficiencies in production; that is, if firm C were not allowed to enter the market for VCRs, the result would be an inefficient mix of outputs.

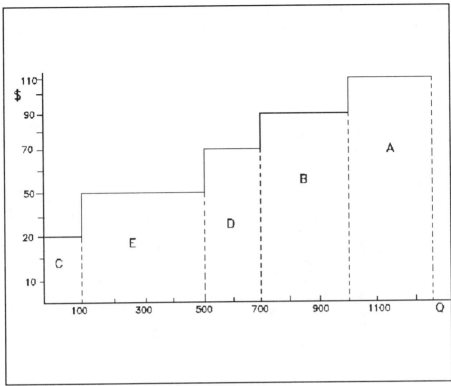

Figure 6-1. The supply schedule for VCRs.

The Role of Profit

The problem of identifying higher-valued uses for resources, as well as of transferring them from lower-valued to higher-valued uses, is a difficult one. The high cost of information, positive transaction costs, and various property relations discussed in the preceding chapters impede the transfer of resources in the direction of greater efficiency. Yet, each and every society must tackle the problems of (i) identifying the best use for some resources and (ii) transferring resources to those uses. Some sort of authority is expected to look after this problem in a socialist state. In capitalism, profit performs this function.

Profits are the earnings per period of time in excess of the opportunity costs of resources used in production. Suppose the interest on government bonds is 8 percent. If a business in which you invested $1,000 gives you $60 after all direct costs are paid, you lost $20. The cost of investing $1,000 in that business must include the $80 you could have obtained by investing in government bonds. If the business yields $90 after direct costs are paid, your profit is $10. In other words, profit is the amount over and above what a resource could earn in the best alternative use. Moreover, the term profit is not reserved for earnings from land, machines, cash, and other "nonhuman" assets. Labor is a source of profit as well.

Profit as an Allocator of Resources

In a private-property, free-exchange economy, each person seeks exchange opportunities at voluntarily agreed-upon terms, given the right of other people to do likewise. The process of seeking beneficial exchange opportunities results in bidding for scarce resources. In the process, resources move to higher-valued uses. The efficient allocation of resources then identifies the end result (equilibrium) of this process: a situation in which no potentially beneficial exchange opportunity (the bidding of a resource away from another use) is left unexploited. The end result might be a pious wish that is never to be attained. Individual taste and income, technology, and many other things modify the equilibrium position. However, the process of adjustment to whatever the equilibrium position happens to be goes on constantly. And it is this process of adjustment, the forces that govern it, and the economic implications that flow from it that explain the working of the capitalist system.

At any point of time the allocation of resources between the pizza industry and the hamburger industry is given, as is the cost of using those resources. Suppose that our preferences change in favor of pizza. The demand price for pizza would rise relative to that for hamburgers. Given the prevailing allocation of resources and the resources' current costs, the rate of profit per dollar's worth of resources in the pizza industry would also increase relative to the hamburger industry. An increase in the rate of profit per dollar's worth of resources in one industry relative to others reveals the community's desire for more of that industry's output relative to other goods.

Through different profit rates for pizza and hamburgers, the community is in effect saying that more resources should be used to make pizza and that fewer resources should be employed to produce hamburgers. To accomplish this there must be (i) a transfer of some resources away from lower-valued uses (hamburgers) to higher-valued ones (pizza), and (ii) a transfer of the right amount of resources. The ability of profit to move resources effectively from lower- to higher-valued uses is predicated on the right of ownership.

The right of ownership provides powerful incentives for owners to seek the most profitable use for their resources. Thus, owners can be expected to respond to differences in the rate of profit among various alternative uses for assets. In our example, resources in the hamburger industry are allowed to be depleted (are not replaced) while the pizza industry bids resources away from other uses. How fast the resources are reallocated cannot be predicted in advance, some inputs are fixed and cannot be readily adjusted to changes in the economic situation. However, the process of adjustment in resource allocation is going to take place. As the resources flow from one industry into another, the community's taste for more pizza relative to hamburgers is being satisfied. This change in the composition of output has two effects. First, the price of pizza falls <u>relative</u> to that of hamburgers. Second, the direct costs of producing pizza increase relative to that of hamburgers. Why? Because the producers of pizza must, in order to make more pizza, bid resources away from other uses, including the hamburger industry. Those two effects combine to reduce the rate of profit per dollar's worth of resources in the pizza industry and to increase the rate of profit per dollar's worth of (remaining) resources in the hamburger industry. When the rates of profit in both industries get to be equal, except for the difference in risk and transaction costs, this process of adjustment comes to a halt.

In a private-property economy, differences in profits signal changes in the community's preference for some goods relative to others. Resource owners, driven by their own interest, <u>respond</u> to this command by transferring resources from lower-valued to higher-valued uses. In the process, differences in profits are whittled away through competition that lowers prices of those goods (thanks to larger supplies) and because of the higher value of resources used in their production. The allocation of resources is then adjusted to suit the community's desired mix of various goods. This tendency for profits to be whittled away via the transfer of resources from one use to another is readily observable.

Many people claim that large firms make more money than smaller ones. General Motors makes more money than an individual Pizza Inn franchise, and a Pizza Inn makes more money than a local TV repair shop. But does GM make <u>more per dollar's worth of resources invested</u> than the TV repair shop? On the average, it does not. Also, many people seem to object when some firms earn large profits. This sort of objection to high profits fails to address the important issue of how to make sure, at the lowest cost possible, that the allocation of resources conforms to the community's taste for various goods. Positive (and negative) profits provide quick, reliable, and low-cost information about desired changes in the composition of output, information to which resource owners are eager to respond. To limit profits would eliminate this vital function they have of guiding the allocation of resources.

INNOVATION AS A SOURCE OF PROFIT

Profit also serves an important function in developing new exchange opportunities (that is, in suggesting new uses for resources).

Suppose a person develops a new product, a new method of producing existing products, a new market, or a new source of supply. Those changes are called innovations, and they offer the community a new exchange opportunity. The community's <u>voluntary</u> acceptance of innovation indicates that it considers the new element beneficial relative to some old ones. Railroads, electricity, Ford's Mustang, and the Beatles are but a few examples of successful innovations. They differ in their impact on society but have one thing in common: they all suggest a change in the use of resources not previously tested in the marketplace. In general, a successful innovation contributes to the community's well-being. It adds to the community's set of choices, it denies the community no alternative that was available to it before, and it gives the community an opportunity to substitute voluntarily a new alternative for an old one.

A successful innovation yields benefits in excess of what the bundle of resources used by the innovator was earning before (that is obvious, otherwise the innovation would be a failure). Positive profits are then created from within the system via a successful change in the use of resources; that is, via the emergence of new exchange alternatives that enough people seek to exploit.

Innovation is a source of profit in the same way that free exchange decreases profits. A successful innovator has a monopoly position that enables him to earn profits in excess of the opportunity costs. Then, the process of adjustment in the allocation and use of resources discussed in the previous section begins anew. Resources flow into the new use and away from old ones. Before too long, the innovator loses his monopoly position because others will follow in the wake of a successful innovation. Eventually, competition erodes profits. Through this process, the community gets the right amount of that which is new.

MONOPOLY AS A SOURCE OF PROFIT

If the innovator could restrict potential competitors from free access to the market, the innovator's profit would be protected. It is therefore predictable that some pressures would be brought to bear on the government to close the market to new entrants. The reasons given for seeking this protection are to encourage innovation (by ensuring profits in the long run), to protect consumers from fly-by-night sellers, to avoid duplication of effort with the attendant waste of resources, and to protect the public interest. All those reasons are a façade that serves only one function: to protect existing producers from competition by new entrants.

Government can, via laws and regulations, create monopoly profits for some by granting them special privileges, licenses to sell, and thus, protection from competition. A predictable outcome of governmental controls is the enhanced importance of competition for political power and influence. In a private-property, free-exchange economy, the producer has incentives to invest in better facilities, better information about consumers' taste, and more efficient methods of production. These investments, in turn, contribute to a more efficient allocation of resources. In a political marketplace, however, the producer invests in generating favorable regulations that grant him special privileges vis-à-vis potential competitors. Those investments tend to perpetuate the misallocation of resources.

Business firms might also be able to protect their profits from competition without any help from political authorities. Predatory pricing, collusion, mergers, and ensuring a high cost of entry, are but a few examples of strategies that existing firms might use to try to convert their profits from innovation, which is a temporary gain, into monopoly profits, which are more permanent.

Predation. Predatory pricing means that a firm sells below costs. Then, after its competitors are driven out, the firm sets a high price. Standard Oil Company is often cited as an example of a firm that employed predatory pricing.

Threatening to employ predatory action could be effective if the firm sells in several markets while each of its competitors sells in only one of those markets. But the practice is costly to the predator. The predator incurs losses now, while gains are deferred. Moreover, gains may be only temporary since new competitors are likely to be attracted by a monopoly price, and the action may have to be repeated. Also, smaller firms can shut down operation, let the predator incur losses, and then reopen when the price rises. Actually, what might appear to be a predatory action may often be competition by more efficient, lower-cost producers. In this case, a law that prohibits predation might, in effect, harm the consumer.

Collusion and Mergers. The acquisition of monopoly power through merger or collusion is another way by which business firms may try to abuse the competitive process.

Collusion is a contract among firms to fix the price of the product they sell. The cost to consumers from effective collusion is very easy to appreciate. The Sherman Act was passed in 1890 to deal with the restraint of trade and conspiracies to monopolize markets. While business firms stand to gain from effective collusion, a member of a price-fixing contract can capture additional gains for himself by violating the agreement. By selling at lower than the agreed-upon price, a firm is usually able to increase its total profits. To illustrate, suppose that ten firms agree to charge $10 per unit of output while the cost of production is $5. Each firm sells ten units and earns $50. If one firm sells fourteen units of output at $9, its total profit would increase from $50 to $56. The temptation to cheat is strong.

If the costs of detecting cheating and enforcing the agreements are high, price-fixing contracts will not be very stable. "Policing" costs are usually high, and consequently, collusions are short-lived. An exception occurs in the case of sales to the government via sealed bids. If a colluding seller does not bid as agreed, the cost of detecting cheating is low, since all the bids are revealed.

In the absence of an enforcement mechanism then, most collusions tend to be short-lived. The colluding firms find it costly to police the agreement and keep out new entrants who are attracted by higher profits. Thus, a merger appears to be a better vehicle for eliminating market competition. The prescription is a simple one. Merge with your rivals into one large firm so as to get a monopoly profit which can then be divided among the merged firms. Unfortunately, new firms will enter if existing firms raise prices above the competitive level. In fact, most mergers that we observe have different objectives, such as a more efficient combination of resources or takeovers by a superior management team.

Legal Closures of the Market. New firms represent a threat to existing firms. Thus, an effective way of preserving profits is to eliminate the start-up of new firms.

However, closing the market to potential competitors requires active cooperation from the government. Firms which, by government authority, are granted exclusive access to the market can be called monopolists. Examples are taxi services in most cities, the medical profession, telephone companies, utilities, liquor stores, and union shops.

The license to operate in a closed market is a property right that has money value. And the difference between competitive and monopoly profits determines the market value of that right. A license grants to its holder the right to be protected from competition. It also denies others the right to compete.

In conclusion, production efficiency is enhanced by (i) assigning resources to private owners, (ii) eliminating (or reducing) constraints on the freedom of contract, and (iii) limiting the role of government to monitoring the game.

SUGGESTED READINGS

Alchian, A. Economic Forces at Work, Indianapolis: Liberty Press, 1977, Part III.

Ferguson, C. The Neoclassical Theory of Production and Distribution, Cambridge: Cambridge University Press, 1969, chapter 1-6.

Machlup, F. "On the Meaning of the Marginal Product," Readings in the Theory of Income Distribution (AEA), Philadelphia: Blackston, 1951.

Maxwell, D. "Production Theory and Cost Curves," Applied Economics, 3, 1969.

CHAPTER 7

THE RIGHT OF OWNERSHIP AND THE FIRM

Methods of Organizing Production

Basically, the process of production can be organized in two ways. In the first, you might enter into a contractual agreement with one person to grow wheat on your land, with another to harvest it, with a third to store it, and with a fourth to sell it. This method of organizing production is called <u>contracting across markets</u>. You negotiate a separate agreement with contractual partners and pay each of them an agreed-upon sum of money in exchange for a specific performance.

Alternatively, you might hire those four men to work for you. In that case, you are the central contractual agent in a team production process. Contractual agreements are still present, but they are different. You pay your employees a specific sum of money (wages) in exchange for the right to tell them what to do, when to do it, and how to do it. This method of organizing production is called <u>the firm</u>. Both methods of organizing production coexist in the real world. For example, General Motors produces many parts that are needed to make cars, but it also buys some from its contractual partners. In a private-property economy, the owners of resources have strong incentives to seek the most beneficial mix of the two methods of organizing production.

Both methods of organizing production are costly. The costs of contracting across markets include identifying the lowest-cost partners, negotiating contracts, renegotiating contracts in order to adapt to changing circumstances, and reducing the probability of opportunistic behavior. However, an important advantage of contracting across markets is that the cost of shirking is borne by the shirking partner himself. He is paid the same amount of money whether he fulfills his side of the bargain in five hours or five days.

The team method of production is costly, too. The employees are paid a contractual wage per period of time regardless of their actual performance. It means that the cost (reduced output of the firm) of shirking is borne by someone other than the worker. Thus, members of the team have incentives to shirk, and the firm must then incur the cost of <u>monitoring</u> its employees. Next, the team method of production requires specialists (managers) to <u>supervise</u> the division of labor up and down the chain of production. Finally, the firm has to pay the cost of <u>metering</u> the performance of <u>individual</u> inputs. The firm's output is an inseparable bundle produced by many cooperating inputs; that is, there is no way to tell who has contributed how much to the total product. Yet, the firm's survival in competitive markets requires a positive relationship between the rewards and productivity of individual inputs.

An important advantage of the team method of production is that it enhances the allocation of inputs to their most valuable uses. The firm is a marketplace within which top management screens resources, estimates their potentials, and evaluates various production techniques. Competition in the labor and capital markets <u>within</u> the firm tends to lower the transaction costs of moving resources to their higher-valued uses relative to external (normal) competitive markets. Armen Alchian comments on the growth of major corporations as follows: "...the wealth growth of [major corporations] derives precisely from the superiority of their internal markets for exchange and reallocation of resources—a superiority arising from the greater (cheaper) information about people and proposals. Many 'knowledge effects' that would be externalistic in an ordinary market are converted into beneficial internalities within the firm; as incentives and rewards to those producing them" (A. Alchian, "Corporate Management and Property Rights," in <u>The Economics of Property Rights</u>, ed. E. Furubotn and S. Pejovich, Cambridge: Ballinger, 1974, p. 142).

The limitations on the supply of managerial skills and the complexities of large operations tend eventually to increase the costs of the team method of production relative to the cost of contracting across markets. Those firms that are successful in adjusting the mix of internal transactions and outside contracts according to their relative costs should have a better chance of survival in competitive markets. And those transaction costs differ from one industry to another. For example, the cost of supervising one hundred waiters in a restaurant is likely to exceed the cost of controlling one hundred workers on the assembly line in a manufacturing plant.

The Unit of Economic Analysis

Conventional wisdom is that a firm decides what its annual objectives are, that the government decides upon an economic policy, and that the local symphony decides to build a new concert hall. However, business firms, universities, and governments do not make decisions. Individuals do. That is why changes in the leadership of business firms, governments, and civic institutions matter. Instead of asking "Why does IBM or the U.S. government or the Dallas Symphony Association behave as it does?," it is more correct to ask "Why does the decision maker in each of those organizations behave in a certain way?" To understand the behavior of any organization, economic analysis has to concentrate on the individuals who make decisions for that institution, the rules under which they make decisions, their incentives, and the costs of evaluating their performance (i.e., transaction costs).

It follows that <u>the unit of economic analysis is the individual</u>. Thus, to conduct economic analysis of the firm in all economic systems one must recognize that: (i) all decisions are made by individuals; (ii) all decision makers have their own objectives; (iii) the behavior of every decision maker depends on the incentive structures under which that person works; and (iv) those incentives are determined by the prevailing property rights in the firm.

Economic Analysis of the Firm

In a private-property, free-market economy there are many types of business firms, such as the single proprietorship, partnerships, corporations, not-for-profit organizations, and government-regulated firms. Clearly, the market for business organizations exists in a capitalist society and provides individual members of the community with a range of choices concerning the types of business firms they are free to form. Competition in the market for organizations weeds out less efficient types of business firms according to industries and production activities. For example, the corporate firm seems better suited to capital-intensive activities, while the partnership seems to do better in services.

This chapter discusses the behavior of two types of business firms in a capitalist economy: the conventional capitalist firm and the modern corporation. The former is the basic type of business firm (the owner-manager arrangement) that is well known from standard textbooks in price theory. Although the importance of the conventional capitalist firm in a modern society has declined somewhat, an understanding of its behavior is essential for economic analysis of any type of business firm across the entire range of institutional arrangements and economic systems. The modern corporation, on the other hand, is the most important and certainly the most characteristic type of business firm in a capitalist society today. Throughout the remainder of this book we will focus on several points that relate to business firms: (i) the objectives of decision makers, (ii) the process through which those objectives are pursued, and (iii) the implications for the community as a whole.

THE CONVENTIONAL CAPITALIST FIRM

What does it mean when we say that a firm is privately owned? For example, suppose Judy wants to have a Bible shop. She rents a building, borrows money from a local bank to buy equipment, and hires several people to work for her. Laura, on the other hand, wants to run a pornography shop. She owns the building, uses her savings to buy equipment, and works alone in the shop. It would appear that Laura owns her business, while Judy has a long way to go to become the owner of the Bible shop. In fact, there is no difference between Judy and Laura. They both own their respective businesses. The ownership of a firm is not about bricks and equipment but about rights. To say that a firm is privately owned means that the owner has a bundle of rights in that firm. Those rights define the conventional capitalist firm.

The first is the right to the revenue of the firm. This is then used to pay all the inputs their contractual prices. Any residual is then retained by the owner. Both Judy and Laura own the residual that is left after they pay cooperating inputs. Judy has to make direct payments for the inputs she is using, while Laura forgoes the income she could have earned by renting the building, equipment, and her labor skills to someone else. This right creates incentives for the owner to monitor the performance of employees, to raise their joint productivity, to reward the employees for their individual efforts, and to use the right mix of the team method of production and contracts across markets to produce the desired output.

The second right in the owner's bundle is <u>the right to hire and fire members of the team</u>. This right presupposes the freedom of contract. The owner can fire employees or sue them for damages arising from a breach of contract. Employees have the same rights. They can "fire" the employer by quitting or suing for damages from a breach of contract. The owner does not, however, have the power to discipline or punish employees. Therein lies the problem with various legal and administrative rules that weaken the owner's right to withdraw from the contract with an employee (i.e., to fire him). By restricting the freedom of contract, those rules in effect raise the cost of production. That is, as the threat of firing is reduced, the owner's ability to monitor the performance of employees and to prevent shirking is impaired.

The conventional capitalist firm's third right is <u>the right to sell the two rights specified above</u>. The right to transfer one's property to others at a mutually agreed-upon price is a basic component of the right of ownership. And the market price of a firm, the owner's wealth in the firm, is the present value of the expected future residuals over the firm's life. The right to capitalize the expected future returns into their present market value is <u>specific</u> to the right of ownership. In our case, both Judy and Laura have the same right to capitalize their future residuals.

The analysis is simple and straightforward. First, we investigate the bundle of property rights that exists under various institutional arrangements; the specific rights in that bundle reveal the allocation of costs and rewards within the firm. Next, we determine the resultant incentive structures and their effects on the behavior of decision makers. Finally, we deduce the implied behavior of the firm and examine the analytical propositions yielded by the analysis against the broad facts of business experience.

The standard theory of the firm has been developed around the owner-manager firm. That model is too well known to be repeated here. However, in order to establish a perspective for our discussion of other types of business firms, let us relate the bundle of rights in the conventional firm to its implied behavior.

The owner-manager of the firm is the decision maker. He is entitled to appropriate the residual, to fire and hire cooperating inputs, and to sell those rights in an open market. Since the residual equals the difference between the firm's revenue and total costs <u>at each different rate of output</u>, the owner-manager must identify the rate of output at which the difference is the greatest in order to maximize the residual. Economic theory has developed a set of analytical tools that formalize the end result of the search for the largest residual. The equilibrium solution shows that the equimarginal principle is satisfied in each type of market (e.g., price searcher's market). Consequently, resources are in their most valuable uses.

The owner-manager has strong incentives to monitor, supervise, and meter the performance of his employees; in exchange for his effort, the owner-manager captures the entire residual. Moreover, the cost of monitoring the employees tends to be low because the owner manages the firm, knows it well, and is always present. The right to hire and fire members of the team thus assures the owner-manager of the best productive effort from the cooperating inputs.

The institutions of capitalism, on the other hand, limit the owner to the residual that is more or less equal to the opportunity cost of his own resources, including labor. As we know from the preceding chapter (and the process is worth repeating in a slightly different context), an above-average residual means that not enough of the kind of output (e.g., X) that is produced by the firm is available in the market. As the price of X goes up, the community is, in effect, saying that it wants more of X relative to other goods. Driven by their desire to maximize their own utility, other owners of resources capable of producing X respond to this request. The effect of these new entries into the production of X is to shift demand schedules of existing firms backward. The market for X is then shared by a larger number of sellers, the price of X falls, and the rate of profit follows suit. Eventually competition erodes all excess profits, the flow of resources into the industry stops, and, most importantly, the community gets the preferred mix of goods.

That is not the whole story. The flow of resources from less valuable into more valuable activity affects resource prices. The prices of the resources that are used in the production of X are bid up, and, consequently, the cost of production schedules shift upward, eating up the difference between revenues and costs. Thus, positive profits generate two responses in a private-property, free-market economy: new entries into the field of production and changes in resource prices. In the process, profits are eroded by competition, because of the lower prices paid by the consumer and higher prices received by resource owners. The owner-manager must then maximize the residual in order to earn his own opportunity costs (i.e., to break even). The objective of profit maximization is the owner's _personal_ objective. To repeat, business firms cannot have their own objectives.

Are resources ever allocated to their most valuable uses? We will never know that. Economic analysis explains how and why the institutions of capitalism create both the freedom and incentives for individuals to interact with each other in ways that transfer resources from lower- to higher-valued uses. It also explains the adjustment process and provides testable implications. However, economic analysis cannot determine with any degree of certainty that resources have ever been allocated to their most valuable uses. To say that capitalism is an efficient system means that its social and economic processes have a strong and observable tendency to move resources toward their best uses.

THE MODERN CORPORATION

Technological developments around the time of the first industrial revolution, improvements in the means of communications, and the emergence of large political entities in place of feudal princedoms made mass production of goods possible, relatively inexpensive, and profitable. However, mass production of goods requires large start-up investments in fixed assets. That is, business firms need large amounts of capital to exploit technological advances and marketing opportunities.

The rule of unlimited liability made the application of new techniques difficult to finance. With each partner held personally liable for the entire debts of the firm, it was too risky to accept additional partners. Every partner could impoverish others through incompetence or dishonesty. Also, an increase in the number of partners raised the cost of monitoring each other. Each owner had to watch the business carefully, so absentee ownership was not prudent. Thus, the rule of unlimited liability restricted an important source of capital: the combining of privately-owned resources or equity financing.

In response to economic pressures from within the system a new legal concept evolved: the law of limited liability. This law limited the liability of each owner to the market value of his investment in the firm. Equity interests were divided into small shares, which were traded in financial markets. The breaking up of equity interests into relatively small alienable shares also made it possible for corporate firms to attract funds from small individual savers. The right to participate in selecting the firm's board of directors was made proportional to the number of shares held by each investor. The corporate firm proved a most effective method of voluntarily pulling together large amounts of capital for long-lived ventures.

The owners of the corporation are entitled to capture the residual, to hire and fire cooperating inputs, and to sell those rights in financial markets. Relative to the owner-manager firm, the legal system makes no changes in the bundle of rights held by the shareholders. However, the economic system does. The ownership of a corporation is dispersed among many shareholders, so individual owners face high transaction costs of monitoring managerial decisions, detecting their weaknesses, and enforcing residual-maximizing behavior. Those costs are responsible for a major difference between the bundle of property rights of the conventional capitalist firm and that of the modern corporation. The owners of the modern corporation find that their right to hire and fire members of the team, and specifically the firm's management, is attenuated. This attenuation of the right of ownership reduces the ability of the shareholders to control the firm's decision makers. This is a significant point because top management can and does affect the shareholder's wealth. The issue can be identified as the effects of the shareholder's bundle of property rights on the behavior of the corporate firm.

Positive transaction costs enable the corporate manager to substitute away from the firm's profit to gain various benefits for himself. In our discussion here we will use the following terms: potential profit, which refers to a price-output combination at which the firm's marginal revenue and marginal costs are equal; reported profit, which is the amount of money reported to the firm's shareholders as the corporation's earnings; and survival (opportunity) profit, which is the amount of money that the resources owned by the shareholders could have earned in another use.

An important consequence of positive transaction costs is that the firm's potential and reported profits might differ. That is so because the manager (i.e., top management) could increase his total compensation at the expense of the firm's earnings by consuming a number of utility-yielding goods, such as expense accounts, plush offices, a large well-dressed staff, pleasant (but not necessarily the most efficient) coworkers, and so on. Positive transaction costs make the consumption of those goods by the manager possible because they are reported as the costs of doing business. The effect of this "indulgence" would be to increase the manager's total income over and above his contractual pay.

However, the manager's on-the-job consumption depends on the difference between the firm's potential and survival profits. The former exceeds the latter when a segment of the demand curve facing the firm lies above its average opportunity cost schedule. The standard competitive model of the firm treats this divergence as a short-run phenomenon because—in a world of zero transaction costs—new entries eliminate the excess profit via size adjustments of existing firms, lower product prices, and higher cost of inputs.

The difference between reported profits and survival profits regulates the rate of new entries. When transaction costs are positive and the manager raises his total income by on-the-job consumption, the reported profits fall short of the firm's potential profits. The flow of new entries is then inadequate to bring about the adjustment in resource allocation that would produce the preferred output-mix, and the flow of resources stops short of the efficient allocation of resources. High transaction costs could then interfere with the role of profit as an allocator of resources. For example, if the firm's demand and the average opportunity cost schedules were $P = 200 - Q$ and $AC = 75 + .25Q$, its potential profit is \$3,125. Assuming that transaction costs are greater than \$3,125, the manager can add to his income \$3,125 worth of nonpecuniary goods and conceal it from the shareholders by reporting the average cost schedule as $AC = 75 + 1.5Q$. In this very simple example, the firm's reported profit would equal its survival profit and the flow of resources to their best uses would be discouraged.

Nonpecuniary goods that the manager can purchase for himself are limited to those activities that could be justified as the cost of doing business. The consumption of nonpecuniary goods is worth something to the manager; it has its money income equivalent. For example, an all-expense paid trip to Las Vegas that cost the firm \$5,000 would generally be worth less than \$5,000 cash to the manager. Leaving tax incentives aside, \$5,000 in cash offers a greater range of choices. The manager could always use the \$5,000 to go to Las Vegas. Should he choose to use the \$5,000 for something else, the message is that a trip to Las Vegas is worth less than another bundle of goods that \$5,000 can buy. Suppose that the manager would prefer to go to Las Vegas rather than receive, say \$250 in cash. Then, the money value of an all-expense paid trip to Las Vegas lies somewhere between \$250 and \$5,000. The cost to the shareholders is \$5,000 in cash. The manager's gain is less than that. Thus, positive transaction costs create incentives for an inefficient redistribution of income within the corporation.

It would appear that attenuation of the shareholders' right to hire and fire members of the team creates, via positive transaction costs, incentives that threaten corporate efficiency by creating: (i) a lower than socially desirable flow of resources into the industry, and (ii) inefficient redistribution of income within the firm. This is only a general conclusion that could be consistent with any outcome. In order to develop it into a theory that is capable of yielding testable implications we must specify the manager's set of opportunity choices, the factors that affect the cost of purchasing nonpecuniary goods, and the factors that control the size of the manager's opportunity set.

The manager's set of opportunity choices with respect to the acquisition of nonpecuniary goods depends on (i) the manager's own estimate of transaction costs, and

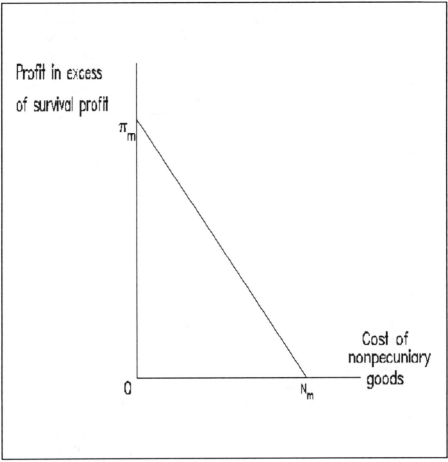

Figure 7-1.

(ii) the difference between the firm's potential profit and survival profit. The lesser of those two determines the maximum the manager can divert to his total compensation. The manager's opportunity set is represented by N_m in figure 7-1. For simplicity, the conversion rate between profits and nonpecuniary goods is assumed to be one. The maximum amount of profit that the manager can take away from the shareholders is then P_m, which will be less than the firm's excess profit when (1) < (2). It could appear that (1) the manager is free to consume N_m worth of nonpecuniary goods, and (2) the dispersion of the shareholding, via higher transaction costs, increases the manager's opportunity set. That is, the dispersion of shareholding tends to push the $P_m N_m$ line farther to the right.

Empirical evidence makes those observations untenable. How do we explain the fact that millions of individuals continue to invest in common shares? Why don't they choose other forms of investment? Why has equity financing not been driven out by investment in fixed claims? Obviously some forces exist within the system that tend to protect the interest of the shareholders. Economic analysis of the factors that affect both the manager's cost of purchasing nonpecuniary goods and the size of the opportunity set supports empirical evidence.

The Cost of Purchasing Nonpecuniary Goods. The OY_n curve in figure 7-2 relates the cost of nonpecuniary goods borne by the shareholders to their money-value equivalent as seen by the manager. The slope of this line reflects the fact that the cost of nonpecuniary goods to the firm exceeds their money worth to the manager.

The manager is paid to increase the wealth of shareholders. Thus, the present value of his future rewards is strongly correlated with his past and future performance. The manager considering the pursuit of objectives other than residual maximization must be constrained by his own estimate of the cost of such action in terms of lower expected future earnings.

In most corporations the manager receives a money bonus for reporting higher than survival profits. It means that the manager has to face a trade-off between higher reported profits and the consumption of nonpecuniary goods. Suppose that the manager's bonus is $B = bP$. At equilibrium, the manager's rate of substitution of income from additional profit for the consumption of nonpecuniary goods is (b). Since (b) is the slope of the $B = bP$ line, the manager will choose a bundle of N in figure 7-2 where the slope of OY_n is equal to (b); that is, where the money value of \$1 spent on nonpecuniary goods equals the manager's income from increasing reported profits by \$1. It follows that if (b) is greater than the increment in income derived from spending N_m dollars on nonpecuniary goods, the utility-seeking manager will move up along the $N_m P_m$ line in figure 7-1.

Let us consider two firms that are equal in everything but the dispersion of shareholding. $N_1 P_1$ and $N_2 P_2$ in figure 7-3 are opportunity sets facing their managers. If (b) equals the slope of the OY_n curve at or before N_1 in figure 7-3, the total amount spent for nonpecuniary goods (and the shareholders' loss of profit) will be the same in both firms. Point A depicts such a situation. The dispersion of shareholding does not lead to greater inefficiencies. Only if (b) equals the slope of OY_n somewhere between N_1 and N_2, say at C, will the managers spend ON_1 and OC, respectively.

Size of the Opportunity Set. The right of ownership and contractual freedom generate market forces that tend to shrink the manager's opportunity set. In financial markets, stock prices reflect the sum total of individual judgments about the future consequences of current managerial policies. Insofar as share prices reflect the present value of the expected future consequences of current managerial policies, market evaluation protects shareholders from a situation in which management has less concern for their wealth. As time goes by, market evaluation of managerial policies might prove to have been wrong. However, the manager knows that his policies and decisions are immediately scrutinized. Market evaluation of the future consequences of current managerial policies

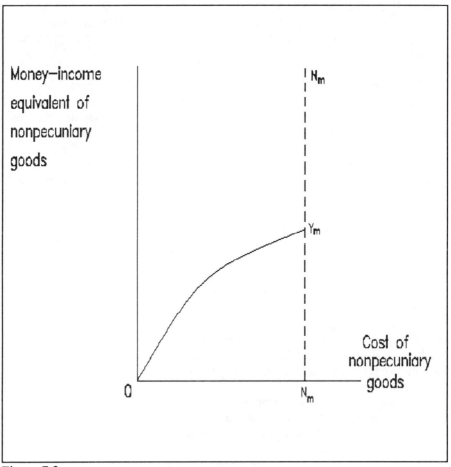

Figure 7-2.

thus provides incentives for the manager to pursue policies and decisions that increase the residual (profit). Thus, the owners' right to sell shares in a market that reflects the capitalized value of current managerial decisions raises the manager's cost of pursuing their own objectives at the expense of profit. Analytically, market evaluation of the future consequences of current managerial decisions shrinks the manager's opportunity set in figure 7-1. A number of scholarly studies have raised the question: Do dispersed ownership firms have a lower rate of growth of shareholders' wealth (allowing for both dividends and capital-value growth) than less-dispersed corporations? In general, no evidence has been found of any significant relationship between the dispersion of shareholding and changes in the wealth of shareholders.

In conclusion, technical advances and large national and international markets make mass production of goods both possible and profitable. However, to exploit those

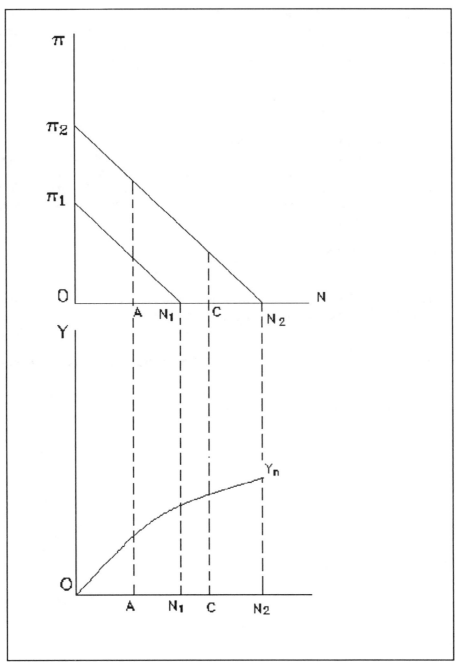

Figure 7-3.

opportunities, large initial investments in fixed assets are needed. The modern corporation has turned out to be the most effective method for pulling together large amounts of voluntary capital. The corporation has survived so well because of anonymous alienability of shares. Anonymity is enabled by limited liability. That is, shareholders need not care who the other owners are. This enables shareholders to sell without requiring the approval of other shareholders. Limited liability then facilitates anonymous alienability which permits investors to share in long-lived investments with returns beyond the time horizon of an investor.

Economic analysis and empirical evidence show that the bundle of property rights in a corporate firm provides some powerful incentives for top management to pursue policies and decisions that tend to maximize the firm's market worth. Market forces at work in a private-property, free-market economy are strong enough to protect both the shareholders' wealth and the tendency for resources to seek their highest-valued uses.

SUGGESTED READINGS

Alchian, A. and Demsetz, H. "Production, Information Costs and Economic Organization," American Economic Review, 62, 1972.

Alchian, A. and Woodward, S. "The Firm is Dead: Long Live the Firm," Journal of Economic Literature, 26, 1988.

Easterbrook, F. and Fischel, D. "Corporate Control Transactions," Yale Law Journal, 91, 1982.

Jensen, M. and Meckling, W. "Theory of the Firm: Managerial Behavior, Agency Costs and Ownership Structure," Journal of Financial Economics, 3, 1976.

CHAPTER 8

THE ATTENUATED RIGHT OF OWNERSHIP AND THE FIRM

There are many types of firms in a capitalist society in which the right of ownership is attenuated. The most significant firms in this class of business organizations are the regulated firm, the not-for-profit firm and the so-called codetermining firm. The regulated firm and the not-for-profit firm are usually discussed in microeconomics and industrial organization classes. The codetermining firm, on the other hand, is much less known and, at the same time, more relevant in the analysis of comparative economic systems. For those reasons, this chapter will discuss the codetermining firm in some detail.

The Regulated Firm

The attenuation of the bundle of property rights that defines ownership of the regulated firm consists of legal restraint on the owners' right to the residual. Regulatory agencies impose a "fair return" criterion on firms such as public utilities. With an upper limit on profits, the managers find it virtually costless to translate the firm's potential profit over and above the "fair return" into consumption of nonpecuniary goods and conceal them from the regulators by reporting higher costs of production. This observation, that has passed a variety of empirical tests, is directly related to the valuation of shares in a regulated industry. The attenuation of property rights in the residual means that the market valuation of the future consequences of current managerial policies is less significant to the shareholders of a regulated firm. Thus, an important factor that raises the price of nonpecuniary goods to the manager of a corporation is absent.

The Not-For-Profit Firm

The types of firms belonging to this category are churches, universities, mutual savings and loan associations, foundations and others. They all have a common determining characteristic: no one can claim the right to appropriate the residual. In other words, the future consequences of current managerial decisions are costly to evaluate and, under such conditions, the managers will use potential profits to obtain nonpecuniary incomes. For example, the home buyer might get the loan approved if he buys insurance from the company owned by the manager of the S&L. Also, the manager of a university's stadium has incentives to create shortages by pricing the best seats below the equilibrium price. He can use the margin between the artificially low price and the market-clearing price to trade favors.

The Codetermining Firm

BACKGROUND OF CODETERMINATION

Many West European countries have joined Germany in actively promoting labor participation in the management of business enterprises. Codetermination is a major post-war social experiment in Western Europe.

Codetermination laws differ from one country to another. However, they all have a common denominator: labor participation in the management of business firms. Labor is represented on the board of directors and is given an active role in decision-making. Where the governing authority of firms is divided into two tiers, as in Germany and the Netherlands, the labor representatives sit on the supervisory board.[1] Where there is a single board of directors, the employees' representatives take their places in that body. Labor unions have been "bribed" into supporting the codetermination movement by having been given either the right to appoint their own representatives on the board of directors, or the assurance that they will be able to control the worker representatives, or both.

Two major explanations for the introduction of codetermination in Western Europe are the enhancement of industrial democracy and the reduction of worker alienation.

The extent to which workers support codetermination is not clear. Codetermination was defeated in Switzerland, the only country in which the issue was put before the voting population. Labor's relative indifference toward codetermination is not too surprising. Workers' interests lie in the rate of growth of their incomes, not in participatory democracy. And the negotiation of collective agreements has been the best understood and historically tested method for influencing the economic and social status of labor.

The major support for codetermination in Germany comes from two groups: the intellectual community and labor union leaders. The support of union leaders for codetermination is predicated on the right—an important property right—to select workers who sit on the board of directors of business firms. In the absence of such a right, labor leaders would actually have incentives to oppose codetermination. Once they have been able to secure this right, labor leaders could use codetermination as a vehicle to increase their political and economic influence. American labor unions, on

---

[1]The supervisory board is the controlling body of the firm--like the board of directors in the U.S.

the other hand, have been less than enthusiastic about codetermination. Commenting on codetermination in Germany, the president of the Machinists Union said:

We have no interest in replacing free enterprise with a Utopian system...And we believe workers can receive a better share of free enterprise at bargaining tables than in Board rooms.[2]

Lane Kirkland of the AFL-CIO was even more blunt in ruling labor unions' support for codetermination:

The American worker is smart enough to know, in his bones, that salvation lies—not in reshuffling the chairs in the board room or the executive suite—but in the growing strength and bargaining power of his own autonomous organizations.[3]

These flat rejections by American union leaders of codetermination suggest that labor is not ready to substitute political decisions for collective bargaining on economic issues.

THE HISTORY OF CODETERMINATION IN GERMANY

Codetermination in Germany finds its source in the philosophical origins of industrial democracy. As early as 1835, Professors Robert von Mohl, Wilhelm Roscher, and Bruno Hildebrand from the University of Tubingen proposed to create "workers' committees" in business firms. They felt that capitalism had failed to emphasize moral issues. Their proposal did not amount to actual codetermination at decision-making levels. The proposal was limited to giving labor the right of hearing. The emphasis was on moral appeals to conscience rather than legal changes.

In 1848, the first elected German Parliament met in Frankfurt. Among other matters, the Parliament intended to pass legislation that was called Reichsgewerbeordnung. That was the first legislative effort to create representation of workers in business firms.

The law did not pass but an interesting development occurred in subsequent years. Many provisions of Reichsgewerbeordnung were voluntarily implemented by a number of firms. The workers and the owners of business firms found it in their self-interest to work out mutually beneficial contractual agreements without resorting to the authority of the state. The point is, of course, that parties to a contract can identify opportunities for exchange, determine their own trade-offs (which are not likely to be the same for all firms) and negotiate terms of exchange at a lower cost than a third party could

---

[2]J. Ellenberger, "The Realities of Codetermination," AFL-CIO Federationist, October 1977.

[3]Ibid.

possibly do it for them. While law applies equally to all firms, voluntary contracts allow the owner and his workers to identify and exploit opportunities that are specific to their firm.

The voluntary emergence of contractual agreements within business firms was eventually arrested by the state. Worker committee laws were enacted in Bavaria in 1900 and in Prussia in 1905. Those laws began the process of exogenous changes in the employer-employee relationship. Instead of endogenous development of contractual agreements that could vary from one firm to another in accordance with their own specific problems, the state began to impose a set of uniform rules on all business firms.

In 1920, the Works Council law was enacted. It profited workers with the right of hearing in social and personnel questions. In 1922, a new law was passed. According to that law one or two employees must be seated on supervisory councils of business firms. It was the first law on codetermination in Germany. The development that began in 1848 with a proposal to establish workers' councils has eventually led to labor participation in the management of business firms.

In 1946, the Military Government passed the so-called Act 22 which reestablished Works Councils. In 1951, the law on the Codetermination of Employees on the Supervisory Boards and Boards of Management of Enterprises in the Coal Mining, Iron and Steel Producing Industry was enacted. The stage was then set for the current phase in the development of codetermination in Germany.

The basic framework of labor participation in the management of business firms in today's Germany is determined by the following three laws:

The Montan Act of 1951

The Works Constitution Act of 1952 (revised in 1972)

The Codetermination Act of 1976

The Montan Act of 1951 covers all firms in the mining and the iron and steel producing industries that employ at least 1,000 workers. The supervisory council of a firm in the Montan industry consists of eleven elected members. The stockholders and the employees appoint four members each. In addition, the stockholders, as well as the employees, appoint an additional external member who cannot be a representative either of a union or of an employer organization nor can he be employed by that firm or otherwise connected with it in some economic way. The eleventh member is jointly elected by all supervisory board members.

The Works Constitution Act of 1952 stipulates employees' rights at three different levels: the personal, the shop, and the decision-making levels of the firm. On the personal level each employee is granted the right to information, hearing, and discussion of issues such as working conditions, hiring, firing, and layoffs. On the plant level, the act prescribes the institution of a works council. The works councils are elected by the employees and vary in size. In general, the function of the worker council is to act as a social agent for the employees. On the decision-making level of the firm, the Works Constitution Act stipulates that in firms that employ more than 500 people, one-third of the members of the supervisory council must consist of labor representatives. The employee representatives are directly elected by secret ballot. They are not appointed by labor unions. Thus, the Works Constitution Act introduced a type of codetermination that is consistent with the conservative Catholic philosophy.

The Codetermination Act of 1976 applies to all business firms that have more than 2,000 employees (about 470 firms). The Supervisory Board has 12 members. Of these 12, six are representatives of the shareholders and six are representatives of the employees. The rights of the German workers today can be summarized as follows: The rights to consultation and collective bargaining on the plant level are ensured by the works council of the firm which is composed of employees only. The codetermination rights on the decision level are supposed to be enforced by the employees' representatives on the supervisory board. The supervisory boards of the firms in the coal, iron and steel industry are subject to equal representation of the shareholders and the employees. German firms with more than 2,000 workers also have an equal representation on their boards, but the chairman who holds the casting vote in cases of a deadlock is elected by the shareholders. The firms with less than 2,000 employees have a minority employer representation on their supervisory boards.

CODETERMINATION AND PROPERTY RIGHTS

Codetermination triggers institutional restructuring that is exogenous to the system. The laws change the prevailing relationship between the shareholders, managers, employees, and labor unions. Consequently, they affect the location of decision-making powers, appropriability of rewards, and the relationship between risk taking and bearing of costs in labor participatory firms. Through those effects, the laws change the way the game is played, especially managerial decisions, wage negotiations, vector of labor compensation (fringe benefits, share of profit, contractual wage, etc.), employment policies, and equity financing. The relevant issue for economic analysis is to look into the effects of the institutional restructuring on the allocation and use of resources in the community.

Whatever the facade of words, terms such as "industrial democracy" and "labor participation" are merely code words for wealth transfers. Codetermination shifts the responsibility for decisions to a group of people who are not at all affected by the consequences of the decisions. No matter what the outcome of the decision is, the worker receives contractual wages—his risk is limited. Codetermination puts stockholders into an uninviting situation—if the corporation makes an investment decision that is successful, the gains are shared with labor. If, on the other hand, the investment decision is not successful, stockholders alone bear the losses. Codetermination violates the risk-reward relationship which, in turn, must raise the cost (reduce the supply) of equity capital.

Involuntary codetermination restricts individuals' freedom to negotiate the most beneficial organizational forms. The freedom of contract means that labor participation in corporate management could emerge out of voluntary contractual arrangements as have many other types of firms. Indeed, there are cases in which codetermination has emerged voluntarily. If codetermination raises the firm's productivity or bestows benefits on labor in excess of stockholders' costs, why do we need <u>laws</u> on codetermination?

Codetermination interferes with the right of ownership. Labor participation in the management of business firms implies the political action of granting labor a voice in areas of decision-making that have traditionally been the prerogative of ownership, either directly or through hired representatives (e.g., managers). What is important to bear in mind is that current decisions about the use of resources have future consequences (measured by changes in the value of resources). Different property rights arrangements imply different assignments of benefits and losses from current decisions. In a private-property capitalist economy the owner bears all the future consequences of his (or hired representatives') current decisions.

Codetermination causes a separation between decision making and risk bearing. In a codetermining firm those who participate in decision-making processes do not bear <u>all</u> changes in the value of the firm's assets. Codetermination then attenuates the right of ownership. Attenuation of ownership means a change in the quality of decisions. Given the workers' time horizon, which is limited to their expected employment by the firm, the labor participatory firm has more incentives to choose investment alternatives and business policies that shift incomes forward and postpone costs. For example, consider two investment alternatives of equal costs. The expected present value of one alternative is $1,000 while the other yields only $750. However if the returns from the first alternative are discounted over a period of 20 years and those of the second over only five years, workers could easily push the management in the direction of choosing the less profitable one. Even in the absence of sharing in the firm's profits, wage negotiations and their perception of job security would provide workers with incentives to prefer business policies that promise larger annual earnings over a limited time period to those policies that maximize the firm's worth.

Codetermination is a costly political reform. Some important costs of codetermination are:

(i)   <u>Monopoly in the market for business organizations</u>. There is no law in the U.S. or Western Europe that prohibits codetermination. If that type of organization were really efficient, it would have emerged contractually. The fact that the law has to mandate the codetermining firm, and to protect it from competition by other types of firms, is evidence of its relative inefficiency.

(ii)   <u>Increased cost of equity capital</u>. The fact that stockholders must be forced by law to accept codetermination is the best evidence that they are adversely affected by it. Labor representatives on the board of directors represent those who have no claim on the capitalized value of assets. A major consequence has to be a higher cost of equity capital to offset lower returns to the holders of stocks and bonds.

(iii)   <u>Changes in the pattern of investment</u>. Labor representatives on the board of directors have incentives to push for investment decisions that promise to maximize near-term cash flow.

(iv)   Reallocation of resources. An increase in the cost of equity capital means that the average rate of return in labor participating firms will fall. The result will be a shift of capital toward non-participatory alternatives such as smaller firms, human capital and foreign investments.

The major effect of codetermination is a transfer of wealth from the stockholders to the employees. This redistribution of wealth has social and economic consequences which arise from the interference by codetermination with the essential characteristics of a private property capitalist economy: the capitalization into the present market-value of foreseeable future consequences of current decisions. This interference with the working of capitalism stems from changes in the prevailing relationship between shareholders; managers, employees and labor unions; incentive structures; and the strength of the link between decision-making and who actually bears the cost or reward from changes in the market value of assets.

SUGGESTED READINGS

McAvoy, P. Regulated Industries and the Economy, New York: Norton, 1979.

Posner, R. "Taxation by Regulation," Bell Journal of Economics and Management Science, 22, 1971.

Stigler, G. "The Optimum Enforcement of Law," Journal of Political Economy, 78, 1970.

Stigler, G. "The Extent of the Market," Journal of Law and Economics, 28, 1985.

Watrin, C. "The Case of Codetermination in West Germany," in Socialism: Institutional, Philosophical and Economic Issues (S. Pejovich, ed.), Dordrecht: Kluwer Academic Publishers, 1987.

Winston, C. "Conceptual Developments in the Economics of Transportation," Journal of Economic Literature, 57, 1985.

CHAPTER 9

THE ROLE OF FINANCIAL MARKETS IN A PRIVATE-PROPERTY, FREE-MARKET ECONOMY

The basic issue we addressed in chapters 5 and 6 was how much of A a person is willing to give up <u>now</u> for one more unit of B <u>now</u>. However, many goods provide services over a period of time. Thus, we must also ask what quantity of A a person would give up <u>now</u> for one more unit of A to be received <u>later</u>. In general, the more we eat today, the less we will have to eat tomorrow.

All societies must face the same set of problems: how to allocate resources between present and future consumption, how to evaluate the goods that provide future services, how to provide an orderly flow of consumer goods between production dates (e.g., wheat between harvests), and how to encourage the growth of wealth. The methods of solving those problems differ from one type of institutional arrangement to another. As one would expect, much depends on who makes decisions about the allocation of resources between today and tomorrow, and who bears the risk of those decisions. For an effective analysis of this situation, it is important to know how different property rights affect these issues.

In a private-property, free-exchange economy financial markets are responsible for performing all those functions. All decisions about the allocation of resources between today and tomorrow are made by either their owners or the people (specialists) they hire for the explicit purpose of making those decisions. The owners bear the risk of changes in the value of their assets. We have already discussed the importance of financial markets in encouraging corporate managers to seek the most valuable uses for resources. This chapter shall briefly explain a few other features of financial markets.

The Rate of Interest and Expectations

In a private-property economy those goods that provide future services are valued in financial markets. The market price of those goods is the present value of their expected future services discounted at the prevailing rate of interest.

The rate of interest is the money price of earlier rather than later availability of nonmoney commodities. Just as the money price of A places a value on the bundle of other commodities that must be forgone, the rate of interest is the rate of exchange between one unit of A now and a bundle of A tomorrow. Earlier availability of goods has value because it offers a greater range of choices than later availability (sometimes called preference for current over future consumption) and an opportunity to use goods now to produce more goods tomorrow (the rate of growth of wealth). Thus, the rate of interest is _positive_ in all societies. However, the effect of the interest rate on (i) the extent of exchange between the present amount of a good and the bundle of future goods for which they can be traded and (ii) the rate of growth depends on prevailing property rights.

The rate of interest is much more than a cost of investment. A change in the rate of interest means a change in the present value of capital goods relative to their costs of production. For example, suppose an asset costing $1,000 has a life expectancy of ten years and promises to return (after all costs) $142 per year. The net productivity of this investment is about 7 percent. At 6 percent interest, the present market value of this project would be $1,045. At 8 percent interest, the value of the project would be $952. The rate of interest is then a means of expressing present prices of capital goods relative to their current costs of production. It is incorrect to think of the rate of interest as being only the rate at which we lend or borrow funds.

Anticipation of future events also affects present prices of assets. Suppose a firm announces a new product, one which is expected to do well in the market. The price of a share of the firm's common stock would increase to reflect the new expectations about the flow of future services. On the other hand, suppose that a firm is located in a country where a political party advocating restrictions on private-property rights is gaining public support. Expectations about the firm's future flow of residual would be revised downward, and the price per share would drop. Also, the shareholders' wealth is influenced by what happens to their firm in the future, whereas the firm's employees have more incentives to be concerned about what happens to the firm now. In order to enhance the employees' interest in future consequences of their present actions, many firms have revised the vector of compensation for their employees by supplementing the salary (wage) system with stock options, profit-sharing, or other benefit schemes.

Since expectations about future events are continuously revised and people's own circumstances are changing, there is constant buying and selling of assets in financial markets. In financial markets, people can purchase basically four types of assets: (i) claims to future amounts of money (bond markets), (ii) claims to capital goods (stock markets), (iii) claims to future consumer goods (futures markets), and (iv) claims to land and buildings (real estate markets). The rights of ownership provide for the transferability of those claims among individuals who have different expectations about the future. Contractual freedom pushes the rate of return implicit in the price of capital, the rate of interest on bonds, and the value of earlier availability of goods (i.e., the community's valuation of future income relative to current consumption) toward an equality by moving activity among different markets. In the process, the extent of exchange is maximized. For example, a person invests $1 and receives $1.20 one year later. The net productivity of investment is 20 percent. If the going rate of interest was 10 percent and the return of $20 was anticipated by some people, the asset would have been quickly revalued to about $110.

An alert reader must have already recognized that the right of ownership and contractual freedom must exist if the expected future consequences of current decisions are to be sold and bought at their present prices; that is, if the capitalization process is to function. Restrictions on the right of ownership and/or contractual freedom would reduce the value of assets and leave some exchange opportunities unrealized. In either case, financial markets would fail to establish "correct" present prices, that is, the prices that reflect current expectations about future events.

The capitalization process controls the rate at which we use our resources. Consider a privately owned tree. The tree is a capital good. It takes resources to produce it, and it is expected to yield returns (increments in the value of lumber in live trees). Throughout the life of the tree, the owner can choose between keeping it alive or cutting it down and investing the proceeds from the sale of lumber elsewhere. Thus, the owner will be influenced by the relationship between the rate of growth of lumber in live trees and the average expected rate of return from investment in other assets.

As long as the rate of growth in the value of lumber in live trees exceeds the rate of interest, the owner will gain more wealth by keeping the tree alive. Since the value of lumber in live trees increases at a decreasing rate (except for a few early years), its rate of growth would approach the rate of interest. The rate of interest might change, however, and approach the rate of growth of live trees. In either case, the owner will have incentive to harvest the tree when the two rates become approximately equal.

Thus, it is not true that human greed consumes our resources too fast. The owner, driven by self-interest, gains by conserving the tree—by capitalizing the future lumber values to present values to determine the best time to harvest the tree. But suppose that no one had private-property rights (ownership) in the tree. Then no one would have any incentive to conserve the tree. I might prefer to wait for the tree to grow but someone else would not. Thus, I have incentives to cut it down without any regard to the relationship between the rate of growth in lumber and the rate of interest.

It is a good exercise in understanding economic processes under alternative institutional arrangements to ask what happened to the buffalo in North America. Why hasn't the same thing happened to cattle? The answer lies in the difference in property rights. The right of ownership creates incentives that channel our "greed" into a search for the most valuable uses for resources. Other forms of property rights have been less successful in generating this kind of incentive.

Conservationists frequently call for governmental controls over the use of some resources. Their argument rests on two points: First, they assert that the actual rate of saving of those resources should be greater, and the state should therefore force us to cut our consumption. Second, they claim that many of us have the wrong idea about the most valuable use for those resources. This argument is simply an assertion that certain people should not have their preferences satisfied.

The Allocation of Consumable Goods Over Time[*]

Suppose the wheat crop (assuming only one type of wheat was planted) has been harvested. Must the farmers store it, gradually selling a bit each month until the next harvest? Farmers do not want to keep so much of their wealth in the form of wheat. They prefer to sell the wheat as soon as it is harvested, letting someone else store it, bear the risk of changes in its value, and decide how much to sell to consumers each month. The millers, who grind the wheat grain into flour, do not want to store a year's supply of wheat in advance. Even consumers refuse to take on this duty, because they do not want to make commitments so far ahead. But there is a very simple way of inducing someone to store the wheat. If people refuse to store the harvested wheat, its price falls. There is an increased prospect of profit in buying wheat at the lower price, storing it, and selling it later at a higher price after some of the wheat is consumed. In a capitalist open-market system, anyone may buy wheat at harvest time in a self-serving endeavor to make a profit by selling it later at a higher price. This is known as speculation.

The market for these transactions is the futures market. That market is character-ized in folklore as a place where speculators gamble on the price of wheat, corn, and so forth, causing prices to fluctuate even more as they are pushed down when farmers sell and pushed up when consumers buy. This folklore about futures markets reflects the fact that many people do not understand the special character of a "futures" contract. An illustration will reveal the crux. Suppose you are a flour miller converting wheat grain to flour. You want your income to depend on efficient milling operations, not on the changing price of unmilled wheat grain. A drop in the price of wheat grain, after you have bought the grain, could ruin you. You can isolate your business income from that risk.

You can buy the wheat yourself before receiving any orders for the flour you will make from the wheat, at the same time placing a side contract with someone else, so that if the price of the wheat goes up (giving you a gain in wealth) you will give the gain to him, but he will compensate you for a drop in value of the wheat you are holding. You are "betting" with him on the value of wheat. In either event, your wealth is unaffected whether the wheat price rises or falls. This means of insulating your wealth from contingent events is called hedging. This is one thing the futures contract does. It is the cheapest known way of separating ownership of the wheat by the miller from his bearing the risk of fluctuations in wheat value.

Perhaps the reason futures contracts are so widely regarded as sheer gambling is that they separate the risk-bearing element so cleanly, efficiently, and openly from the use

[*]From University Economics: Elements of Inquiry, Third Edition, by Armen A. Alchian and William R. Allen © 1972 by Wadsworth Publishing Company, Inc. © 1964, 1967 by Wadsworth Publishing Company, Inc. All rights reserved. Reprinted with permission of the publisher.

of the wheat, and therefore appear to be only devices to satisfy hungry speculators, bent on profiting from unanticipated changes in supplies or demands.

Who determines the rate at which the harvested stock of wheat is consumed? No one. Some thing does, and that thing is the current price of wheat relative to expected future prices.

Past experience, the prime source of knowledge, provides the basis for expectations of what the price of wheat will do between harvests. And the closer the current price is to future price expectations, the more will speculators be willing to sell now, because profit prospects of holding wheat are diminished.

The present (spot) price of wheat is affected by the consumption demand and the supply of wheat coming into consumption channels from storage. If current consumption demand should increase, the current spot price of wheat will rise and reduce prospects of profits from storing wheat, thus inducing storers of wheat to sell more wheat to consumption channels. The relationship between the current "spot" price for wheat and the price that is expected in the future affects the rate at which wheat will be released from storage into consumption. And the prices (futures prices) of current contracts for future deliveries of wheat reflect beliefs and predictions about the future price. Why? People make contracts to deliver or to accept delivery in the future and will pay or be paid in the future at prices agreed upon now. This means that the prices now agreed upon for future delivery are predictions of what the price will be in the future; no one would purchase and store wheat today at a price higher than what he thinks it will be in six months. Nor would anyone sell wheat forward (that is, contract to make future delivery) for a price less than he thought it would be in the future.

Suppose it is now September, and you can buy wheat (in 5,000-bushel lots) for $2 a bushel for immediate delivery—on the "spot." Today's spot price of wheat is $2. Today, you also can make a futures contract for delivery of wheat upon payment of $2.10 per bushel next May. The price of $2.10 agreed to now, but to be paid in May, is called the May futures price (formed in September of the prior year). The difference between the two prices (spot and futures) usually covers storage, insurance, and interest costs of holding wheat in the interim, because of competition among speculators.

Futures prices in today's futures markets provide predictions of what the spot price will be in the future. If anyone can make a better prediction of next May's spot price of wheat, he can quickly reap a fortune. For example, suppose the present futures price for May is $2.10, a price lower than a trader believes will actually exist in May of next year. He could place a bet in this futures market that the currently quoted May futures price is too low and that next May's spot prices will be higher. The process for placing this bet is to buy now a futures contract for, say, 5,000 bushels of wheat at $2.10 a bushel—to be delivered to him and paid for next May. He agrees to this contract now in September at the currently quoted May futures price of $2.10 per bushel. Then he nervously waits until May; if the spot price next May is higher than $2.10, he can take delivery of the wheat and resell at the higher price, reaping the difference as a profit. If the price is lower, he suffers a loss.

Of course, for every buyer of a contract for future wheat, there must be a seller who promises to deliver wheat in the future. That seller may believe the spot price in the future will be lower than the current futures price, and, if _he_ is correct, <u>later</u> he can buy wheat at the lower spot price in the future and deliver it to the buyer for the currently agreed-to higher futures price. That seller may also be a <u>hedger</u>.

We are now in a position to see how higher demand, higher spot prices, and a consequent faster rate of consumption out of inventories has an effect on futures prices. As the hedging inventory holders sell their wheat for current consumption at a more rapid rate, they have less wheat to hedge, so they therefore want to cancel (buy back) their commitments to speculators to deliver wheat in the future. The increased demand to buy back futures contracts, as hedgers reduce their inventories, raises futures prices, which restrains hedgers' willingness to sell so much current wheat.

We have an answer to our question of who bears the risk of value changes of the wheat between harvests. Under the incentive of increased wealth anyone can shoulder this risk—not because he <u>intends</u> to perform some socially useful function (rationing wheat from harvest to harvest). Private interest motivates this method—a method not consciously designed or motivated by the social storage purpose but one discovered by a trial-and-error selective process and not widely understood by members of society, not even by many of the speculators and farmers.

Do the speculative markets, to which everyone has access, predict future prices more accurately than some other possible scheme? The organized futures market in onions was abolished by federal law in 1959. Among those who wanted the markets closed were firms that specialized in assembling, storing, sorting, and distributing onions to retailers. Without an open futures market, information about onion conditions was less widely dispersed; insiders, such as these processors, can benefit by their more exclusive access to information and opportunity to buy and sell onions. How they managed to induce enough members of Congress to vote for that legislation is a question for your professor of political science. However, as it happens, this prohibition provided a fine opportunity to compare the behavior of prices of onions with and without futures markets. The record is clear. With the organized futures markets for onions, the forecasts were more accurate than when they were closed. In particular, spot consumers' prices varied less between crops with open speculative markets than did those without them. In other words, the forecasts of future prices—the futures prices—influenced spot prices more accurately toward what was going to happen, avoiding large fluctuations when spot prices respond to unforeseen events.

How should the consequences of forecasting errors be borne? It has been contended that only experts should be allowed to make speculative decisions; this would avoid the errors made by less-informed people. To this contention there are several responses. First, if experts are now better informed than the consensus of the markets, they could easily become wealthy very rapidly by speculating. Furthermore, experts' superior information would help move the present spot and futures prices in the "correct" directions. Second, there is the problem of finding experts. Although the government may employ a group of specialists, the specialists are not necessarily superior forecasters. The predictions of "experts" differ. If, despite these inherent difficulties, a group of experts were responsible for making forecasts and controlling the storage rates, who bears the losses when the forecasts are erroneous? In other words, how are the consequences of ignorance about future events to be allocated among people? Should we require that all people, regardless of individual wishes, bear, in proportion to their taxes, the changing wealth values of the stocks of stored commodities? If the speculative activity were a voluntary arrangement with open futures markets, those who want to bear more of the risk can hold more of their wealth in the form of goods to be stored, and those who want to be relieved of those risks can own other forms of wealth. This arrangement points up one fundamental attribute of a capitalist system: It permits individuals to adjust their patterns of risk bearing, as well as their pattern of consumption. If you wish to avoid the wealth changes of certain goods, you can choose to own other goods. You can concentrate your risks on a few particular goods or on a large class of goods. Complete avoidance of risk is not possible, but with open markets and private-property rights people can choose the types of risk they can best live with.

People differ in their attitudes or willingness to bear the risk of losing wealth because of price fluctuation. Given these differences, each individual can move to a preferred position, if he will let the risks be borne by those who are more confident about a price increase or are more willing to bear risks inherent in the uncertainty of futures prices. Of course, he will have to pay them to bear those risks, but if they regard carrying such risks as less burdensome than he does, the cost will be less than if he bore the risks himself. Abolishing futures markets raises the costs of performing the storage function, because it prevents those who are more willing to bear these risks from doing so and forces the less willing persons to bear these risks.

Sometimes it is mistakenly believed that speculation can be avoided by legally imposing fixed prices on commodities. This is identical to painting the thermometer to avoid a fever. Price controls do not prevent shifts in demand or supply. Instead, they merely restrict individuals' ability to adjust (by exchange) to differences in interpersonal values among goods as well as among risks.

The Growth of Wealth

Economic growth is the rate of change in GNP from one year to another. It measures the increase in the value of output that is available to the community. The rate of growth is often expressed in constant prices and on a per capita basis in order to eliminate the effects of inflation and the growth of population, respectively. An increasing flow of goods makes people better off. It is thus important to investigate the effects that alternative institutional structures have on the rate of economic growth.

The idea of economic development has dominated both the aspirations and the public policy of most countries since the end of World War II. Yet, only a few countries have been able to accomplish anything in this area. A number of reasons have been offered to explain the observed differences in economic development. Most developing countries attribute their economic problems to a lack of resources or the shortage of capital or to exploitation by their former colonial masters. After several decades of being sovereign nations, most developing countries are in much worse economic shape than they were in the years following their independence. So, the exploitation argument for economic backwardness is being abandoned.

A view that developing nations have an inadequate resource base was behind the United Nations resolution known as the New International Economic Order. The purpose of this resolution was to institutionalize the transfer of resources from the developed to developing nations (from the North to the South). The New International Economic Order was a poorly conceived attempt to translate a privilege of applying for foreign aid and technical assistance into the right to demand it.

Empirical evidence does not support the contention that the availability of resources ensures a high rate of economic growth. Much seems to depend on what people do with whatever resources they happen to have. If an inadequate resource base is responsible for poverty in India, why is a resource-poor country like Japan doing so well? If overpopulation is a problem in China, why are people in Hong Kong so much better off? The Soviet Union is surely better endowed with resources than Belgium, but its leaders are having a rather hard time clothing, feeding, and housing their people. For centuries the Texas plains were among the most uninviting areas of the world but within a century have become one of the most affluent regions on earth.

It is also difficult to accept the argument that the shortage of capital is holding back economic development in Eastern Europe, Africa, and Asia. Capital is a very mobile resource which is continuously looking for higher yield opportunities. The flow of capital from the developed to developing nations has not been sufficient to equalize marginal yields. The reasons cited for this insufficient flow are political instabilities, currency controls, restrictions on the freedom of contract, and attenuation of property rights. Moreover, many developing countries have, in the name of economic growth, overtaxed their people, cut back on current consumption, mortgaged resources to foreign banks, and imposed "forced" savings to finance political objectives.

Empirical evidence suggests a simple observation. Those countries that have shown respect for the right of ownership and freedom of contract have done better than other countries regardless of their respective availability of resources, high or low rates of savings, or growth-oriented economic policies. The differences in economic develop-ment seem to arise from the interplay between institutions and the flow of innovation.

Property Rights and Innovation

Innovation could be the development of a new good, the opening up of a new market, a new source of supply, or a new method of production. By injecting a novelty into the flow of economic life, the innovator offers the community a new choice. The voluntary acceptance or rejection of the innovation reveals its evaluation by the community. Thus, voluntary acceptance of innovation is a major source of economic development. Unfortunately, innovation cannot be planned. Business firms and governments cannot decide to have three innovations per month. Innovation is triggered by the individual, who must perceive an opportunity to do something that is new, be willing to face the risk of introducing a novelty into the system, and have the power to carry it out. The issue of economic development thus boils down to the expected effects of alternative institutions on the pool of those who are free to innovate and have access to financial markets.

Since innovators do not come from a specific social class, the larger the number of people who have the freedom to innovate, the higher is the probability of increasing the flow of innovation, all other things being the same. Three important factors determine the pool of people who are free to innovate: the right to choose the method of organizing production, the right to acquire resources, and the right to use them. In a private-property, free-exchange economy, all people (except, for example, convicts and mental patients) have the right to acquire resources and to use them to pursue any lawful activity, including innovation. The owners of resources (or their hired managers) can choose from a variety of organizational structures ranging from small proprietorships to large corporations, and from cooperatives to not-for-profit firms. A private-property economy places no restrictions on the freedom to innovate. However, the right of ownership has been attenuated in many activities, thus interfering with the owner's right of exclusive use of an asset or its transferability. Codetermination laws in Germany prescribe a definite method for organizing production in large firms. License requirements for entry into many occupations are quite common in Western Europe. The regulation of pharmaceutical products in the United States offers an example of the consequences of restrictions on the right to use one's assets. Karl Brunner wrote:

> The tragically crippled and deformed babies resulting from the use of thalidomide by pregnant women influences . . . regulatory policies. The measures implemented raised the costs of development for new products by a large factor. . . . Innovation declined by a sharp margin and the appearance of new drugs sharply contracted. . . . A policy addressed to minimize the probability of bad products maximized at the same time the probability of NOT having useful drugs. (K. Brunner, "The Limits of Economic Policy," in Socialism: Institutional, Philosophical and Economic Issues, ed. S. Pejovich, Kluwer Academic Publishers, 1987, pp. 41-2)

It would be difficult to argue that regulatory policies have no benefits, but they do impose some heavy social costs. Restrictions on the method of organizing production raise the cost of equity capital in financial markets. License requirements reduce the number of people who have the right to acquire resources. Protectionism and monopoly privileges limit one's right to use resources. In general, the attenuation of property rights restricts the freedom to innovate and raises the cost of venture capital in financial markets.

A successful innovation yields benefits in excess of what the bundle of resources used by the innovator was earning before. Positive gains are created within the system through the emergence of new exchange opportunities and institutional forms that enough people want to exploit. In financial markets, the innovator can choose to appropriate the expected future benefits from his investment in one lump sum now. The manager of a firm captures the benefits of innovation in the market for managers, where his current performance determines his future income. Also, the threat of a hostile takeover has, through financial markets where the price per share is determined, an effect on the corporate manager. It raises his cost of choosing routine (safe) invest-ments. To alleviate the threat, the manager must continuously search for new investment opportunities.

Codetermination in West Germany attenuates the right of ownership because it raises the cost of equity capital in financial markets. Unlike the shareholders, who have an unlimited time horizon (because of the capitalization process), the workers can capture the benefits only as a stream of periodic payments and only for as long as they stay with the firm. They have incentives to push for safe, routine investments. In 1984, G. Benelli, a Swiss economist, found that the variations in returns on shares in industries that have been affected by codetermination have been the lowest compared to other industries within and outside West Germany.

Freedom to acquire and use resources is not the same thing as having the actual power to get them. I have the freedom to acquire resources, but I might not be able to obtain funds to carry out my innovation. Thus, efficient financial markets in which new ideas are evaluated and accepted or rejected by profit-seeking individuals are essential for economic development. They match the quantity of financial assets demanded with the quantity supplied, at prices that reflect contractual agreements on various issues, including risks and uncertainty. The ability to acquire an asset in financial markets depends on the borrower's having enough resources (including the market evaluation of his expected profits) to pay for it and on the lender's having a bundle of rights in the asset that he is willing to transfer, at a price the borrower is willing to pay.

In a capitalist economy, individuals evaluate a novelty in competitive markets. The freedom of contract incorporates their individual judgments about the novelty into relative prices, which, in turn, tell us whether or not the innovation has enriched the social opportunity set.

In conclusion, all societies must allocate resources between today and tomorrow, evaluate the goods that provide future services, ration consumable goods over time, provide financial means for investment projects with varying degrees of risk, and price the consumer's preference for present over future consumption. In a private-property, free-market economy those essential functions are performed in financial markets. To understand the working of a capitalist economy, it is essential to understand financial markets.

SUGGESTED READINGS

Greenspan, A. "Commercial Banks and the Central Bank in a Market Economy," paper presented at Spaso House, Moscow, October 10, 1989.

Hirshleifer, J. Price Theory and Applications, New Jersey: Prentice Hall, 1984, chapter 14.

McCloskey, D. The Applied Theory of Price, New York: McMillan, 1982, chapter 26.

Posner, R. Economic Analysis of Law, New York: Little Brown & Co., 1986, chapter 15.

PART THREE

THE SOVIET-TYPE ECONOMY

CHAPTER 10

THE HISTORY AND DEVELOPMENT OF THE SOVIET UNION

THROUGH THE 1980S

The Soviet Union is the largest country in the world. It spreads over two continents, covers almost one-sixth of the world's land surface, and is two and one-half times as large as the United States. The Soviet Union occupies more than half of Europe and about two-fifths of Asia. The total population in the Soviet Union is about 300 million.

The Soviet Union or, more correctly, the Union of Soviet Socialist Republics (USSR), was known as the Russian Empire or simply Russia until the 1917 revolution. Even today it is not unusual to hear many people refer to the Soviet Union by its traditional name, Russia.

The Soviet Union has more than one hundred nationality groups. National groups in the USSR have their own languages, traditions, customs, and culture. Unlike the U.S., which is also rich with many national groups, the Soviet Union has never been called a "melting pot." National groups in the Soviet Union live in well-defined regions; even young people do not easily move away from their homes to other areas of the country. The Soviet people prefer to stick with their own kind.

The administrative divisions in the Soviet Union reflect the importance of ethnic origin. The country is divided into fifteen Union Republics, twenty Autonomous Republics, eight Autonomous Regions, and ten Districts. Each of these administrative units is named after the area's dominant national group. Many other national groups are too small to have an administrative area of their own.

There are fifteen major national groups in the Soviet Union. Those fifteen national groups account for about 90 percent of the total population, with Russians being the largest national group. Slavic peoples (Russians, Ukrainians, and Belorussians) make up more than three-fourths of the total population in the country. (Table 1 lists all major national groups.)

Density of the Soviet population varies from one area of the country to another. In some parts of the Soviet Union, such as Moldavia and the Ukraine, the number of people per square mile exceeds 200. Some parts of the country are virtually empty. Siberia covers about 43 percent of the USSR and has about five people per square mile.

Table 1. Population by Union Republic (1979 Soviet census figures)

Republic	Population (Millions)	% of Population Russian
Russian Soviet Federated Socialist Republic	137	83
Ukrainian	50	21
Uzbek	15	11
Kazakh	15	41
Belorussian	10	12
Azerbaijan	6	8
Georgian	5	7
Moldavian	4	13
Tadzhik	4	10
Kirghiz	4	26
Lithuania	3	9
Armenian	3	2
Turkmen	3	13
Latvia	3	33
Estonia	1	28
TOTAL Soviet Union	263	52

History of Russia Before 1917

THE KIEVAN STATE

The first Russian state was established in the ninth century around the city of Kiev. The Kievan state grew fast and reached its "golden era" in the period from 980 to 1050. Accomplishments of the first Russian state during that period were many. The first law code in Russia was enacted, diplomatic relations were established with many European princes, and Christianity became the state religion. The introduction of Christianity had profound social implications in the Kievan state. The Russian Orthodox church quickly became a strong integrating force for all the different Slavic groups. It contributed to the development of the arts and literature in Russia. Artists and architects came from Europe to build and paint churches, and monks began to write books and chronicles in

Slavic languages. The Russian Orthodox church also became the repository of Russian tradition and culture.

The source of prosperity of the first Russian state was trade. As trade routes shifted to the eastern Mediterranean (especially after the Crusades), however, the importance of Kiev as a major trading center declined. The decline of trade brought the golden era of the Kievan state to an end.

In 1228, Genghis Khan's Tartars began their conquest of Russia by defeating Russian princes in a major battle. When the Tartars entered Kiev in 1290, their conquest of Russia was completed. Russia became a part of the Tartars' empire called the Golden Horde. The Tartar rule in Russia lasted two centuries, until Prince Ivan III threw them out of Russia in 1486.

THE RISE OF MOSCOW

The first known mention of Moscow goes back to the mid-twelfth century when the city was a small military outpost. Unlike Kiev, Moscow prospered during the Tartar rule; its princes got wealthier and its territory grew larger. In 1330 the Russian Orthodox church moved its seat to Moscow. From that time on, Moscow rather than Kiev became the center of religious life in Russia and a repository of its culture and tradition.

The first Moscow ruler to be crowned the "Tsar of Russia" was Ivan IV (1547-1584), better known as Ivan the Terrible. Not all was bad in Russia during the years of Ivan the Terrible, however. He was a social reformer and a successful warrior. In the 1550s, Ivan enacted a law code which seated local representatives in administrative bodies of local governments and in courts. As a warrior, Ivan conquered western Siberia, and reached the Caspian Sea.

In order to wage his wars, Ivan needed a permanent army. He created such an army by simply exchanging land for a man's promise of military service, whenever called to arms, for life. These professional soldiers had to buy their own weapons, horses, and support several foot soldiers. Professional soldiers could neither sell the land they received nor will it to their heirs. However, their sons were expected to step into their fathers' shoes and continue to serve in the army in exchange for the right to exploit the land. In this manner, Ivan created not only a professional army but also a new self-perpetuating elite.

It soon became obvious to Ivan that his professional soldiers were spending more time in the army than at home working their fields. A serious economic problem had arisen. To deal with the problem Ivan passed a series of laws which eventually tied peasants to the land as serfs. That is how serfdom became the economic foundation of Russian social life and military power.

The period of Russian history following Ivan's death in 1584 and extending until 1613 is referred to as the "time of troubles." In 1613 Mikhail Romanov was crowned as tsar. That event marked the beginning of the Romanov dynasty that ruled Russia until the 1917 revolution.

RUSSIA UNDER THE ROMANOVS

During its rule of about three hundred years, the Romanov dynasty produced eighteen tsars. Some Romanovs were outstanding rulers while others were rather weak. However, they all had one common trait: they believed in autocracy, the ruler's divine right to absolute power.

Peter I, Catherine II, Alexander I, and Alexander II were among the most able tsars from the Romanov dynasty.

Peter I (reigned 1696-1725) was the first important tsar in the Romanov dynasty. He wanted to westernize Russia. Thus, in 1698, he went on a long tour of Germany, Holland, England, and Austria. Peter was deeply impressed by the industrial, military, and cultural achievements of Western European nations. In fact, he returned to Russian with more than a thousand European technicians and scientists. They helped Peter build factories, ships, and buildings. Peter also introduced European manners, clothing, and other customs in his court. One of his major accomplishments was the construction of Russia's new capital, Petrograd (now known as Leningrad). The city was built on swamp land at a tremendous cost in money and human suffering.

In order to finance his development programs and wars, Peter raised taxes and passed laws that tied serfs more tightly to the land on which they toiled. Militarily, Peter defeated Sweden and gained vast new territories, including a part of Finland. For all his accomplishments Peter was named "Peter the Great."

Catherine II (reigned 1762-1796) was a German princess who assumed the throne when her husband, Peter III, died. Catherine was intelligent, educated, and beautiful. She was a first-class administrator and the first educated tsar of Russia. Catherine patronized literary works, education, and the theater, and during her reign Russia became a major world power. Yet, like all other tsars from the Romanov dynasty, she did not tolerate opposition.

Catherine imposed censorship on foreign literary works, banning Voltaire's books from Russia, for example, and introduced repressive measures against the more liberal intellectuals. She was quick to put down revolts against her regime. For example, Pugachov, the leader of a major peasants' revolt, was captured after several bloody battles, put in an iron cage for public display, and then executed.

Catherine streamlined the empire's administration, divided the entire country into provinces, and for each province appointed a governor who reported directly to her. The result was that Catherine had better and more direct control over the affairs of her empire while higher social classes were drawn into local administration.

Alexander I (reigned 1801-1825) was an able man who encouraged education, modernized state administration, and streamlined Russian bureaucracy. His military achievements were also considerable. He defeated Napoleon and was the first Russian tsar to cross Europe and enter Paris at the head of an army. However, like all other Romanovs, Alexander repressed liberal intellectual ideas. In 1820, he banished the famous Russian poet Pushkin to the remote town of Ekaterinoslav.

Alexander II (reigned 1855-1881) was a good tsar. His major accomplishment was a partial emancipation of the serfs in 1861. More than 20 million serfs became landowners in the early 1860s. Alexander lifted restrictions on foreign travel, relaxed censorship of literary works, and allowed many intellectuals (including Dostoevsky) to return from Siberia. He also improved the system of education in Russia, reformed the Russian courts, introduced (on a limited scale) trial by jury, and promoted self-government by local representatives in Russian cities and villages.

Yet Alexander II was unyielding on the subject of his right to rule absolutely, and he was impatient with those who criticized his rule and quite severe with those who openly opposed him. He was assassinated in 1881.

Nicholas II (reigned 1894-1916) was the last Russian tsar. His firm belief in autocracy accelerated political activities in Russia. In 1895, the Socialist Revolutionary Party was organized and became the first Russian political party. The Social Democratic Workmen's Party was organized in 1898, and in 1903 the party split into two factions: the Bolsheviks and the Mensheviks. Both factions had socialism as their objective, but the two groups disagreed on the means by which socialism should be brought to Russia. The Bolsheviks believed in immediate change and in using violent revolution to achieve it while the Mensheviks favored a slow evolution toward socialism. The Bolsheviks were led by Lenin. On November 7, 1917, he and Leon Trotsky led the Bolshevik troops against the Winter Palace. The provisional government surrendered to the Bolsheviks, and its ministers were sent to jail. On July 18, 1918, Lenin ordered Nicholas II and his family to be shot. The Soviet rule over the country began.

The Lenin Years

The November 1917 revolution put the Communist Party in power, yet it took Lenin several years to consolidate its rule over Russia. He had to deal with the ongoing war in Europe, military interventions from outside, domestic opponents, and numerous social problems.

The Communist rule was unstable and threatened by powerful enemies. To survive, Lenin entered into negotiations with Germany and signed a peace treaty in March 1918. This treaty, which is known as the Brest-Litovsk treaty, was very unfavorable for the Russians, but Lenin had no choice but to pay this price in order to stave off the German army. Under the terms of the treaty the Russians agreed to withdraw from Finland, the Baltic states, and parts of the Ukraine and Caucasus. Lenin also transferred the capital of Russia from Petrograd to Moscow, which is located deeper inside the country.

British, Japanese, American, and Polish troops were sent to Russia to fight the Red Army. However, the objectives of the foreign interventionists were limited, their numbers were inadequate, and they lacked decisive and daring leadership. This foreign intervention was never a serious threat to Lenin; the major threat came from inside Russia. In many regions of the country the Communist regime was opposed by regular troops and local populations. The heaviest fighting took place in Siberia, Ukraine, and along the Don River, where the Cossacks fiercely fought against the Red Army. Lenin called all his domestic opponents by the same name: the White Guard. However, those troops were a divided lot and the Red Army was able to deal with the White Guard factions one at a time. By 1922, all major pockets of resistance to the Communist rule were destroyed by the Red Army.

The Communist regime was also opposed by various segments of the Russian population. To deal with that kind of opposition Lenin organized the Soviet secret police and gave it virtually unlimited powers. Within a year, the Cheka, as the secret police were originally called, arrested and shot without trial about 8,000 people. According to Solzhenitsyn, the Cheka quickly outperformed the Romanovs, who had permitted only 894 executions to be carried out from 1826 to 1905.

In March 1921, Lenin turned to the problem of his authority in the Party. He got the Party to decree that no individual member be permitted to criticize Party leadership. This decree eliminated the last vestige of democracy from the Party and made it into a monolithic institution. The act said that decisions announced by the leadership must be accepted by all members of the Party and carried out without further debate. It changed the Marxist "dictatorship of the proletariat" into the Leninist "dictatorship of the Party leadership."

The combination of war, terror, and Lenin's social policies reduced Russia's economy to ruins. Industry, which was run by inexperienced members of the Party, came to a standstill. The ruble (Soviet currency) became worthless. The peasants consumed what they could produce and refused to deliver food to the cities. The result was the famine of 1921-22, during which millions starved to death.

Lenin had to do something to stave off complete chaos. In 1921 he introduced a set of economic policies that came to be called the New Economic Policy, or NEP. NEP represented a major retreat for Lenin. It restored private property and denationalized trade and small-scale industry. Managers of state-owned firms were instructed to maximize profits, while wages and salaries were set by market forces. This return to a sort of free enterprise economy lasted seven years. During that period Russia recovered from war and famine, and signs of general prosperity became numerous.

Khrushchev's reference to the New Economic Policy is quite revealing. He said:

> In essence, the New Economic Policy meant the restoration of private property and the revival of the middle class, including the Kulaks. The commercial element in our society was put firmly back on its feet. Naturally this was, to some extent, a retreat on the ideological front, but it helped us to recover from the effects of the Civil War. As soon as the NEP was instituted, the confusion and famine began to subside. The cities came back to life. Produce started to reappear in the market stalls, and prices fell.[1]

It is remarkable to have a Soviet leader tell us that a return to capitalism was all that the country needed to get back on its feet.

---

[1]E. Crankshaw, ed., Khrushchev Remembers (Boston: Little, Brown, 1970), p. 20.

Lenin suffered several heart attacks in the early 1920s, and they triggered a power struggle in the Soviet Union. He died in 1924. After Lenin's death, the struggle for power began in earnest. Stalin emerged victorious to become the most powerful ruler of Russia, more powerful than any tsar had ever been.

The Stalin Years

Stalin exhibited a unique ability to outmaneuver his opponents, and by 1928 he was in complete control of the Communist Party. Of course that meant he was in full control of the Soviet government. However, it was not enough for Stalin to subordinate his opponents. He wanted to destroy them physically. And that is what he did in the 1930s, when all his rivals, would-be rivals, could-be rivals, and countless other people perished. By the mid-1930s, he had become an absolute and much feared ruler.

The so-called Stalin Constitution was enacted in 1936. It recognized three social classes in the Soviet Union: workers, peasants, and the intelligentsia. In the late 1920s, Stalin abandoned the New Economic Policy and began a drive to industrialize the country through comprehensive economic planning. In 1928, the First Five Year Plan was announced. It was followed by the Second Five Year Plan in 1933, the third in 1938, and a series of five year plans after the end of World War II. The most fundamental feature of each five year plan has been a strong emphasis on the development of heavy industry.

Stalin's decision to collectivize Soviet peasants was a pragmatic one. Politically, collectivization of land was an expedient way for Stalin to establish full control over Soviet peasants. Economically, it gave him full control over the distribution of food. Peasants resisted collectivization by slaughtering animals and refusing to work the fields. The 1932-35 famine was the predictable outcome of Stalin's agricultural policies. Faced with an inadequate supply of food, the Soviet government opted to feed industrial workers at the expense of peasants. The government simply forced peasants to deliver to state warehouses as much food as they did before the famine. That is how and why the famine caused the most starvation in rural areas, where millions of peasants perished.

By the end of 1940 Stalin had received intelligence reports about Hitler's decision to attack the Soviet Union. However, he still needed time to equip and train the Red Army. For that reason he tried very hard until the last day to appease Hitler. But the war began anyway, on June 22, 1941, and within a few days the Red Army was in a full and disorderly retreat.

The German plan was to capture Leningrad, Moscow, and the Ukraine before the Russian winter set in. For the time being it looked as if Hitler's objectives were to be attained. The German advance into the Ukraine was swift and irresistible. On September 17, the Germans entered Kiev and their armor divisions surrounded four Soviet armies. Eventually, the Germans captured about 600,000 Soviet soldiers. By the end of October, the Germans were within fifty miles of Moscow. However, Stalin stayed in the city, and on November 7 (Revolution Day) he reviewed the Red Army troops. The setting was quite dramatic and morale-boosting. The troops that marched by Stalin came from the front, or were on the way to the front. Stalin spoke to the troops about the "enemy at the gates of Moscow" and told them:

> The war you are waging is a war of liberation, a just war. May you be inspired in this war by the heroic figures of our great ancestors, Alexander Nevsky, Dimitri Donskoy, Minin and Pozharsky, Alexander Suvorov, Michael Kutozov...."

This invocation of the great ancestors appealed to the Russian national pride and to their love for the country. Stalin's glorification of Russia had a tremendous psychological effect on the people's morale and their willingness to fight. Many historians claim that snow and bitter cold saved Moscow. That might be so, but it is also true that the Russians put up great resistance.

The end of the war found Soviet troops in Poland, the Baltic states, Hungary, Yugoslavia, Czechoslovakia, Bulgaria, Romania, East Germany and Austria. Communist governments were quickly installed in all those countries except Austria. In addition, Stalin incorporated the Baltic states and parts of Poland into the Soviet Union. He compensated the Poles by giving them an equal share of East German territory.

When the war ended Stalin had to face a difficult choice: either to maintain open and friendly relations with the West or to close down the frontiers. The first choice held economic advantages because the post-war economic situation in Russia was desperate. The second choice had a clear-cut political advantage; Stalin wanted to stabilize his hold over Eastern Europe. An "open door" policy toward the West would have made that effort quite difficult. He opted for the second alternative and closed down the frontiers. The Cold War developed and marked the last years of Stalin's rule, until his death in 1953.

POST STALIN YEARS

Stalin's death signaled the beginning of a power struggle among his lieutenants. Somewhat unexpectedly, Khrushchev was able to outmaneuver all other candidates, and by 1956 he was clearly the top man in the Soviet Union. In fact, he felt secure enough to use the 20th Congress of the Communist Party (1956) to deliver a vicious attack on Stalin. Khrushchev blamed Stalin for bloody purges, for labor camps, for mass murders, and for ignoring some convincing and reliable intelligence about German preparations for war with Russia. Of course, Khrushchev was part of Stalin's inner circle and had to have been fully aware of everything that happened under Stalin. Yet he chose to attack his former master for the crimes that they, in effect, had committed together.

Khrushchev tried to eliminate some of Stalin's harshest policies. He stepped up the construction of apartments for workers and relaxed labor discipline by not prosecuting workers for tardiness, absenteeism, and shirking. Artists and writers were also given a greater scope of freedom, resulting in some outstanding films (The Ballad of a Soldier) and literary works (Solzhenitsyn's One Day in the Life of Ivan Denisovitch). Khrushchev never relaxed the Party's control over the lives of Soviet and Soviet bloc citizens. It was Khrushchev who built the Berlin Wall in 1961. The Wall became a living, visible, and unchallengeable monument to oppression.

In 1964, Khrushchev was forced to retire, and the top job in the Soviet Union was captured by Leonid Brezhnev. Brezhnev turned out to be less tolerant of artists, writers and intellectuals in general. He arrested many intellectuals, imposed stricter controls over their works, and forced a few to leave the country. In general, historians are likely to judge the Brezhnev years as a partial return to Stalinism. In effect Brezhnev ushered the Soviet Union into the 1980s with the political and economic system that was built on the foundations created by Lenin and Stalin.

Suggested Readings

Pejovich, S. A Report Card on Socialism, Dallas: Fisher Institute, 1978.
Zaleski, E. Stalinist Planning for Economic Growth, 1933-1952, Chapel Hill: University of North Carolina Press, 1980.

CHAPTER 11

BASIC INSTITUTIONS OF THE SOVIET-TYPE ECONOMY:

STATE OWNERSHIP

The basic institutions of socialism in the Soviet-type economy are: (i) state ownership in productive assets, (ii) central planning of resources, and (iii) one-party political monopoly. Those institutions set the Soviet-type economy apart from other social systems. They generate incentives and transaction costs that have specific and predictable effects on the behavior of decision makers, the allocation of resources, and the flow of innovation.

State Ownership in Productive Assets

The term state (or public) ownership is merely a façade hiding the true owner. The Politburo of the Soviet-type Communist Party is the owner of most of the nonhuman resources in the country. The Politburo is a self-perpetuating elite to which new members are appointed through personal connections and from which they depart by death or in political disgrace.

In theory, local units of the Communist Party send their representatives to the Party Congress, which is supposed to be held every five years. There, the delegates elect the Central Committee of the Communist Party, which is the highest governing body of the Party. The Central Committee, in turn, elects the Politburo, the highest executive organ of the Party.

In practice, the procedure has been turned upside down. The Politburo selects members of the Central Committee, and the latter control who represents the local party units at the Party Congress. Until the mid-1980s, the slate of candidates proposed by the leadership had been automatically and unanimously approved by the delegates.

The Politburo makes all important decisions that affect the life of each and every citizen in the Soviet-type economy. Those decisions are formally approved by the Central Committee and turned over to the Soviet bureaucracy for implementation. The Politburo is then the most powerful body in the Soviet-type system. For all practical purposes, it is above the law.

The Politburo's property rights include (i) the right to choose the mix of outputs, (ii) the right to determine the allocation of total income (pecuniary and nonpecuniary), and (iii) the right to control entry into and exit from the Soviet hierarchy. This and the next two chapters discuss the social, political, and economic consequences of this bundle of rights in the Soviet-type system.

Sources of the Politburo's Power

The right of ownership in productive assets is a major source of the Politburo's political power. The most significant consequence of state ownership is the marriage between political power and economic wealth. Individuals can thus acquire economic wealth only by joining the ruling group; they lose it if they are dismissed from the group.

State ownership provides the ruling group with two important sources of utility: the right to appropriate a large share of output for its own consumption, and the right to allocate the remainder. Thus, the Politburo needs economic monopoly in order to maintain its political monopoly.

The Politburo's political objectives determine the allocation of resources and the choice of outputs. Two factors support the implementation of the Politburo's preferences: state ownership and centralized planning.

Price theory breaks down the total effect of a change in the price of a good into the income effect and the substitution effect. Similarly, the total effect of a change in property rights could be conceptually broken down into the allocation effect and the productive efficiency effect. The former is about the effect of a change in property rights on the choice of output along the production frontier. The latter is about the effect of a change in property rights on the size of the social opportunity set. In general, the allocation effect of changes in property rights is associated with changes in incentive structures while the efficiency effect reflects changes in the costs of transactions. Thus, the analysis of the allocation effect of state ownership in this chapter is merely a useful first step in explaining the total effect of changes in property rights. The issue of efficiency in production will be addressed in the next two chapters.

THE CHOICE OF OUTPUT

The social opportunity set defines the associated costs of all the different choices in the existing set. By trading one bundle of goods for another, the community moves along the production frontier. This is the choice of output trade-off. Given state ownership, the Politburo controls the choice of output along the production frontier in two ways. First, the economic plan is the Politburo's choice on the production frontier. Without its sanction not a single economic plan can be changed. Second, the Politburo has veto power over entry to and exit from the Soviet ruling group (the nomenklatura). A member of the nomenklatura who questions the Politburo's economic policies risks a reduction in social status, flow of income, and other nonpecuniary benefits. The survival strategy for members of the nomenklatura is, then, to identify and respond to the Politburo's preference.

From the very first day of the Soviet state, the major objective of the Politburo has been to strengthen and enhance its political and economic power. It is then important to identify some of the most durable factors that have played an important role in influencing the Politburo's choice of output during the seventy years of Soviet rule.

The Demand for a Religion. Soviet leaders have legitimized their economic and political monopoly by professing their strong belief in the dialectics of history and the inevitability of communism (see chapter 3). According to Marx, capital formation and technical changes are two basic instruments servicing the "laws of history."

The Demand for Influence in the Third World. The Politburo's drive for political monopoly requires that socialism be accepted as a viable alternative to capitalism. Since the standard of living in Soviet-type countries has never been much of a marketing point, communist propaganda has argued that in exchange for more consumption today, capitalism brings recessions, unemployment, and low growth rates, whereas socialism means scientific planning for full employment and steady growth. Socialism, in other words, means a high rate of capital formation.

The Demand for Political Equality With the West. The goal of "equal" economic status with the capitalist West has led the Soviet Politburo to make large investments in heavy industry and military technology.

The Collectivization of Agriculture. Because collectivization means farming on a large scale, heavy agricultural machinery has been needed, pushing the Politburo in the direction of a high rate of capital formation and pushing redundant peasants into the cities to work in factories.

Those and similar factors have been instrumental in the Politburo's choice of output. Throughout the long period of the Soviet rule, the Politburo has been very consistent in setting aside a large percentage of the Soviet GNP for capital formation, with an especially strong emphasis on investments in the capital goods sector.

The Limits of the Politburo's Power

The Politburo's power to invest in capital formation is limited by its perception of the maximum price the community is willing to pay so that the ruling group can pursue its political and economic objectives. Let us explore that limit by reference to a standard neoclassical analysis of the short-run equilibrium in the capital market.

The (SS) curve in Figure 11-1A shows the assumed supply of existing capital in the community. The demand curves (DD) show that the stock demand for capital follows the price of capital; this price is defined as the present value of the flow

100

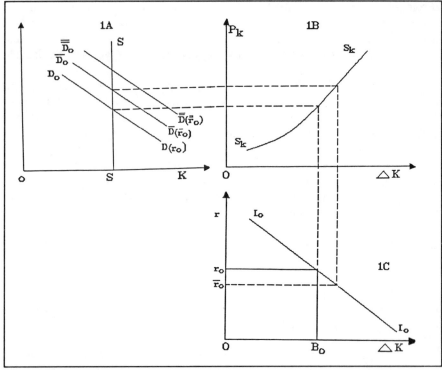

Figure 11-1.

of expected earnings from the existing capital stock discounted at the relevant rate of interest. Given the rate of interest, the current price at which the public is willing to hold the existing stock of capital emerges. This price is determined in the capital market where the rate of interest is equated to the percentage return from the capital stock.

Should personal preferences change toward a greater desire for future income, the price of both the stock of existing physical assets and bonds would increase and the rates of return from nonhuman assets would fall. The stock demand curve for capital would shift to $(D_0 D_0)$, and the rate of interest implicit in the relative prices of capital goods would fall. The equilibrium rate of interest (r_0) falls to $(\bar{r}_0)$. In other words, all the various rates of interest would be brought into equality by switching activity among different markets.

The production market for capital goods is shown in Figure 11-1B. The curve $(S_k S_k)$ is the flow supply curve of capital goods. Given this schedule, the rate of output of new capital goods by capital-producing industries is determined for each given market price on the vertical axis. The producers are assumed to equate the marginal supply price to the market price of capital goods. The rate of investment decision becomes the rate of output decision of supplying firms. The important simplifying assumption is that

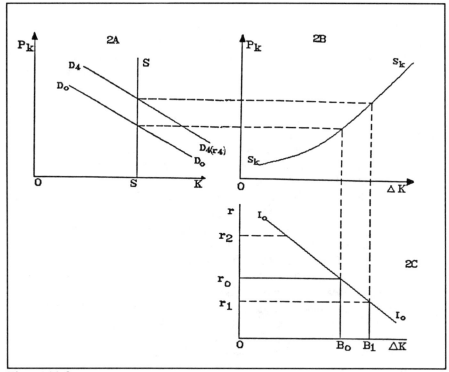

Figure 11-2.

the demand flow for new capital goods is perfectly elastic at the level of the <u>current</u> <u>price</u>. Thus <u>new capital goods</u> can be sold at the going price. It should also be noted that the scales on the horizontal axes in Figures 11-1A and 11-1B are different.

Figure 11-1C shows the rate of output of new capital goods as a function of the rate of interest. The investment function (I_0I_0) is a market equilibrium curve and not a demand curve for investment. The rate of interest and the marginal efficiency of investment are equal at each given point on the I_0I_0 curve.

The rate of real income diverted to gross investment is (OB_0) in Figure 11-1C. The equilibrium rate of interest (r_0) brings into equality the rates of return from capital goods and bonds, the community's valuation of future income relative to current consumption and the interest rate implicit in relative prices of capital goods.

In a Soviet-type economy, the ruling group can allocate one dollar's worth of resources for investment in fixed assets without any depreciable reduction in its own consumption. The cost is borne by the community at large. That is, from the point of view of the ruling group, the cost of purchasing additional capital has fallen, while the benefits, pecuniary as well as nonpecuniary, have risen. Given its growth orientation and the power to allocate the increment in output, which is an important source of utility (and political power), the ruling group's demand for new capital goods has to exceed the rate which would prevail if individual members of that group had to bear the cost of investment (through a reduction of their own consumption). Going back to Figure 1C, the ruling group will increase the rate of capital formation beyond (OB_0).

Each additional dollar invested beyond (OB_0) increases the community dissatisfaction by interfering with its time preference, and this dissatisfaction is a real cost to the ruling group. The ruling group then has incentives to increase the rate of capital formation up to a point such as (OB_1) in Figure 11-2C, where its own gains from the last dollar invested equal its own costs from violating the preferences of the community (i.e., from increasing other people's costs). Given the rate of investment (OB_1) and the marginal efficiency of investment (r_1), the implicit price of the stock of existing capital can be approximated by the (D_4D_4) schedule.

The rate (r_1) brings into the equality only the marginal productivity of capital and the ruling group's valuation of the community's future income relative to the community's current consumption. It does not reflect the community's valuation of future income relative to current consumption.

State ownership of resources also means the absence of financial markets. It means that the set of choices open to the members of the community for converting their current income into wealth is limited to savings deposits, investment in human assets, and purchase of durable goods such as cars. Given the community's time preference and the regulated rate of interest on savings, the demand for knowledge in the Soviet-type economy must exceed that prevailing in a private-property, free-market economy. And that is true. The importance that Soviet youth attach to education reflects the simple fact that human capital is the only type of earning assets they can own and use to earn a rate of return above the rate of interest on savings deposits. It does not mean that they are more (or less) interested in education than young people in the West.

Given the property relations, the community's saving schedule (that is, the rate of income which citizens in the Soviet-type economy make available for capital formation), is perfectly inelastic above the regulated rate of interest. It follows that the saving schedule cuts the (I_0I_0) schedule in Figure 11-2C at some rate of interest above (r_0), say (r_2). Thus the state has to generate forced savings in order to finance planned investment.

In summary, the (B_0B_1) distance in Figure 11-2C shows the allocative effect of a change in the form of ownership in capital goods, while the vertical distance between (r_1) and (r_2) reflects the effect of state ownership on the difference between the ruling group's and the people's time preferences.

State Ownership and Incentives to Innovate

Suppose a technical innovation introduces a new choice into the system. An uncertainty about the community's response to the innovation means that it has unintended consequences and an unpredictable outcome. This is the common result of all innovations. Thus, innovating activity could be treated as a trade-off between a wider range of choices with unpredictable outcomes on the one hand and "routine" activities within the existing set on the other. One set of property rights may then be superior to another set, not because it happens to be technically more efficient in terms of the standard trade-off along the production frontier but because it encourages the flow of innovation with the expansion of the opportunity set.

State ownership has a specific and predictable effect on the flow of innovation. In the Soviet-type economy all innovations have to be approved at the level of the nomenklatura. The manager is free and, in fact, encouraged to propose an innovation to bureaucratic superiors. However, there is a world of difference between one's right to propose innovation and the right to implement it. The problem is that state ownership provides neither managers nor their superiors with much incentive to innovate. Let us mention a few reasons for this lack of incentives.

Under a regime of state ownership, decisions to innovate cannot be individual decisions. Members of the nomenklatura who perceive opportunities for innovation must first sell their ideas to colleagues and then to superiors. The same goes for managers of Soviet-type firms.

Innovation, being a nonroutine activity, is a risky venture. Incentives to innovate then depend on the appropriability of benefits. In the Soviet-type economy, individuals who believe in specific innovations find that their own costs of pushing the new ideas through the bureaucracy are high relative to the benefits. If the innovations succeed, the innovators will share the benefits with superiors. If the innovations fail, superiors will blame the innovators.

In conclusion, the nomenklatura does not receive market signals and, therefore, cannot make sound judgments about alternative projects. Balcerowicz, a Polish economist, argues that it does not even matter whether the nomenklatura is aware of new technical opportunities. He writes: "The development of special institutes for the diffusion of technology cannot be an efficient means for inducing innovativeness under the Soviet-type economy and is not a substitute for a fundamental change in the incentive structures."[1]

Suggested Readings

Ioffe, O. and Maggs, P. The Soviet Economic System: A Legal Analysis, Boulder, Westview Press, 1987, chapters 1-3.

---

[1]L. Balcerowicz, "The Soviet-Type Economic System and Innovativeness," Institute for Economic Development, Warsaw, 1988, paper No. 19, p. 12.

CHAPTER 12

BASIC INSTITUTIONS OF THE SOVIET-TYPE ECONOMY: ECONOMIC PLANNING

A major consequence of state ownership is that it permits the Politburo to choose the mix of outputs that is consistent with its political requirements and other preferences. Analytically, the allocation effect of state ownership is like a movement along the production frontier, from the mix of outputs preferred by individual members of the community toward the one agreed upon by members of the Politburo. In the Soviet-type economy, economic planning is the method by which the Politburo's choice of outputs is implemented. The purpose of this chapter is to describe the mechanism of economic planning and its consequences.

The Mechanism of Economic Planning

Economic planning means that vertical relations, that is, administrative orders, are dominant with respect to horizontal relations, that is, contracts. In other words, the terms of contractual agreements are mostly non-negotiable; exchange of consumer goods therefore takes place at government-regulated prices.

An order from the planning authority replaces voluntary agreement and determines the quantity and the quality of the good to be produced and how it will be produced. All decisions concerning the level and character of the economy flow from the top leadership through various bureaucratic channels down to productive units. The sum total of those administrative orders is the economic plan.

In the Soviet-type economy, the central planning agency (Gosplan in the USSR) and its subordinate bureaucratic units are merely executive agencies. They provide economic and technical solutions for decisions and directives issued by the Politburo.[1] That is,

---

[1] The structure of the Soviet-type bureaucracy tends to change in response to many factors, such as purges, the Politburo's search for more efficient political controls, and serious economic failures, so it will not be discussed here. The important point is that its role is always the same: to provide technical expertise for the implementation of the Politburo's choice of output, to prepare annual and long-term plans, to monitor their execution, to set and control prices, and to ration the use of raw materials and intermediary goods.

they translate the Politburo's choice of outputs into production targets for all productive units in the country.

The planning bureaucracy begins its job of preparing the annual production plan by sending preliminary production targets, via its hierarchical structure, to the industries and firms in every region. Those preliminary production figures are based on the past performance of productive units, new capacities, new priorities, assumed changes in productivity, and other indicators. Productive units and their respective industries must send back their comments and suggestions for modifications of preliminary targets. Predictably, they tend to understate their production capacities and overstate their need for inputs.

A major problem facing the planning bureaucracy is that production targets should, in the aggregate, neither exceed nor fall short of the country's productive capacity. The target plan should be on the production frontier. And that is easier said than done. The Soviet Union produces millions of goods and has about 500,000 producing firms of one kind or another.

In an economy in which administrative commands replace voluntary contracts, supplies are not purchased in open markets. When distribution and consumption do not occur in an open market, a large and expensive bureaucracy is needed to artificially channel distribution and consumption. The relationships between producers on the one hand, and their suppliers and customers on the other are bureaucratic rather than economic in nature.

Business firms are the lowest units in the Soviet planning hierarchy. They are answerable directly to their higher bureaucratic superiors, who monitor their compliance with the plan, evaluate the attainment of production priorities, and are empowered to administer rewards and punishments. Moreover, business firms cannot seek alternative suppliers. The supply plan is therefore the most essential part of the economic plan in the Soviet-type economy.

SUPPLY PLANNING IN THE SOVIET-TYPE ECONOMY

In a market economy, business firms bid for supplies in the market. To allow firms to do the same in a planned economy could easily disturb the plan's objective and frustrate the will of the ruling elite. Thus, economic planning must eventually lead to the planning of supplies. In the Soviet Union, Gosplan controls the allocation of about 2,000 inputs, while various ministries and lower level bureaucracies allocate another 38,000 inputs. In total, the Soviet bureaucracy thus controls the allocation and use of about 40,000 inputs.

Sizable bureaucracies have been established to administer supply planning. In theory, firms are told what inputs they will get, in what quantities, and when and from whom to expect deliveries. In practice, supplies arrive late or never. They also come in the wrong quantities and specifications. The result is that even a small deviation from the supply plan can easily cause a chain reaction throughout the system. Suppose that a firm that produces screws and bolts fails to deliver them on time to other firms. The rate of output of those firms is immediately affected. And in turn, enterprises that depend on those firms' outputs become affected. And so on.

So-called material balances play a key role in preparation of the supply plan. Soviet planners draw material balances for all products in physical units. The balance for each input shows its sources (inventory, current production, imports) and uses (inventory, current production, exports). On the basis of material balances and production targets, the supply plan determines the allocation of inputs to individual enterprises. Again, several layers of bureaucracy are involved in this process.

Business enterprises provide information to their administrative supervisors about technical coefficients that relate inputs to outputs. On the basis of those reported production functions of business firms, past performances of enterprises, expected (planned) changes in productivity, and the knowledge that the managers of business firms never tell the whole truth, the Soviet planning bureaucracy develops the supply plan. The final figures are far from perfect, however, because the number of interdependent relationships that must be integrated into the plan is too great.

The job of correcting even a minor mistake in the plan is enormous. Suppose that planners detect that the production of screws is lagging behind the planned rate. Clearly, they must increase the allocation of coal, steel, iron, and so on to the firms producing screws. But to do that, they must reduce the allocation of coal, steel, iron, and so on to other firms. And they must then reduce the planned rate of output of these firms, as well as other firms that depend on them, and so on. Every time a mistake in the plan is noticed, the supply and production plans for a number of industries must be revised. Because these modifications inevitably are needed, in effect the plan is constantly revised and brought in line with the business firms' actual performance. Thus, in the course of the year, the plan and the economy's actual performance eventually converge, and at the end of each year the Soviet press can honestly report that the annual plan has been fulfilled.

It is clear that revisions and adjustments in the plan must result in lower output targets for many firms and industries. To take care of this, the ruling elite designates certain sectors of the economy as low-priority areas. And for this purpose consumer goods industries have consistently been assigned the task of bearing the cost of miscalculations, inadequacies, and inconsistencies in the plan. Put another way, centrally planned systems need a buffer to absorb mistakes in the plans. In the Soviet Union, the consumer has served that function.

ADMINISTRATIVE CONTROLS IN THE SOVIET-TYPE ECONOMY

For at least two reasons, Soviet planners must closely monitor the performance of productive units. First, to make adjustments in the economic plan, Soviet planners must have information about its shortcomings, miscalculations, bottlenecks, supply problems, and so on. Second, planning without control could easily frustrate the Politburo's objectives. It would be like planning a candy-free diet for a six-year-old boy. Unless his parents take on the cost of controlling him, the boy's real diet will almost certainly frustrate the parents' "plan." One important device for monitoring the execution of the plan in the Soviet Union is the financial plan.

The Soviet firm's financial plan is the monetary equivalent of its production plan. Like the budget of a government bureau in the U.S., the financial plan of the Soviet firm identifies its receipts and expenditures by categories. Unlike the budget, it specifies both the firm's contractual partners and the terms of exchange. Suppose that a firm is told to produce 1,000 television sets per month and deliver them to specified retail stores at $100 each. Assume also that the firm's supply plan allocates to it 1,000 wooden boxes at $30 each, 10,000 screws at 25 cents each, $20,000 for wages, and a total of $40,000 for other inputs. The firm's planned revenue is $100,000 and planned expenditures are $92,500. Depending on the Party's priorities, the firm's planned receipts are equal to, greater than, or less than its planned expenditures. In our case, the surplus is $7,500, and it is used to subsidize other (higher-priority) firms and governmental activities.

All transactions of Soviet business firms are done through the bank, which transfers funds from one account to another. Because all payments must be made through the bank, the bank checks those payments against the firm's financial plan. The Soviet firm cannot withdraw cash to make payments to its contractual partners. Such payments would escape the planners' control over the firm's transactions and could interfere with fulfillment of the plan by other firms.

The financial plan thus serves two major functions. By controlling the flow of receipts and expenditures of business firms, the bank can detect miscalculations and bottlenecks in the plan and alert the appropriate planning bureaus. Also, the bank serves a watchdog function. Any deviation from the plan by a firm could easily interfere with the leadership's objectives for the economy. Suppose that the manager of a firm uses more resources than the plan called for, or produces the wrong assortment of goods. His actions will have a chain reaction throughout the system. If he uses more resources than he was supposed to, shortages of those resources will appear elsewhere and affect the fulfillment of the plan. If he produces the wrong assortment of goods, business firms which use his output as intermediary goods will be affected. It is thus important to the government to make sure that the firm's managers do as they are told. The financial plan helps the state facilitate this type of control over enterprises. It also helps the government reduce, if not eliminate, deviations from the plan by business firms.

PRICE CONTROLS IN THE SOVIET-TYPE ECONOMY

The financial plan could, under some circumstances, complicate the planners' job. Suppose that the price of screws rose from 25 cents to 35 cents. The firm's budget of $2,500 would then not be sufficient to purchase 10,000 screws. The firm's payment of $2,500 to its suppliers would give no assurance to the bank that the firm has received all the screws it needs to produce 1,000 television sets. The planners' cost of monitoring the execution of the plan would therefore increase.

Because stable prices are important to Soviet planners, planners make them stable by administrative decisions. With few exceptions, most prices in the Soviet Union are set by the government and are rarely changed. Soviet prices are not meant to determine who gets what and who does what. Soviet citizens cannot raise their money offer to bid a good away from other claimants.

Administratively controlled prices are by definition stable prices. Does that mean there is no inflation in the USSR? Not at all. It only means that inflationary pressures reveal themselves differently in the United States than in the Soviet Union.

Suppose that everybody in the United States has an extra $100. What will people do with that extra income? They will spend at least some of it. Suppose that, among other things, they want to buy more beef. As consumers' demand for beef increases, grocery stores discover that their inventories of meat are being decreased. So, grocery stores will call slaughterhouses and ask them to ship more meat. In order to ship more meat to grocery stores, slaughterhouses will call cattle raisers and ask them to ship more cattle. However, ranchers might not be able to satisfy immediately this increased demand for cattle. Even in Texas it takes time to breed larger herds. The result is that not enough meat is available at the old price. As the price of meat is bid up, the excess demand for beef is reduced. The average of all prices goes up.

Suppose now, for the purposes of discussion, that everybody in the Soviet Union has an extra $100 to spend. Grocery stores will discover that they do not have enough beef to satisfy all their customers, so managers will call planners and ask them for more beef. Since everything is tightly planned in the Soviet Union, planners will say that all the beef has already been allocated. Now some buyers who like beef a lot might be willing to pay more in order to induce others to give up some beef; however, the price of beef is set by the state and cannot be changed. Soviet consumers do not have the choice of trying to get more beef by raising their offer. At the old price, the supply of beef is not sufficient to satisfy the increased demand. What can the Soviet consumer do? Get up early and try to get to the store before others do. But others will do the same thing. A predictable outcome is that a long queue will form in front of various stores. Those who are willing and able to wait longer than others will get more beef. Some others might try to work out a deal with the grocer. They might offer to pay him some extra money for beef. It is, of course, illegal for the grocer to accept bribes. But it is safe to assume that some do. At any rate, long queues in front of different stores are the predictable consequence of administratively controlled prices.

Economic Planning and the Social Opportunity Set

Economic planning in the Soviet-type economy affects the social opportunity set primarily through the costs of transactions. Transaction costs are the costs of making an exchange and protecting the institutional structure. They depend critically on the rules of the game.

In the Soviet-type economy, the substitution of the bundle of goods which is preferred by the Politburo for the one that would more accurately reflect the preferences of the community raises transaction costs on two accounts. First, the costs of making annual and long-term plans are quite high. Second, the Politburo's choice of output distorts the valuation of resources by the only source of human value--the individual persons in a society.

The costs of transactions that are specific to the Soviet-type economy are the volume of human and nonhuman resources employed to (i) prepare economic plans, (ii) monitor their execution, (iii) maintain and protect the rules of the game, and (iv) cheat and lie to bureaucratic superiors. Those costs limit the expansion of the social opportunity set in response to a technical change and even contribute to a contraction in the social opportunity set.

TRANSACTION COSTS AND AN EXPANSION OF THE SOCIAL OPPORTUNITY SET

Figure 12-1 derives from the writings of North and Wallis[2] and illustrates the relationship between transaction costs and economic growth. The total cost of an activity includes both production costs and transaction costs. The former are the costs of all the resources required to change inputs into outputs, while the latter are the costs of all the resources required to transfer property rights from one economic agent to another. By modifying North and Wallis' arguments slightly, we can use them to look into the effects of transaction costs on economic growth in the Soviet-type economy.

The demand curve for transactions is derived from the demand for the firm's output. The supply schedule reflects the prices and productivity of the transaction inputs.

In a private-property, free-market economy, the firm's response to technical change is to increase the scale of its operations at each price. The demand for transactions then shifts from, say, DD to D'D' in Figure 12-1.

As the firm increases its level of operations, transaction costs will increase along the SS schedule because of additional purchases of less-productive inputs from the transaction industries and/or additional transaction services produced within the firm. However, with larger outputs, the firm might be able to reduce transaction costs per unit of transaction by re-organizing production (e.g., the firm could internalize some contracts across the market). While incurring higher transaction costs is necessary in order to capture the potential benefits from technical change, modifications in methods of organizing production tend to make the supply schedule more elastic. It is important to note that the privately owned firm has both the right and the incentives to adopt the lowest-cost method of organizing production at each level of operations. Thus, the movement from A to A represents an expansion of the social opportunity set.

---

[2]D. North and J. Wallis, "Measuring the Transaction Sector in the American Economy," in Long-Term Factors in American Economic Growth (S. Engerman and R. Gallman, eds.) Chicago: University Press, 1987.

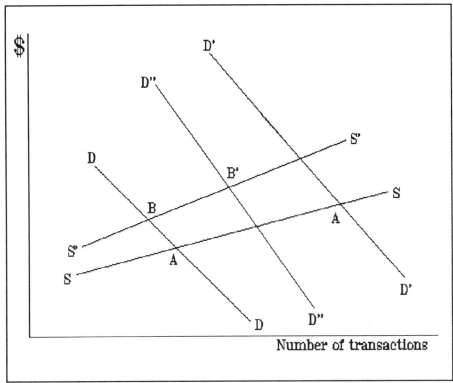

Figure 12-1.

Let us assume that a similar innovation occurs in the Soviet-type economy.[3] The Soviet manager has the <u>incentive</u> to underestimate the effects of innovation on the productivity of inputs in the firm. The firm's administrative superior knows that. However, the absence of competitive markets raises the cost of evaluating the manager's report. Suppose they agree that the technical change has shifted the demand schedule for transactions to D"D". The firm gets a new output target and the additional allocation of supplies necessary to produce it. However, the Soviet manager has no <u>right</u> to reduce transaction costs by switching to more efficient methods of producing transaction services. Soviet planners might have <u>incentives</u> to adopt more efficient methods, but they do not have the benefits of market signals (since prices are not scarcity prices) for evaluating the alternative methods of organizing production at different levels of output. The outcome could be interpreted as a more inelastic supply schedule of transactions S'S', which means that in the Soviet-type economy technical

---

[3]Soviet prices are not scarcity prices. Thus, Figure 12-1 cannot be used for quantitative comparison of DD and D"D". Its purpose here is to depict the effects of alternative institutions on innovation.

innovation would produce a smaller expansion of the social opportunity set than it would in a private-property, free-market situation.

TRANSACTION COSTS AND A CONTRACTION OF THE SOCIAL OPPORTUNITY SET

The economic plan leaves little room for discretionary decisions by firms. Vertical orders determine which factory is going to build bicycles, how many bicycles will be built, to whom they are to be sold and at what prices, and which suppliers of parts the bicycle factory must depend on. The Soviet manager is required to transmit to superiors a bundle of detailed information about the firm. But, in transmitting the firm's plan from the top to the bottom of the Soviet planning hierarchy, the firm's administrative superiors are exercising their administrative authority over the firm rather than responding to the flow of information and initiatives from the manager. The flow of information up the bureaucratic ladders and the flow of orders down to the bottom of the Soviet hierarchy is the essence of economic planning in the Soviet-type economy.

The transaction costs of assigning output targets to business firms, while simultaneously equating expected supplies with their planned uses and ensuring that each firm receives only the minimum in supplies needed for producing its output target, are enormous. They amount to huge expenditures of real resources. Thus, even if economic planners were able to prepare and execute a flawless plan, the social opportunity set would not expand as much as it could have in an institutional environment with lower transaction costs.

That statement cannot be readily tested, however, since flawless plans are not the norm. Mistakes in the plan are common and predictable. For example, Sovietskaya Rossiya, a Soviet newspaper, complained on October 15, 1987, that "70% of machine building factories were failing to meet delivery deadlines, were slowing down the operations of hundreds of their customers, and creating problems in many branches of the economy." Soviet newspapers and magazines are full of similar stories. And to correct the mistakes in the plan requires the expenditure of even more resources. It follows that the Soviet-type economy creates transaction costs that are specific to one of its basic institutions: economic planning. Those transaction costs, in turn, reduce the social opportunity set.

Given the staggering transaction costs of delivering the Politburo's choice of output, Soviet planners have been very cautious with the supply of money. They know that any deviation from the minimum money supply needed to carry out real transactions specified in the plan could reduce the volume of planned transactions and/or support additional transactions, of which the ruling elite might not approve. They also know that it is difficult to calculate the "proper" quantity of money. So they have sought help in imposing additional restrictions on business firms. For example, business firms are not allowed to keep cash balances subject to holding preference; they make all payments to other firms by transferring budgetary balances from one account to another. Also, each firm is required to deposit all cash receipts promptly. Those and similar restrictions are bound to raise even further the costs of transactions. The shortage of supplies and the shortage of consumer goods are two observable consequences of a reduction of the social opportunity set. The former is a predictable outcome of high transaction costs of the Soviet system of planning. The latter reflects the Politburo's decision as to who should bear those costs. Moreover, the shortages in the Soviet-type economy are not a simple matter of economic inefficiency that more talented people and/or better policies could alleviate. A reduction in the social opportunity set is a predictable consequence of economic planning, which in turn is a predictable consequence of the Politburo's choice of output. And the Politburo's choice of output is a predictable consequence of the prevailing property rights in the Soviet-type economy.

The Politburo needs economic monopoly to protect its political monopoly. In an excellent book on the Soviet-type system, Ioffe and Maggs write: "In a society that subordinates the economy to politics, the criterion of efficiency must be found in the degree to which the structure of the economic system guarantees the unlimited dominance of the political rules."[4]

CHEATING AND LYING

Soviet-type planning provides incentives for a lower agency to report false figures to a higher agency. The only major constraint on cheating of this type is the cost of audit. The absence of market signals makes transaction costs of monitoring reports by subordinate units higher in the Soviet-type economy than they would have been in capitalist economies, where price competition and financial markets sharply reduce those costs.

In the Soviet Union, an army of inspectors is employed by the Soviet Bureau of Weights and Measurements and other agencies to monitor the execution of the plan. Yet the cost of inspecting all goods, monitoring the use of all inputs, and overseeing all technological parameters at each and every production and distribution center for adherence to the plan would be exorbitant. Thus, managers who make false reports run a low risk of getting caught; the cost to them of a false report is relatively low. Most cheating and lying occurs when firm managers (i) alter the mix of outputs, (ii) alter the quality of output, and (iii) choose production numbers randomly. The first two offenses are changes in the mix of outputs and inputs which are reported as increases in the value of output. The third offense, which is called pripiski, is simply lying about production figures. A major audit in 1981 found that about one third of audited reports in the Soviet Union contained some distortions.

It is safe to say that the costs of transactions in the Soviet-type economy reduce the price of cheating and lying and thus further reduce the social opportunity set.

---

[4]Ioffe and Maggs, The Soviet Economic System, Boulder: Westview Press, 1987, p. 6.

Suggested Readings

Ioffe, O. and Maggs, P. The Soviet Economic System; A Legal Analysis, Boulder: Westview Press, 1987, chapters 4, 6-8.

Nutter, G. W. "Markets Without Property: A Grand Illusion," in Money, the Market and the State (N. Beadles and L. Drewry, eds.), Athens: George University Press, 1968.

Schroeder, G. The System Versus Progress, London: Centre for Research into Communist Economies, 1986.

CHAPTER 13

BASIC INSTITUTIONS OF THE SOVIET-TYPE ECONOMY:

THE POLITICAL AND ECONOMIC MONOPOLY OF THE POLITBURO

The Contract Between the Politburo and the People

Lenin argued in 1921 that politics must inevitably have priority over economics. To argue differently, he said, was to forget the ABC's of Marxism. He was able to convince his cohorts that the Party should be organized along the lines of democratic centralism. Under democratic centralism, members of the Party are free to voice their opinions on any issues while it is being debated. However, once the Politburo makes its decision on an issue, members of the Party must carry out that decision without any further criticism. In this manner, Lenin transformed the "dictatorship of the proletariat" into the "dictatorship of the Politburo." The Politburo's decisions became the law of the land. Thus, the Soviet-type economy is essentially a political phenomenon, where the advantages of political stability and political monopoly outweigh the disadvantages of economic inefficiency.

The Politburo's power is not without limits. Chapter 11 analyzed those limits with respect to the interaction between the preferences of the Politburo and the rate of investment. Briefly, it said that the Politburo's power depends on the extent to which its members perceive that they can violate the preferences of the community in order to pursue their own.

A major constraint on the Politburo's power then is its perception of the minimum bundle of rights which members of the community expect to have in return for their sacrifice of economic, civic, and political freedoms. That is, a lesser bundle of rights could increase the people's dissatisfaction over and above the cost of protesting in a tightly controlled police state. This bundle of rights is the opportunity costs of the people. The following rights figured most prominently during the Brezhnev years: economic equality (outside the ruling group), economic stability, guarantee of employment, undemanding work pace, and a slow but steady rise in living standards. The bundle included a critical promise, based on the official ideology, that a not-too-distant generation will enjoy both the life of material abundance and all those freedoms that preceding generations had to give up so that the Party could take the people along the path of Marxism.

Clearly, the total relationship between the Politburo and the people was not voluntarily chosen by the latter. It is useful, however, to think of this relationship as the social contract between the Politburo and the people. The overwhelming power of the Politburo determines the nature of the contract, while the opportunity costs of the people define its terms. A change in the contract would mean a change in the system, while a change in the terms of the contract would mean a change in the opportunity costs of the people. The latter could explain various pressures for reforms since Gorbachev's rise to power in the mid-1980s, provided that we are able to identify the circumstances that have affected the opportunity costs of the people. We shall return to this point in the chapter on perestroika.

Political Structure in the USSR in the Late 1980s

The implementation of Gorbachev's reforms requires the support of the prevailing political structure in the Soviet Union even as the reforms attempt to alter that structure. To understand the obstacles to glasnost and perestroika, it is necessary to briefly review the Soviet political structure at the end of the 1980s.

FORMAL POLITICAL STRUCTURE

The purpose of the Communist Party was to maintain and strengthen the political and economic monopoly of the Politburo. The Party's professional apparatus exercised the monopolistic power it held with strong vertical organization. The central committee was at the top of the hierarchy, then republic committees, regional committees, district committees and, finally, town committees. The professional apparatus relied on the rank and file for active support in implementing the Party's decisions in all enterprises, farms, government agencies, institutes, and associations.

The Party controlled all the aspects of social, political, and economic life in the Soviet Union. In elementary schools, children joined the Pioneers. They had to attend lectures and meetings where they were taught how to love and respect what the Communist Party had done for the country. In their teens, children became eligible to join the Young Communist League, in which they were taught about Marxism, about their duty to listen for and report hostile remarks, and about the shortcomings of capitalism. When Soviet youths joined the labor force, they were pressured to attend voluntarily numerous meetings at which the Party's decisions were discussed, praised, and supported. When Soviet seniors retired, they were expected to attend similar meetings, from which telegrams of praise and support were sent to the leaders.

At the same time, the Party took good care of its members. The best jobs in every field were reserved for them. Party members got promotions easier and faster than other members of the labor force. Thus, there were incentives to join the Party. The Party would pick and choose, however, taking in only those people who had the right personal connections and seemed most likely to follow orders faithfully.

The Soviet government had numerous structures and offices similar to the legislative, executive, and judicial branches of the U.S. and other western governments, but together they served the Party. The Party had to approve all appointments in the government, so it controlled all branches of government, which would then implement Party decisions.

The Supreme Soviet (the Soviet parliament) had two divisions: the Soviet of the Union and the Soviet of Nationalities. The former is similar to the House of Representatives in the U.S., while the latter is more like the Senate. The Supreme Soviet elected the Chief of State and the Soviet Councils of Ministers, which together constituted the executive branch of the Soviet government. Union Republics elected their own Supreme Soviets, which were organized along the same lines as the Supreme Soviet. At local levels, regions, districts, and towns elected their own local soviets. The Supreme Soviet also appointed the Supreme Court judges, as did the Supreme Soviet of each republic. Lower court judges were appointed by regional, district, and town Soviets.

All Soviet citizens were issued identity cards, which had to be carried at all times. Members of collective farms did not receive identify cards, however. This policy effectively, and ironically, tied Soviet farm workers to the land in much the same way serfs were tied to their medieval feuds. Through this government restriction the Party controlled the flow of people between rural and urban areas of the country.

INFORMAL POLITICAL STRUCTURE

Up to the time of this writing (1990), members of the Politburo had the common objective of enhancing and perpetuating the social contract (i.e., the institutional structure) upon which their power rests. To pursue this objective, they had to work as a team.

However, members of the Politburo do not have tenure. To leave the Politburo means to lose both political power and economic benefits. Thus, members of the Politburo had strong incentives to seek ways to enhance their own positions within the top leadership. They had to be alert to internal alliances within the Party summit. They also had incentives to appoint friends and "cronies" to important positions in the Party and government.

The latter set of incentives led to some important developments in the political structure of all Soviet-type economies. Pursuing those incentives, members of the Politburo created their personal "courts." Then, pursuing the same set of incentives, members of the court gathered around each top leader formed their own "courts" at republic and district levels of the Soviet power structure. In this manner, a number of informal channels of influence developed in Soviet-type economies. Predictably, those private courts were in competition with each other for power and influence.

A critical consequence of the existence of those competing informal channels of influence was that the bureaucracy became less concerned about the substance of policies handed down the ranks and more interested in discovering who made them and who was pushing them. The speed of implementing policies and decisions, especially those that tended to hurt a cluster of bureaucrats, was determined by the perceived balance of power between competing courts. Also, information, exchange, and decisions usually followed the channels inside those courts, circumventing the official structure. Ministries, industries, agencies, and/or firms affected by a decision circumvented its consequences by seeking adjustments, interpretations, and revisions through their own, or a friendly, court. Informal channels have also created a market for "insider" information about decisions debated at higher levels of government. Finally, bargaining for limited funds between competing claimants (ministries, industries, and firms) is usually carried out by competing courts.

Writing about informal courts in Poland in the late 1970s, Jan Kowalski said:

> ... some top politburo member can give an order without feeling constrained by laws... Whether his orders will be actually executed remains question-able.... One day in a speech by the first party secretary E. Gerek ... orders were given, without any reference to the legally binding five-year plan, to halt numerous investment projects. Regional and sectoral officials used all their available channels ... to defend "their" investment projects.... In the end the aggregate resource constraint of that period diminished the overall level of investments. But instead of a planned "maneuver" a survival of the fittest mechanism governed the investment cuts.[1]

The history of purges in Soviet-type economies is evidence as good as any of the existence of competing courts. Whenever a member of the party summit died or "retired" from power, members of his court were quickly "retired" too. The existence of those courts explains why Stalin, who replaced his politburo several times, had to purge such a large number of people. The only difference between Stalin's purges in the 1930s and more recent ones has been the method by which members of various courts were retired. Stalin preferred gulags and Brezhnev used mental wards. Gorbachev seems to favor corruption charges.

THE SOVIET BUREAUCRACY

The Communist Party was the single most important source of recruits for the Soviet bureaucracy. From being a small group of believers in the inevitably of socialism (300,000 members in 1917), the Party was, by the end of the 1980s, transformed into a mass organization of more than 17 million members who were willing to serve the nomenklatura in exchange for higher incomes, social advantages, and other nonpecuniary privileges. Although Party membership was not a guarantee of success in life, lack of it guaranteed a person the life of an ordinary Soviet citizen. Exceptions from this rule did exist, but mostly for artists, athletes, and scientists.

---

[1]Jan Kowalski, "Rational Expectations in Centrally Planned Economies," in Socialism: Institutional, Philosophical and Economic Issues, S. Pejovich ed., Kluwer Academic Publishers, 1987, pp. 187-8.

The Soviet bureaucracy filled a huge gap between the Party summit and ordinary citizens. In the late 1980s, it was hierarchical, with sharply defined rights and responsibilities. With respect to the economy, the lowest levels of the bureaucracy collected technical and economic information with which to begin the process of planning. At the end of the process, the bureaucracy informed enterprises of what the production targets were, who would supply inputs, and who would buy the output. The middle levels collated information received from subordinate units, performed preliminary technical and economic analyses, and later distributed the targets and orders formulated at the top to their subordinate units. The top levels of the Soviet bureaucracy received the information collated at the middle level, prepared economic and technical solutions for directives issued by the Politburo, and upon approval of the economic plan, monitored its overall implementation. Entry into the bureaucracy was coveted by young men and women, and loyalty to superiors was generously rewarded.

A segment of this entrenched bureaucratic establishment consisted of the nomenklatura, the "ruling class" in Soviet-type economies. By the end of the 1980s, the Soviet nomenklatura comprised close to one million people. It is important, however, to distinguish this economic ruling class from the Soviet "elite," which included artists, athletes, poets, and other celebrated people who did not have influence on political and economic affairs.

Even within the nomenklatura strong class distinctions existed. The top category included the leaders of the Party, the Komsomol (the Young Communist League), the trade unions, and other social organizations. The second category included heads of the state administration and their deputies. The third group consisted of key people in the economy, in education, and in scientific institutions.

In a brilliant book titled Nomenklatura (Doubleday, 1984), Michael Voslensky compared the social structure of the nomenklatura to a cone with a number of concentric rings which represent the boundaries between the various levels of the nomenklatura, from the district committees at the bottom to the Politburo at the top. The Politburo was not only the top of the nomenklatura's social structure but also its master.

The nomenklatura has three general sources of wealth. In monetary terms, the salary of a bureaucrat of the lowest rank was approximately twice as large as the average salary in the Soviet Union. And a nomenklaturist was paid five times as much as the lowest-ranking members of the bureaucracy. The so-called approved benefits were the second source of wealth for members of the nomenklatura. Those benefits included their access to special shops, special restaurants, special hospitals, special resorts, state-owned dachas, and car pools. Those establishments provided members of the nomenklatura with goods and services that were nonexistent in public stores, and at very nominal prices as well. Finally, the tolerated benefits increased the total compensation of members of the nomenklatura. Those benefits included patronage, good jobs for family members and close friends, influence to get things done, travel abroad, tickets for various entertainment events, and so on.

The relationship between the Politburo and the nomenklatura had an aspect which is specific to the prevailing property rights in Soviet-type economies: a strong interdependence between the Politburo and the nomenklatura. The survival strategy for members of the nomenklatura is to demonstrate loyalty to the Politburo, because in appointments and promotions, the trade-off between competence and loyalty strongly favored the latter. At the same time, an important survival strategy for the Politburo was its own loyalty to the nomenklatura. Khrushchev's demise in the 1960s is a case in point. He promoted economic and other policies that might have been popular with Soviet citizens but not that popular with the nomenklatura.

Only at the level of the Politburo, however, was loyalty not enough. Members of the Politburo had to produce some real results in order to meet the opportunity costs of the people and to protect their political and economic power from would-be contenders. The absence of real results was less costly to the nomenklatura. Thus, it was possible for the Politburo and the nomenklatura to react differently to the same class of problems, the latter being more inclined to resist institutional changes. The absence of economic signals in the Soviet-type economy meant that the Politburo's costs of monitoring the nomenklatura had to be higher than the shareholders' cost of monitoring corporate managers in a free-market, private-property economy. Thus, the nomenklatura could, within its perception of the costs of transactions, sabotage the Politburo's decisions. We shall return to this point in the chapter on Gorbachev's reforms.

Suggested Readings

Voslensky, M. Nomenklatura, Garden City: Doubleday, 1984.

CHAPTER 14

THE BEHAVIOR OF THE SOVIET-TYPE FIRM

We know from the three preceding chapters that the Soviet-type firm operates under the following conditions:

   a.   The manager is the main link between the firm and the planning bureaucracy.

   b.   The firm's production plan specifies its output quota and the quantities of most variable inputs to be received by the firm, and it designates the suppliers of those inputs.

   c.   The firm has a financial plan which is the monetary equivalent of its production plan. A bank supervises the use of budgeted funds, extends short-term credit when approved expenditures exceed planned receipts, and oversees the firm's operations.

   d.   The firm's performance is evaluated on the basis of the achievement of the gross output target and the realization of the average planned costs and profits.

   e.   The firm hires labor services in the market, but the production plan determines the size of the firm's wage fund. Also, the relative wages for different skills are set administratively.

   f.   The government allocates new capital goods to enterprises and transfers existing ones from one enterprise to another. The firm pays no rent on capital goods in its possession; however, it cannot sell them, rent them, or change their quality. Thus, the firm bears no cost for having "too much" capital.

The prevailing property rights in the Soviet-type firm suggest a pattern of behavior for its manager. Since the manager's tenure on the job, promotions, and monetary rewards depend on his ability to deliver the planned production quota, the output variable plays a crucial role in his formulation of policy. The production target assigned to his firm makes the manager desirous of accumulating both fixed assets and variable inputs, for accumulation assures the manager of survival in case of production difficulties, late deliveries of supplies, etc.

The Manager's Incentives

The mechanics of accumulating fixed and variable assets differ. The manager views capital goods as a free reserve and concentrates on convincing the planning bureaucracy of his firm's urgent need for additional capital to achieve the given output quota. By contrast, the firm's accounting costs of production vary with the acquisition of additional variable inputs. Thus, the manager who wishes to accumulate variable inputs must convince the state that the firm's production function has less efficiency than it actually possesses.

It follows that the manager of the Soviet-type firm has the following utility function:

$$U_t = f(q_t, S_t; Q_t),$$

where (q_t) is the output of the firm in period (t) and the parameter (Q_t) represents the firm's planned output quota for period (t). (S_t) is a measure of the stock of inventory of a specific variable input accumulated by the manager over time and held back from active use in period (t). To simplify our discussion of the behavior of the Soviet-type firm, we shall consider a period of time during which the state does not change the quantity of capital in the firm's possession.

The rationale for including the stock variable (S_t) in the preference function rests on the existence of uncertainty in the Soviet-type economy. Since input allocations are frequently delivered late, or not at all, or with the wrong specifications, the firm's possession of unplanned reserve stocks serves to obviate production crises. While managers who fail to fulfill their production plans may be able to justify a shortfall to the state, they would be in a better position if they were able to produce the required output consistently on schedule. Reserve stocks provide the manager with insurance; having a safe, ready supply of inputs will enable the manager to meet future output targets even when planned resource allocations are not received.

Given property-rights relations in the Soviet-type economy, it is clear that the manager seeks to maximize his utility function subject to the firm's production function and the expected deliveries of variable inputs. The behavior of the manager has to reflect the manager's subjective forecast of the firm's supply situation over his time horizon. The greater the deficiency anticipated by the manager between official input allocations and actual deliveries, the more weight he is likely to place on the stock variable (S_t), and conversely.

The Manager's Survival Set of Choices

Once the planned output target (Q_t) has been achieved, there is some trade-off of current production (q_t) for stock accumulation (S_t). We can define (S_t) as the expected delivery of (S) in period (t) plus the previously accumulated stock of this input minus its current use. In practice, the manager is hardly ever able to accumulate inventories of all desired inputs and has to rely on "informal" channels to trade surplus items with other managers.

An important question is how the manager can accumulate units of the variable input when the flow of the input to the firm is legally controlled and the official allocation is based on the planned output. Given his perceptions of the planning bureaucracy's cost of acquiring information about the firm's true production function, the manager's job security is enhanced if there is an opportunity to convince the state that his firm has a relatively low technical efficiency. That is, he reports the firm's production function as

$$q_t = (v_t; Ko, m),$$

while the true production function is

$$q_t = f(v_t; Ko, n),$$

where (q) is the flow of output per period (t), (v) is the variable inputs flow, (Ko) is the stock of capital that has been given to the firm by the state, and (m) and (n) are technological parameters. The difference between the two production functions is that (n) is greater than (m).

The Soviet manager controls the magnitude of the gap between the two functions by falsifying the true production capabilities of his firm. However, there are definite limitations on the extent to which the manager can misinform government authorities. First, if the manager's report shows a significant departure from average industry norms (which are understated to begin with), the government's suspicion is likely to be aroused. Second, the possibility is always present that other functionaries at the firm will make reports to the state that contradict the manager's testimony.

The Soviet manager then has to reach a decision about the reported production function on the basis of his willingness to take risks, his knowledge of the true production function, and his estimate of the costs of transactions that the state must bear in order to make a detailed audit of conditions at his firm. While different managers tend to reach different solutions for reported efficiency, the potential gains from falsification of the production relation make it unlikely that anyone will report the true production function.

Given the costs of transactions in the Soviet-type economy and the manager's incentive-penalty structure, the manager is able to create a set of opportunity choices for himself. The origin of this set lies in the difference between the firm's approved and true production functions. Figure 14-1 describes the situation.

The approved production function determines the firm's output quota (Q_1) and its allocation of inputs (S_1). Then, given the firm's true production function, the manager can choose to produce no more than his output quota and accumulate stocks $(S_1 - S_2)$ for future emergencies. In this case he forgoes the rewards he could receive for overfulfillment of his production quota. Conversely, the manager can choose to overfulfill his output quota (Q_2) by increasing the flow of inputs to current operations. In this case the manager adds nothing to his inventories and, in effect, trades future security from stocks for current monetary gains from additional input.

The set of opportunity choices open to the Soviet manager includes the two extreme output-inventory policies (A and C) and all intermediate points lying between these two extremes on the firm's true production function. Contrary to the intent of the

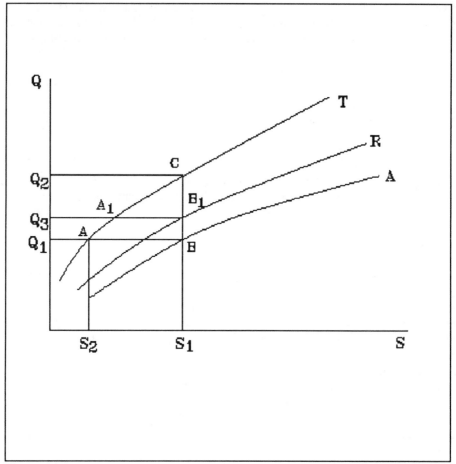

Figure 14-1.

government's planning procedure, the Soviet manager is able to secure for himself a set of discretionary choices. And the manager's ability to <u>create and preserve</u> that range of <u>choices</u> is his primary key to survival in the Soviet-type economy. The behavior of the Soviet-type firm can be then explained as the result of the process in which the utility maximizing manager seeks to <u>ensure his survival</u>.

The Behavior of the Soviet-Type Firm and the Economy

The difference between the approved and true production functions enables the Soviet manager to accumulate stocks essential for his survival. The unreported stocks are generally limited to those inputs, including labor, which the plan allocates to the firm. The manager will also, if and when it is possible, report smaller than actual output to the state and retain some finished goods for future uses.

The difference between the approved and true production function benefits the state as well. The unreported stocks permit the firm to meet its output quota and contribute to the mix of outputs considered desirable by the leadership. Thus, the firm's unplanned inventories tend to reduce the effects of waste and inefficiencies of the Soviet-type economy. However, it is important to note that unplanned inventories contribute mostly to more efficient use of resources to produce the planned output.

Let us use two examples to illustrate the Soviet manager's response to the incentive-penalty system in the Soviet-type economy.

Some years ago, the Schekino Chemical Combine was designed by the state to serve as a laboratory for testing new economic concepts. The factory's designated goal was to increase output by 80 percent in three years while its wage fund was frozen at the original level. Given the wage fund, the average wage was then tied to the level of employment. The firm's output target was attained in two years while its staff was reduced from 8,000 to about 7,000 workers. Clearly, the firm held an unreported inventory of labor. Then, the firm was handed a new system of rewards and the manager found himself in a different position. The excess of labor turned from an asset into a liability. The manager economized on the use of labor, and the result was reported to the state as a jump in the reported productivity of labor. An important lesson from the Schekino experiment is that it would be a major error to evaluate economic reforms on the basis of the economy's performance shortly after new institutional arrangements are introduced into the system.

More recently, the state leadership indicated that its tolerance of informal activities by managers has its limits. Under investigation for bribes, a manager from Bratsk argued that he operated in difficult conditions which arose in connection with the imbalances in the plan, i.e., delays, low delivery discipline, etc. The situation called for unconventional methods in resolving problems, including using the goods sent to Bratsk for production purposes to create a pool of needed reserves.

The ability of the manager to accumulate reserves is limited only to those supplies he actually receives. Suppose the manager of a firm needs only two inputs, X and Z. The plan (i.e., the approved production function) promises to the firm 100 units of X and 100 units of Z. The manager needs (i.e., the true production function requires) 80 units of X and 70 units of Z in order to produce the planned output target. The firm also receives its quota of X on time. But what if the firm does not receive its entire allocation of Z, such that its total supply of Z (including reserves) is not sufficient to cover the deficit? It then appears that the ability of the Soviet manager to accumulate stocks via false reporting to the state is necessary but certainly not a guarantee that the firm will fulfill the plan.

The manager who does not get his allotment of Z can eventually explain his shortfall to the authorities. However, the manager can do much better for himself if he somehow delivers the required output. The manager therefore views his reserves of supplies in still another way. In addition to providing the manager with security against future shortcomings in the system of planning, the unreported stocks are also his source of purchasing power. He can trade those stocks with other managers in what are known in the Soviet-type economy as informal markets. True, the cost of information about exchange opportunities is greater and the extent of exchange less than what it would be if the manager could maintain cash balances subject to holding preference. Yet, some trade occurs and as long as it does, resources move toward higher-valued uses as defined by the plan. This is yet another way the Soviet manager, acting in his own self-interest, reduces waste and inefficiencies of the plan.

Sooner or later, the manager of the Soviet-type firm is likely to increase the firm's output beyond Q_1 in Figure 14-1. He has two reasons for producing more than his quota. First, an excess of output over and above the firm's production quota would give the manager a monetary bonus as well as an improved standing with administrative superiors. Second, the firm has limited storage capacity as a constraint.

However, overfulfillment of the quota has costs for the Soviet manager. Each time he produces more than quota, the state is likely to approve a revised production function for the firm. For example, suppose the firm produces at point A_1 on its true production function in Figure 14-1. The manager then reports the output-supply combination B_1 and takes credit for the difference between B and B_1. But there is a price he has to pay. In response to the manager's above-plan performance, the state would revise the firm's production function (R in Figure 14-1) for the next planning period. The manager would receive the same supply of input S and be expected to produce output Q_3.

An important effect of this new production function is a reduction of the manager's range of opportunity choices, from AC to A_1C. Eventually, the firm's approved production function would approach its true production function. If and when this happens the manager would find that his survival depends on the behavior of external suppliers.

As long as the Soviet manager perceives that his survival depends on the existence of his discretionary range of choices, he will be eager to preserve it. In reality it means that he must raise the firm's total product curve in Figure 14-1 and conceal the shift from the state in order to offset the effect of a revised production function on his area of discretion. It follows that the Soviet-type economy creates incentives for the manager to search for cost-saving innovations, provided the manager can choose the rate at which the effects of those improvements are made known to the state. Incentives like these and the manager's ability to use them stave off the convergence of the approved and the true production function of the firm. Moreover, the manager's incentive to generate and promote innovative behavior benefits the economy as a whole. The extent of this innovating activity is an empirical question that is hard to investigate. However, the evidence that those incentives exist is the fact that after so many years of planning, the

Soviet manager is still able to trade current output for additional reserves of variable inputs.

Suggested Readings

Furubotn, E. and Pejovich, S.   The Economics of Property Rights, Cambridge: Ballinger, 1974, Chapter 14.

Schroeder, G. "The Implementation and Interpretation of Innovations in Soviet-Type Economies," The Cato Journal, 9, 1989.

Winiecki, J. The Distorted World of Soviet-Type Economies, Pittsburgh: University of Pittsburgh Press, 1988.

CHAPTER 15

PERFORMANCE OF THE SOVIET-TYPE ECONOMY

As we have seen in chapters 11 through 14, the Soviet-type economy creates some unique incentives and transaction costs. Those incentives and transaction costs, in turn, contribute to a misallocation of resources. We have identified three sources of economic inefficiencies in the Soviet-type economy:

a. misallocation of resources, arising from the difference between the "planned" mix of outputs and the allocation of resources toward outputs preferred by the community. The ruling elite's economic preference includes forced industrialization, while the community's valuation of present relative to future consumption is ignored. Analytically, we interpreted this difference as the movement along the production frontier.

b. misallocation of resources, arising from a contraction in the social opportunity set. Negative incentives and high transaction costs are major reasons for this source of economic inefficiency.

c. waste and inefficiency attributable to the high cost of gathering the vast amount of information required for central planning.

It is important to recognize the difference between the first two problems and the last. Problems (a) and (b) represent the price the community has to pay so that the ruling group can pursue its political and economic goals. The third problem affects the execution of the plan itself and reflects inefficiencies that create the difference between the planned output and actual results. As we have seen in chapter 14, survival strategies of the Soviet manager tend, within some definite limits, to reduce those specific inefficiencies.

Those three sets of inefficiencies affect both the quality of life in the Soviet Union and the quantitative performance of its economy. The former is important because statistics alone do not tell the entire story.

The Quality of Life in the Soviet-Type Economy

The quality of life in an economy depends on a variety of factors, such as the accessibility of education, the housing situation, the availability of good health care, the supply of consumer goods, the assortment of agricultural products, and the extent to which people have to resort to illegal means to support themselves. Let us briefly review the set of choices open to Soviet citizens with respect to some of those factors.

EDUCATION IN THE SOVIET UNION

The accessibility of elementary, secondary, and technical education is about the same in the Soviet Union and the United States. However, the accessibility of higher education differs greatly between the two countries. Upon completion of secondary education, a Soviet youngster can apply for admission to an institution of higher learning. About 20 percent of the applicants are accepted. Those who are not accepted enter the labor force or enroll in specialized technical schools to learn a skill.

A comparison is sometimes made between the free university education in the Soviet Union and the rather costly higher education in the United States. This kind of comparison misses an important point. Higher education in the Soviet Union is tuition-free and available to only about 20 percent of the high school graduates. They are selected on the basis of their grades in high school, scores on the college entrance exam, and the personal connections of their families. In addition, most students in Soviet universities receive stipends.

In the United States, higher education is also free for a small group of high school graduates who qualify for various scholarships. In that respect, the two countries are very much alike. However, some form of higher education is available to all other high school graduates in the United States at a price. The correct comparison is, then, between the American youngster who can get a university education at a cost and the majority of high school graduates in the USSR who cannot get it at any cost. Statistics reflect this difference. The number of students in the United States and the USSR per 10,000 population was 517 and 181, respectively, in 1986.

HOUSING IN THE SOVIET UNION

The population in the Soviet Union is almost evenly distributed between urban and rural areas. Moscow is the seat of the Soviet government, and its population is close to 8 million. In the center of Moscow stands the Kremlin, an ancient fortress and a symbol of Soviet power. The red brick wall around the Kremlin was built by Ivan III some five centuries ago. Just outside the wall is Lenin's tomb and a strikingly beautiful church, St. Basil's Cathedral. The church was built by Ivan the Terrible, who, according to a Russian legend, ordered the architect's eyes burned out in order to make sure that he would never design a more beautiful building for anyone else.

The most affluent and powerful Russians live in downtown Moscow. Within minutes from the center of downtown Moscow are old residential areas that look much the same as they did in 1917. Farther out are the Moscow suburbs, which are quite different from suburbs in the United States. Instead of residential homes with carefully tended lawns, Moscow is virtually surrounded with high-rise apartment buildings which house more than 2 million people. Those apartments look sturdy but are, in fact, poorly constructed. The typical apartment has two or three rooms. It is designed to conform to the official standard of nine square meters of housing space per person.

Leningrad is the second largest city in the Soviet Union. It is a showplace of old Russian grandeur and has the look of a beautiful European city.

Smaller cities in the Soviet Union have few paved streets. The homes are mostly small cottages accommodating several families. The shortage of housing is quite acute because small cities have less influence when it comes to gaining funds from Moscow. It is not unusual to see two or three TV antennae on the roof of one house. They indicate the number of families sharing the house.

Russian villages all look alike. Homes are small, plumbing is nonexistent, and sanitary facilities are primitive. The family laundry is often done at a nearby creek. The center of the village usually has a general store, a church that is used as a storehouse, a school, a library, and the collective farm's headquarters. The life of a villager is difficult and dull.

The housing situation in the Soviet Union is thus quite critical. Some estimates suggest that about half of all housing in the Soviet Union is without running water or sewerage. Yury Krotkov, a Soviet defector, described his Moscow apartment as follows:

"Our apartment contained eleven rooms. It had one kitchen with eight gas-rings, three bells (one general, and two individual), a telephone in the corridor which was in constant use, a bath, and a lavatory, which only the fastest were able to get to in the morning (the others stopped in at the public lavatories on their way to work). There were eighteen in the apartment, besides myself. Seven families, seven meters for electricity, seven tables and cupboards in the kitchen, and seven launderings a month, since none of my neighbors used the state laundries. This was not because they did not like them, but because they were economizing. There was not a single washing machine in the apartment; we had never even heard of a clothes dryer. But there were three television sets and two radios. Furthermore, all eighteen people ate at home. They never went to even the cheapest cafeteria, much less a restaurant. Again, it was because of the expense."[1] The housing situation in the Soviet Union has not changed in the last twenty years.

Housing units in the Soviet Union are built by the government, cooperatives, and the private sector. The government housing program is financed from administrative budgets and the firms' own funds, which is also government money. The share of housing financed by the government amounts to about two-thirds of the housing space produced annually in the Soviet Union. Monthly rent incomes are not expected to recover the cost of investment. Moreover, rental payments are estimated to cover only about one-third of the cost of maintenance.

Cooperatives are associations of Soviet citizens who are permanent residents of a given locality and who want to improve conditions. Members of a cooperative have to

---

[1]Y. Krotkov, The Angry Exile, London: William, Heinemann, 1967, pp. 125-127.

make a down payment of as much as 40 percent of the total purchase price of a building share and pay the balance over twenty years. In addition, the members have to pay for the maintenance of the building. The individual who invests in cooperative housing does not become an owner of the apartment. He has the right to live in it, but the cooperative owns the building.

Privately built homes are usually found in smaller cities and rural areas. Those homes are small, often built without plumbing, and located on unpaved streets.

Argumenty i Fakty (Arguments and Facts), a Soviet weekly paper, published some interesting statistics on the housing situation in the Soviet Union in 1988, including the number of people who were on a waiting list for housing in the capitals of the Union republics and other major cities. The city with the longest housing queue in absolute terms was Moscow, with 344,800 families on the waiting list; in proportional terms, Ufa, a large industrial city, had 36 percent of all families waiting for better housing. Table 15-1 gives the "list norm" for several cities, that is, the maximum amount of living space a person can have and still be eligible for rehousing. Although Soviet leaders promised back in 1920 to secure nine square meters (100 square feet) of housing space per person, they are still a way off from fulfilling their promise.

HEALTH CARE IN THE SOVIET UNION

Free medical care is a central element in the Soviet welfare system. When Soviet citizens get sick, they go to a clinic, where they are treated free of charge. The word "free" must be understood, however. It means that services are not paid for by the consumer at the time when they are consumed. The cost is borne by all citizens via the taxes they pay. In fact, health expenditures per capita in the USSR are about 34 percent of those in the United States.

Like everything else in the Soviet Union, medicine and medical care exist on many levels. There is medicine in the Soviet Union that is up to the best international standards. There are many good doctors. But as far as "free" medical care is concerned, it is the scourge of the citizenry.

Suppose 50 people show up for office hours at a neighborhood polyclinic. The doctor will have five hours to see them. That's about six minutes per patient. During those six minutes the patient must undress and dress and tell the doctor what's bothering him; and the doctor has to prescribe something and fill out the "hospital list," the document that excuses the patient from work.

In Soviet hospitals beds are jammed into the corridors (sometimes so tightly that there is no walkway), next to the elevators, and next to dining rooms.

THE CONSUMER IN THE SOVIET UNION

The Soviet-type economy's institutions rule out what has come to be known in the West as consumer sovereignty. Soviet consumers are free to spend their income in any way they choose. However, their freedom of choice is limited to those goods that the

Table 15-1. Housing conditions in capitals of the union republics and other large cities

	Average Per Capita Living Space (m^2)	Families & Single People on Waiting List Early 1988	Percent of Families on Waiting List	"List Norm" (m^2)
Alma-Ata	8.9	49,700	15	6
Baku	7.9	68,700	26	5
Dnepropetrovsk	9.7	74,200	20	6
Kazan	9.2	112,900	34	7
Kharkov	9.7	113,400	23	5.5
Kiev	9.6	208,400	26	5
Kuibyshev	9.2	114,300	29	7
Leningrad	10.6	282,900	20	5.5
Minsk	8.9	134,600	28	6
Moscow	10.7	344,800	12	5
Novosibirsk	9.0	111,600	25	8
Odessa	8.5	80,400	23	4
Riga	10.8	75,700	26	5
Rostov-on-Don	10.0	74,100	23	6
Sverdlovsk	9.2	130,600	31	6.5
Tallinn	11.8	25,400	16	6
Tashkent	8.2	60,100	12	7
Tbilisi	9.5	59,000	19	5
Ufa	8.0	118,800	36	8
Vilnius	9.7	36,300	21	5

Source: _Argumenty i fakty_, No. 32, 1988, p. 5.

One square meter = 10.7 square feet

ruling elite has decided to produce for the general public. Let us briefly compare basic responses of the private-property and Soviet-type institutions to consumers' preferences.

Suppose that an American consumer wants a pocket calculator. He goes to a store and asks for it. The seller might or might not have the calculator. But the seller's survival depends on selling things that people want to buy. So, the merchant will order calculators from the manufacturer. The manufacturer will consider the merchant's order as a command, because his survival depends on producing those things that his merchant customers demand. However, to produce calculators he might need to borrow money. The lender in financial markets will respond positively to the manufacturer's demand for a loan. His survival also depends on providing funds for production of marketable goods. In a private-property market economy, consumers get what they want.

Suppose that the consumer in the Soviet Union also wants a calculator. The seller is not going to worry whether he has calculators in stock or not. He only has incentives to worry about the goods that he is required to produce. At best, he might pass on information about the consumer demand to his superior. And the survival of the firm's superior does not depend on what the consumer wants, either. It depends on what the leadership wants. The leadership will eventually learn about the consumer demand for calculators. It might even order some calculators to be produced. But (and it is a very important but) the ruling elite does not have to take the demand for calculators as a command. Given the leaders' objectives and preferences, the Soviet consumer will get whatever the leaders think is in their interest for him to have.

Clearly, the gap between the people's purchasing power and the assortment of available consumer goods is a major problem for economic planners in the Soviet-type economy. The plan is supposed to balance the total value of "planned" consumer goods with the total of "planned" wages. However, it is a difficult objective to accomplish. The consumer goods sector routinely fails to meet output quotas. Soviet managers are more interested in their production quotas than in consumer tastes. Perishable goods are frequently delivered too late to be consumable. Informal markets for supplies create "unplanned" purchasing power. The best evidence of the discrepancy between the supply of consumer goods and actual purchasing power is widespread rationing of sugar, meat, butter, and other staple items.

According to the calculations of John Tedstrom, the total value of consumer goods produced in 1989 was about 426 billion rubles, or 28 billion rubles above the output produced in 1988.[2] However, inflation was responsible for about 9 billion rubles of the increase in the value of output and another 10 billion resulted from increased sale of alcoholic beverages. In the same period, an additional 64 billion rubles ended up in the hands of consumers, an increase of about 13 percent. According to Tedstrom, an increase in savings accounts from 297 billion rubles in 1988 to 338 billion rubles in 1989 could be attributed to the excess purchasing power. The Soviet consumer lives in

---

[2]J. Tedstrom, "An Economy Out of Control," Report on the USSR, February 16, 1990, pp. 1-5.

a world of long queues for all sorts of consumer goods, high-priced black markets, and "closed" shops where the Soviet elite buy goods at low prices and without long lines.

INCOMES IN THE SOVIET UNION

Ruble for ruble, the income of a low-ranking bureaucrat is about twice as large as the average wage in the Soviet Union. High-ranking members of the Soviet bureaucracy are paid about five times as much as an average worker. However, money incomes amount to only part of the Soviet elite's total, nonpecuniary incomes. Members of the nomenklatura have access to special shops, restaurants, resorts, country houses, and hospitals where goods are available to them without waiting and below cost.

Soviet workers are classified in eight categories based on several factors, including skill, experience, and job difficulty. The average monthly wage in the Soviet Union rose from about 160 rubles in the mid-1980s to about 220 rubles in 1989, reflecting double-digit inflation. The range of wage rates varies from one industry to another. In the mid-1980s, the range was from 80 rubles to 150 rubles per month in the lowest-paying food industry. The top wage in the highest-paying coal mining industry was 326 rubles per month. In general, the earnings of managerial and professional personnel are higher by about 24 percent; the earnings of wage earners by about 22 percent.

The important question is, What does the wage buy? One method for comparing the standard of living in different countries is to ask how long an average worker has to work in order to purchase various bundles of goods. Table 15-2 shows the number of hours of work required by average wage earners in Washington, D.C., and Moscow to purchase some selected goods. The table understates real prices in the Soviet Union on three grounds: the goods are not of the same quality, the goods are not always available, and the cost of waiting in line when the goods are available is not included in the statistics.

SOVIET AGRICULTURE

The agricultural sector accounts for about one fifth of the Soviet GNP and employs about 22 percent of the total labor force. In comparison, the agricultural sector in the U.S. contributes about 3 to 4 percent of the total GNP and employs about 2 percent of the labor force.

Soviet agriculture consists of three sectors: state farms, collective farms, and private plots. The main productive unit of the state sector is known as the Sovkhoz. The Sovkhoz is governed by the same rules that apply to other state enterprises and has its production and financial plan like any other firm in Russia. Its employees, however, are paid a wage that is not strongly linked to their performance. In the early 1980s there were about 15,000 state farms in Russia. They made up about half the total agricultural area in the Soviet Union.

The main productive unit of the collective sector is the Kolkhoz. There were about 33,000 collectives in the early 1980s. The average Kolkhoz has about 15,000 acres, about 450 households, some 60 tractors, 1,300 cattle, and 1,600 sheep and goats. In

Table 15-2. International income comparisons

	Hours Work	
Item	**Washington**	**Moscow**
Bread (1 kg)	16	17
Ground beef (1 kg)	37	123
Sausages (1 kg)	33	160
Cod (1 kg)	61	47
Sugar (1 kg)	9	58
Butter (1 kg)	55	222
Milk (1 liter)	6	22
Cheese (1 kg)	100	185
Eggs (10)	8	55
Potatoes (1 kg)	7	7
Cabbage (1 kg)	9	12
Carrots (1 kg)	11	19
Apples (1 kg)	10	92
Tea (100 g)	10	53
Beer (1 liter)	11	16
Vodka (.7 liter)	61	452
Cigarettes (20)	9	15
Weekly Basket (hours) (Family of Four)	18.6	53.5

Source: "What's the Difference?" National Federation of
Independent Business, 1982.

theory, the major differences between the Kolkhoz and Sovkhoz are that the Kolkhoz has collective rather than state ownership, and elected rather than appointed management. Given the overall control by the Party, however, those differences do not really matter. The Kolkhoz has to deliver a predetermined quota of its output to the state at low prices. This is really a tax in kind. What is left after the tax is shared by the collective farmers in accordance with the number of days each of them spent in the fields. Some of the output is consumed directly by members and some is sold in farm markets, with the proceeds shared by the collective farmers. Thus, the total income of collective farmers consists of payments in kind and monetary compensation. In general, farmers' incomes are below the average earnings of industrial workers.

The private sector consists of household subsidiary plots (about an acre per household) and household livestock holdings. Both collective and state farms' households are entitled to such plots. They do not have the right of ownership in that land—just the right to use it. On those plots households can grow anything they want for their own consumption or to be offered for sale in collective farm markets. Those plots account for only about 3 percent of the total agricultural area in the Soviet Union, yet they make a significant contribution to the total output in agriculture—about 33 percent of the Soviet Union's total agricultural output. On the average, private lots supply about 44 percent of the total income in cash and kind received by collective farm families.

The Quantitative Performance of the Soviet Economy

This section will offer a few selected statistics on the performance of the Soviet economy. They basically confirm the analysis of the effects of the Soviet-type institutions on the economy.

In the late 1980s, Soviet economists accused state statistical agencies of disseminating inaccurate data and falsifying statistics. The CIA's estimate of the Soviet economy has been criticized for the Agency's "bias." However, Aganbegyan, an economic advisor to Gorbachev, Khanin and Selyunin published their "adjusted" growth rates for the Soviet economy, which turned out to be worse than the CIA's figures.

Table 15-3. The average annual rate of growth

	1961-1970	1971-1980	1981-1985	1984	1985	1986	1987	1988
U.S.	3.8	2.8	3.0	7.2	3.4	2.7	3.7	4.4
USSR	4.9	2.6	1.9	1.5	.8	4.0	1.3	1.5

Source: Handbook of Economic Statistics, Washington, D.C.:
CPAS 89-10002, 1989, p. 33.

Table 15-4. USSR: Percent distribution of Soviet GNP at factor cost, by end use

	1960	1970	1975	1980	1984	1985	1986	1987	1988
Consumption	54	52	52	53	53	54	53	53	54
Investment	22	25	28	30	32	32	33	33	33
New Fixed	17	20	22	23	25	25	26	26	26
Administration and Other	24	23	20	17	15	14	14	14	13

Source: Handbook of Economic Statistics, Washington, D.C.: CPAS
89-10002, 1989, p. 60

Table 15-5. Alternative measures of Soviet economic
growth (average annual growth in percent)

	Official Soviet Statistics	Selyunin-Khanin Estimates	CIA Estimates
1951-60	10.3	7.2	5.1
1961-65	6.5	4.4	4.8
1966-70	7.8	4.1	5.0
1971-75	5.7	3.2	3.1
1976-80	4.3	1.0	2.2
1981-85	3.6	0.6	1.8

Source: Revisiting Soviet Economic Performance under
Glasnost: Implications for CIA Estimates,
Washington, D.C.: SOV 88-10068, 1988, p. 11.

Suggested Readings

The best source of current events in the Soviet Union is a weekly publication by Radio Liberty: <u>Report on the USSR</u>, Oettingenstrasse 67, D-8000 Munich, West Germany.

CHAPTER 16

TOWARD THE END OF THE SOVIET-TYPE ECONOMY

The Nature of Reforms in the Soviet-Type Economies

The rise of Mikhail Gorbachev to the top of the Soviet power structure in the mid-1980s triggered (perhaps coincided with) a series of reforms in the Soviet-type economies. These reforms caught the world by surprise. But the institutions of the Soviet-type economy are so loaded with disincentives and high transaction costs that they simply had, at some point in time, to generate pressures for changes from within the system. Some major observable circumstances that brought about those reforms were:

(i) Loss of faith in the inevitability of socialism. The performance of capitalist economies has refuted the Marxist belief that socialism is a superior system, which will inevitably triumph over capitalism. Thus, the present value of the cost of "building" socialism increased relative to the people's perception of the present value of promised future benefits.

(ii) Loss of faith in the ability of the ruling elite to fulfill the terms of the implicit social contract with the people. All Soviet-type economies have been deteriorating, their leaders have failed to improve living standards, and pockets of unemployment have appeared in most of those countries.

(iii) The younger generations in countries with Soviet-type economies are more pragmatic, better educated, and more aware of the quality of life in capitalist countries than those that grew up in the immediate post-revolutionary years. New generations have a much higher preference for current consumption over a hazy vision of things to come.

(iv) The ruling elite in the Soviet-type economies has recognized that high rates of capital formation are not a guarantee of high rates of economic growth.

In chapter 13, we defined the total relationship between the Politburo and the people as a social contract. We said that the power of the Politburo determines the nature of the contract, while the opportunity costs of the people affect its terms. In exchange for the Politburo's political and economic monopoly, the people in the Soviet-type economies were promised economic equality (only outside the ruling group), economic stability, guaranteed employment, a wide range of social welfare programs, an undemanding work pace, and a slow increase in living standards. A change in the contract would then be a change in the system, while a change in the terms of the contract could be interpreted as evidence of a change in the opportunity costs of the people.

The former happened in East European states toward the end of the 1980s. Those countries are now in the process of trying to replace the Soviet-type economy with a new set of institutional arrangements. Political changes in Eastern Europe have created an institutional vacuum in that part of the world. Thus, for the first time in decades, East European countries are in a position to choose their own institutional arrangements. In making those choices, East European countries are being influenced by a number of factors, including their respective philosophical heritages, the strength of the entrenched nomenklaturas, the inbred demand for welfare programs, and the balance of power among emerging political parties. While positive economic analysis cannot predict institutional developments in Eastern Europe, it can assist the East European people in evaluating the consequences of their choices.

While the social contract is being changed in Eastern Europe, Gorbachev is trying to save the Soviet-type economy in the USSR by adjusting the terms of the contract to changes in the opportunity costs of the people.

The Gorbachev Reforms in the USSR

A clear distinction should be made between glasnost and perestroika. Glasnost is about political changes that could be made within the Soviet system. Perestroika is about institutional changes in the system.

Glasnost is a reality in the USSR. For the first time since 1917, Soviet citizens are granted some limited civic and political freedoms. A number of issues, such as the quality of life in the country, national disputes, lying and cheating by the Soviet propaganda machine, widespread corruption, and shortages of consumer goods, are being widely discussed in the Soviet Union. Soviet citizens seem less worried about talking to foreigners. Soviet scholars attending academic meetings do not feel compelled to be of the same mind in political and economic issues. The Soviet government has relaxed the process of issuing exit and entry visas. The Soviet consumer also has crossed the threshold of fear. For example, by the end of December, 1989, a "special" store in the city of Yaroslavi received a shipment of Panasonic video cassette recorders. The crowd put the shop under siege. On the morning of the sixth day of siege, the first lucky consumer emerged with a VCR in his hands.

However, glasnost is not on a steady course. By the end of 1989, the Soviet government had reversed some of its earlier concessions and clamped down on others, including the video industry, publishing activities, and the manufacture of religious items. It also suspended many provisions in the law on state enterprises and the right of cooperatives to set their own prices. Finally, in March, 1990, a law was enacted that gave Gorbachev and his cohorts extraordinary powers to rule the country. Gorbachev proclaimed this law to be a step toward a greater democracy while refusing, at the same time, to discuss the Baltic states' demand for political independence.

In assessing glasnost, the real issue is not the number of concessions made by the ruling elite but the cost to the Politburo of retreating from glasnost. As of 1990, there is no legal mechanism in the USSR capable of preventing the Party from switching glasnost off. The passage of time is, however, bound to raise the leaders' costs of retreating from glasnost.

Economic Analysis of Perestroika

The purpose of perestroika is to save the Soviet system by changing the terms of the social contract. Changing the terms of this "contract" means changing Soviet institutions. The implementation of perestroika would modify property rights relationships, redefine the location of decision-making powers, and affect the benefits of the nomenklatura. From the standpoint of the Politburo and nomenklatura, perestroika could be costly reform.

The most important question about perestroika is, What does it take to implement economic reforms in the Soviet Union? To answer that question this chapter applies property-rights analysis to the following three objectives of perestroika: (i) making business firms more efficient, (ii) increasing the supply of inputs and consumer goods, and (iii) reducing the power of the Soviet bureaucracy.

To recapitulate, institutions are the legal, administrative, and customary arrangements (rules) that structure repeated human interactions. Different institutions create different incentives and transaction costs. It is through their own incentives and transaction costs that institutions have specific and predictable effects on the behavior of economic agents. The behavior of economic agents, in turn, determines economic outcomes.

PERESTROIKA AND BUSINESS FIRMS

Perestroika has been proposed to change the behavior of Soviet managers by relating their rewards to the firm's profitability. Profitability has been defined as the ratio of profits to the stock of capital. The reformers' hope is that this accountability measure would give managers more incentives to pursue innovating activities, to seek efficient production techniques, and to improve the quality of output.

In addition to announcing its intentions, the Politburo has to find a way to implement them. In this case, to make profit incentives work, perestroika has to change the Soviet manager's property rights in capital goods.

In the Soviet Union, the nomenklatura allocates capital goods to business firms, transfers existing capital goods (via administrative edict) from one enterprise to another without compensation, and decides what to do with investment funds. The Soviet firm cannot sell, rent, or modify capital goods in its possession. It can only use them to produce (and overproduce) its prescribed output target. Since the firm pays no rent for the use of capital goods, the Soviet manager naturally considers capital goods to be a free reserve. There is no penalty for having too much capital (relative to the firm's output target), and that excess capital comes in handy in frequent breakdowns and emergencies. It follows that Soviet managers have incentives to press administrative superiors for more capital. There is evidence that either through successful underreporting of their firm's production functions or through political pull, most managers have been able to acquire an excess of capital (and many other inputs, including labor) relative to their prescribed output targets and true production functions.

By making the manager's rewards depend on the firm's profitability, perestroika would change the penalty-reward system. Accumulated reserves of capital would become a liability rather than an asset. The emphasis on profitability would make managers cost-oriented. They would have incentives to minimize holdings of capital, or accept an increase in prescribed output targets. However, the prevailing property rights in capital goods would render the manager's incentives legally inoperative. Managers would want to control not only their replacement capital but also new additions to the firm's stock of capital. But to grant Soviet managers this property right, the Politburo and nomenklatura would have to give up their own property right of controlling output produced by capital goods industries.

The Politburo has two alternatives. It can leave Soviet managers frustrated in pursuing their new incentives, or it could give managers a right similar to usus fructus: the right to use an asset belonging to someone else or to rent it to others or to return it to the owner, but not to sell it or change its substance. If the Politburo chooses the first alternative, perestroika will fail. If it follows the second path, it would have a chance. The statement "would have a chance" means that the agency problem in the USSR must not be ignored. Recent reports from the USSR speak of new laws approved by the Politburo that have disappeared into the Soviet bureaucratic jungle.

PERESTROIKA AND THE PROBLEM OF SUPPLIES

An important objective of perestroika is to alleviate the shortage of supplies (inputs) and the shortage of consumer goods. To accomplish those objectives, the Soviet Politburo has approved several major reforms which should be expected to lower the costs of transactions.

Perestroika and the Shortage of Supplies. Perhaps the costliest problem facing Soviet planners has been that of assuring business firms of a timely and adequate supply of inputs. Perestroika has proposed three reforms to deal with this issue: free contracting for supplies (inputs), price reform, and long-term leases.

Free contracting for inputs means that voluntary horizontal relations among enterprises would replace vertical administrative orders in the Soviet economy. However, free contracting for supplies presupposes competitive markets. In addition to divesting the nomenklatura of an important source of its influence and income, the emergence of competitive markets would require two institutional changes in the Soviet economic system. First, because the output of one firm is the supply of inputs for another, the Soviet manager's right to choose for whom to produce must be accompanied by the right to decide how much to produce. This means that the Soviet planning bureaucracy would have to relinquish control over the volume of output produced by business firms. Second, the implementation of free contracting for supplies would also require a change in Soviet financial institutions. To negotiate contracts with other enterprises the Soviet firm must be given the right to hold and use cash balances, as well as the right to negotiate short-term credits.

Relating the manager's rewards to the residual of the firm provides some efficiency-oriented incentives. However, to evaluate alternatives, the manager must know the opportunity costs of the inputs used by the firm. In the Soviet Union, the value of goods and the real cost of producing them are simply not known. To change that situation requires scarcity prices. But price reform is still in the distance. Consumer prices are supposed to be decontrolled sometime in the mid-1990s.

To deal with economic problems in Soviet agriculture, the Politburo announced a new long-term lease program. Under the program the government will lease land, livestock, equipment, and all other state-owned means of production to Soviet farmers. Soviet leaders seem to think that long-term leases of state-owned resources can duplicate the incentives of private ownership. It could be true, but only if institutions played no part. But they do and, in this case, for at least two reasons. First, the leasing arrangements do not address problems such as land pricing, obligations to meet the economic plan (under unknown price conditions), access to short- and long-term bank credit, the availability of inputs such as fertilizers, and state taxation. According to the Soviet Analyst of February 21, 1990, the Ministry of Finance has yet to provide lessees with a new tax system. Without knowing how they will be taxed, farmers have no guarantees of a certain future. Moreover, the branch offices of the ministry are doing their best to stifle the program by reorganizing whole collectives when the demand for leases appears.

Second, unless the would-be farmholders are given the right to transfer the leased resources to other farmers (or individuals) at scarcity prices, the long-term lease program would have no mechanism for moving resources from less-efficient to more-efficient users. Thus, a fifty-year lease of state-owned resources in the Soviet Union cannot, without some institutional modifications, approach the results of private ownership.

Perestroika and the Shortage of Consumer Goods. The "second economy" is supposed to alleviate the shortage of consumer goods and increase the range of choices available to Soviet citizens. The law on state enterprises of 1987, the law on cooperatives of 1988, and the recent debate on the law on property ownership of 1990 are attempts to allow individuals, within well-defined and controlled frameworks, to engage in private exchange so that they can provide the population with products that are in short supply. Those laws have faced considerable opposition from the very beginning from bureaucrats who see them as illegitimate offspring of the system, from hooligans who have discovered that it is inexpensive to terrorize cooperative members and their patrons, and from ordinary citizens who complain about the high prices charged and high incomes earned by "private" cooperatives. In 1989 the Council of Ministers restricted various cooperative activities. Those restrictions reinforce uncertainty about the future of one's private investment in the second economy.

The Soviet institutional structure creates problems for the second economy and its participants. An individual operating in the second economy has incentives to produce goods that are not highly visible, but uncertainties about the future of the second economy mean that all decisions must be based on a short time horizon. The development of the second economy also depends on the extent to which the state economy is willing to provide it with the necessary supplies. It is highly unrealistic for individuals in the second economy to expect that state enterprises and banks would provide them with a steady flow of supplies, tools, and credits their operations require.

The institutional change that would generate a steady flow of inputs and a variety of consumer goods would be the creation of a capital market and a competitive banking system. And this change would necessitate further privatization of resources.

PERESTROIKA AND THE NOMENKLATURA

The implementation of reforms depends on the Politburo's trade-off between its benefits from correcting economic problems via institutional changes and its costs of upsetting the nomenklatura. Gorbachev seems to be uncertain about the costs associated with various trade-offs. He said at the 27th Party Congress: "We set ourselves the aim of enlarging the autonomy of enterprises" and then in the same speech, "we set ourselves the aim of strengthening the role of the center in implementing the main goals of the Party's strategy." This is clearly a statement that refuses to make a choice. The entire text in the blueprint of proposed reforms published in Pravda on June 27, 1989, is an equivocation, a typical committee product full of contradictory statements, sophomoric economics, and political compromises. For example, the document says, "It is essential to abandon administrative and high-handed methods and move on to economic management methods" and then, "the attainment of strategic goals of the economic policy of the Communist Party calls for the creation of a central guidance system."

The strength of the nomenklatura's opposition to reforms depends on the benefits it stands to lose. In general, the relevant cost of any specific institutional change is the effect of that change on the power and privileges of a cluster of bureaucrats. From the standpoint of the nomenklatura, the only costs that count are those which are borne by members of the ruling class. Social costs and social benefits related to the general public receive little consideration in Soviet decision making, and the power of the Soviet bureaucracy to (quietly) sabotage any reform is considerable.

Given the Politburo's cost of monitoring the nomenklatura, the latter has exhibited several methods for neutralizing economic reforms. For example, the nomenklatura keeps returning the proposals and directives to the Politburo with opinions and questions raised by experts. The law on property ownership of February, 1990, is an example. In February, 1990, the Soviet bureaucracy was able to water down the law on private ownership, arguing that the term "private" is offensive to the Soviet people, and that it would revive the "exploitation of man by man." During the same month, the bureaucracy was able to restrict the right of state enterprises to engage in foreign trade by imposing licensing controls. Also, internal trade barriers, in the form of restrictions on retail sales to people other than local residents, were enacted in many parts of the Soviet Union. The nomenklatura also keeps the proposals for economic and social changes in various committees for more "thorough" analysis of their "side effects." Finally, the proposals are frequently moved at a snail's pace through the bureaucratic channels.

A second method the nomenklatura may use to neutralize economic reform is to try to shift the cost of economic reforms to the Soviet consumer. As we pointed out earlier in this chapter, the principle of profitability is supposed, via a change in property rights in capital goods, to lower the costs of production in Soviet enterprises. An alternative course of action for the nomenklatura is to keep property rights in capital goods the same and to let the firms raise their prices. The firms would then turn out to be profitable irrespective of their production inefficiencies. The cost of economic reform would be borne by the consumer, while the Politburo would be given evidence that economic reforms are working.

The jury is still out on the fate of perestroika. Writing for the January 26, 1990, issue of the Report on the USSR, Philip Hanson, a noted Soviet expert, concluded his analysis of perestroika saying that "in 1989, the Soviet economy probably became, on balance, more centrally controlled than before."

In April, 1990, Gorbachev ruled out Polish-style economic reforms and "delayed" the introduction of market prices. According to a report published in the New York Times[1], this decision was made because the government does not have the popular support for such drastic change. N. Petrakov, Gorbachev's personal economic advisor was quoted as saying that "people accept rationing coupons and standing in line—especially during work time—but not price increases." S. Shatalin, an economist in Gorbachev's cabinet justified the decision to defer price decontrols—the most essential ingredient of economic reform—as follows: "In the Soviet Union Gorbachev's opponents would be quick to exploit any unpopular economic measure to challenge our government. The opposition to market reforms is coming this time not from government ministries (i.e., the bureaucracy] but from politicians who play on the moods of the masses." Yet, recent local elections throughout the Soviet Union have demonstrated remarkable support for reform-oriented candidates.

It is naive to simply assume that a speech by Gorbachev, and/or a Politburo's resolution, and/or a decree on a new policy are enough to change the Soviet economy. Economic analysis of Soviet institutions and economic processes makes this point quite clear. To implement a change in the system, Soviet leaders must modify that country's institutions so that they can embrace the novelty. That is, economic analysis of Soviet reforms in the USSR should concentrate on spelling out the institutional adjustments that

---

[1]"Gorbachev Delays Economic Plans," New York Times, April 25, 1990, pp. 1 and 7.

each announced economic change requires, and after a period of time has elapsed, consider the results.

The jury is also out on Gorbachev's attempt to rewrite the contract with the people. It is difficult for him to know the extent to which the opportunity costs of the Soviet people have changed. Should Gorbachev's perception of changes in the opportunity costs of the people exceed those of the nomenklatura, he might be in trouble. On the other hand, the system might be in trouble if he failed to estimate those changes correctly.

Suggested Readings

Hewett, Ed. Reforming the Soviet Economy, Washington, D.C.: Brookings Institute, 1988.
Pejovich, S. "A Property Rights Analysis of Perestroika," Communist Economies, 2, 1990.
Schroeder, G. "An Anatomy of Gorbachev's Economic Reforms," Soviet Economy, 3, 1987.

APPENDIX

ECONOMIC DEVELOPMENTS IN HUNGARY AND POLAND

While announced economic changes in the Soviet Union represent an attempt to make the existing system more viable, Hungary and Poland have moved away from the Soviet-type economy. Those two countries are now in the process of searching for institutional arrangements. Thus, it is too early to evaluate their systems.

The purpose of this appendix is to present the current thinking of top decisionmakers in Hungary and Poland, with one important warning: the papers should be recognized for what they are—a search for a new set of institutions. The subsequent laws and regulations that transform intentions into reality will tell us more about the true direction of change in those two countries. As it was pointed out before, the divergence between intentions and reality is predictable for many reasons, such as (i) the basic intentions are bound to have unintended and unexpected consequences that will force the leadership to modify the components of the system as time goes by, and (ii) the implementation of those intentions into real life is in the hands of the bureaucracy, which is likely to have its own interpretations of the leaders' intentions.

Hungary

SUMMARY OF DEVELOPMENTS IN THE HUNGARIAN ECONOMY, IN 1988[2]

The record of events in the Hungarian economy of 1988 represented a definite step towards sustainable macroeconomic equilibrium and structural improvement. The country managed to lessen its reliance on external savings by cutting the deficit of its current account vis-a-vis the rest of the world. The improvement of the external balance was, to a great extent, achieved by concerted Government policy actions enforcing tight conditions on the domestic markets, which had the cost of zero growth of gross domestic income and an unusual drop of the level of real household consumption. At the same time, the increased tightness of macroeconomic policies pressed Hungarian producers to sell their products on external markets, which was intended to be an efficient incentive for structural modernization. In fact, exports of manufactured products to convertible currency areas picked up dramatically, which was also helped by exogenous factors, including buoyant domestic demand in developed economies. During the year, the Government continued the implementation of its medium-term reform program through, most importantly, a sweeping tax reform, sizeable cuts in subsidies from the state budget and consecutive steps to liberalize the determination of consumer prices. A fundamental deregulation of individuals' traveling abroad also took place, which had significant macroeconomic and structural effects already in 1988.

The macroeconomic targets for 1988 included first of all the cut of Hungary's convertible currency current external deficit to USD 500 million (from USD 846 million in 1987). Although some shortfall against the target was actually registered, the outcome was a cut of the deficit to USD 592 million (2.1 percent of GDP), substantially close to expectations. With exports running by 9 percent and imports dropping in real terms, the trade balance was in a surplus of USD 370 million, an improvement of USD 675 million over the previous year. However, gains in the trade balance were partially offset by more than tripling travel expenditures under the new passport regulations.

Following several years of lively international borrowing activity, Hungary cut its reliance on new external financing in 1988. Gross external borrowing for medium- and long-term dropped to USD 2.3 billion (USD 3.1 billion in 1987 and even more than that earlier). New loans and bond issues were contracted in a balanced situation on the market. During the year, Hungary also borrowed from multilateral agencies, including the IMF and the World Bank. The overall balance was roughly in equilibrium, the stock of international reserves reached a comfortable level (USD 2.2 billion) at the end of the year.

On non-convertible currency external accounts, Hungary had a large structural current payments surplus in the last couple of years. As the country's net external position

---

[2]Prepared by the National Bank of Hungary for the Conference on Hungary into the Nineties, Budapest, November, 1989.

against non-convertible currency regions was estimated to turn over into positive, the maintenance of substantial surpluses on a regular basis became less desirable by 1988. The problem was accentuated by a more than 3 percent terms of trade gain and the traditionally high level of the country's surplus on the service accounts, most notably tourism. However, the Government succeeded to stabilize the level of CMEA exports by cutting financial incentives and to raise the volume of imports from the CMEA by 4 percent. This contributed to the moderation of the need for imports from convertible currency areas and lessened the exports of Hungarian savings through pressing down the non-convertible currency current account surplus to USD 203 million.

Throughout the year, the rate of economic growth was subordinated to external adjustment in the framework of the Government's macroeconomic policies. To curtail domestic demand, tight financial policies were enforced on both the fiscal and the monetary areas. Through sizeable cuts of budgetary subsidies, the efficient management of the new taxes and mid-year measures on both the revenue and the expenditure side, the deficit of the state budget was cut in 1988 to 1.4 percent of GDP from nearly 3 percent of GDP in 1987. Monetary control by the Bank was substantially activated, as tight management of the level of global reserves in the banking system was enforced through central banking refinancing policies. At the same time, central bank interest rates and administered interest rates for households credit and deposit facilities were raised several times in 1988. With the gradually increasing level of interest rates on the market and the decreasing reliance of the state budget on monetary financing the growth of domestic credit by the banking sector slowed down to 5 percent in 1988 from 11 percent in 1987, and the expansion of broad money to 2 percent in 1988 from 8 percent in 1987. To promote external adjustment, the forint was devaluated by 6 percent against convertible currencies in July. With all the above means, final domestic demand was pressed down by 2.3 percent in real terms, which forced many producers to switch their sales to external markets. The volume of GDP remained at the 1987 level.

The structural reform measures introduced in 1988 implied a high risk of macro-economic instability. First, in replacement of various selective taxes, simpler and more equitable systems for a value-added tax and a personal income tax were introduced at the beginning of the year. The fundamental change in the taxation structure involved a great degree of uncertainties in the state budget, and the price as well as the wage system. Second, a substantial portion of consumer and producer price subsidies was terminated at the same time, which caused the level of consumer prices to increase by 8 percent overnight on January 1, 1988. To lessen the risks involved and avoid a possible escalation of the inflationary process, a temporary general price-freeze was enforced up to March 31, and a stringent system for wage taxation was maintained throughout the year. Although the price system was substantially liberalized later in the year, financial policies managed to contain domestic demand. Consumer price inflation was an annual 15.7 percent, slightly higher than targeted.

In the course of 1988, the implementation of Hungary's bankruptcy legislation was further enforced. Restructuring operations were pursued at the sectoral (e.g., coal mining, ferrous metallurgy) as well as the individual enterprise level. A number of large firms were restructured organizationally and financially, some of them were split into medium-size units, which were converted into joint-stock companies. The liquidation ratio was gradually increasing in the circle of smaller size units. Registered unemployment increased to an annual average of 15,000 people, 0.3 percent of the active population.

PRIVATIZATION IN HUNGARY[3]

After twenty years of half-hearted and cautious economic reforms, characterized by achievements and failures, aspirations and hesitations, progress and retreats, it is now clear that Hungary has recently embarked on a historic experiment to implement a global and profound, indeed, revolutionary change of its political and economic system.

The essential objective is to change the whole political and economic system by creating a workable market economy as well as a genuine parliamentary democracy based upon a multiparty system.

It seems that the quiet revolution aiming at the establishment of a new political and economic system is steadily progressing despite all the problems and difficulties involved in such a historic change. These problems are aggravated by the economic crisis essentially due to the unworkability of a social and economic system termed as "existing socialism" and characterized by a heavy debt burden in hard currency, by domestic government debt and also in a more general sense by a debt towards the national health, education, and the environment.

It is confirmed by historic experience that a centralized economic system, a state-controlled or planned economy is incompatible with a democratic political system. (Examples to the contrary—i.e., a totalitarian political system living together with a market economy—are to be found, but their number is diminishing.) It is also demonstrated by experience that a truly decentralized economic system based upon not a bureaucratic, hierarchical coordination but upon market mechanisms cannot be established without independent and external owners, in other words, without private ownership. This is perhaps the most important lesson taught by the Hungarian economic reforms which were started in 1968 and which tried to create a market-oriented economy without essentially changing the ownership structure. This created a number of fundamental contradictions that eventually resulted in the failure of the reforms. (However, the reforms were characterized by some successes as well, particularly in terms of a gradual changing of people's thinking and the preparation of the system as a whole for more radical change.) The Hungarian experiment demonstrates that, indeed, private ownership is a fundamental prerequisite for the establishment of a workable market system.

---

[3]Prepared by Janos Martonyi, Professor of Law and Commissioner for Privatization in Hungary, for The Karl Brunner Symposium on Analysis and Ideology, Interlaken, June, 1990.

The conclusion to be derived from these two tenets verified by historic experience is that private ownership cannot be dissociated from political democracy and its basic human values.

For all the above reasons Hungary has to reshape radically its present ownership system; in other words, we have to undergo a global and radical process of privatization. It will be a process of historic importance, the final result of which is very little disputed. There appears to exist a general consensus that the privatization process will, ultimately, have to result in an economy where the role of private ownership—individual or associated (corporations, cooperatives)—together with different forms of communal property, funds and foundations, will be predominant and where the state property will be relegated to a minority status and restricted to some special areas, such as public utility and perhaps some strategic industries.

However, the actual development of this process and the exact outcome of it, including the proportions of this or another ownership type or form, should not be predetermined or prefixed for any ideological reasons whatsoever. Although the end result will be influenced by criteria related to political or moral values as referred to above, the fundamental criterion to be followed in this process will have to be economic efficiency. It is essentially the increase of efficiency that has to guide any successful privatization process and that has to be the primary criterion of measuring its success or failure.

As regards the ways and means of achieving the above objectives, the opinions are far more divergent. One of the most important underlying questions to which most of the controversial issues are related is what should be the responsibility and function of the state and its role in bringing back the society to normal evolution, and, more specifically, what role the state has to play in the transformation of a state-controlled economy into a market economy. Is this role to be restricted to deregulation and liberalization, leaving essentially the task of recuperation to a kind of "autotherapy" of society, to its self-generated, spontaneous forces? Or, on the contrary, should the state play an active role in this operation "back to normal"? The answer to this question is that the state cannot avoid its responsibility for the control and direction of the transition; it has to guide, and it has to play an active role.

The forms and techniques of this intervention, in other words, the short-term and long-term legislatory, regulatory, or administrative measures to be taken are the central factors of the Hungarian privatization policy. To understand the implementation of this policy we need a brief review of the existing legal, economic and social framework of state-owned enterprises (SOE) in Hungary.

In the traditional, Stalinist system SOE's are closely linked to the state administration; they form part, as a matter of fact, of a hierarchical, bureaucratic system based upon subordination. In this model, the functions of the state as an owner of the means of production and the functions of the state as a regulator (or as a public authority) are amalgamated and the enterprise is absorbed by the all-pervading and dominating power of the Party-State.

From the earliest days of this Stalinist system, enterprises had an inherent drive to detach themselves, at least to some extent, from this "paramilitary" structure and to correspond to economic necessities qualitatively different from those of state administrations. The concept of "self-accountancy" was soon invented, contractual forms were reintroduced, although all this remained of a purely formal nature. One of the main objectives of the economic reforms of the late sixties in Czechoslovakia and Hungary was to increase substantially the degree of legal and economic autonomy of the SOE's and to free them, to the greatest possible degree, from the state as an all-powerful owner. In Hungary the progressive decentralization of the economic decision making started essentially with the introduction of the so-called "New Economic Mechanism." This began in 1968 and culminated in 1984 with the separation of the SOE's (or at least the basic form of them) from the state as an owner. The separation became almost complete with the introduction of the so-called self-governing enterprises. With the introduction of this concept the exercise of the ownership rights of about 75 percent of all SOE's was delegated to the elected enterprise councils. It became soon apparent that the self-governing enterprises are not only managed and controlled, but also de facto owned by the managers of the enterprise; in other words, the enterprise has become a kind of "self-owning" entity. All strategic decisions, including the establishment of secondary companies and transferring the enterprise's assets into that or those companies, or the selling or leasing of the enterprise's assets, are made by the management of the enterprise. The proceeds from these transactions belong to the enterprise which can freely dispose of them. Also, the enterprise may transform itself as a whole into a joint stock company or limited liability company by a decision brought by the enterprise council. The terms and conditions of the transformation of self-governing or self-administered as well as of state-administered SOE's into joint stock or limited liability companies are contained in the Transformation Law (Act XIII of 1989) adopted by the Parliament in May, 1989. The purpose of this much-disputed legislation was to facilitate the corporatization of state-owned enterprises (which have no corporate structure) based upon the principle of global legal succession.

The SOE's not belonging to the self-governing category are the enterprises under the control of public authorities, i.e., ministries or local councils (state-administered enterprises). Here, again, the degree of autonomy of the enterprise is very high (this kind of enterprise can also establish secondary companies, etc.), but the ownership rights are not delegated to the enterprise. Until recent legislation the decision on the transformation of the enterprise as a whole into a joint stock or limited liability company fell in the competence of the public authority ("founding organization") under the control of which the enterprise is operating. Since March 1, 1990, it is the newly-established State Property Agency that has the powers to transform, indeed, to corporatize the state-administered enterprises.

In Hungary the most important legal device of privatization is at present the total or partial transformation of SOE-s into joint stock or limited liability companies. Self-governing SOE's in most cases opt for a partial transformation, this solution being more favorable for them in financial terms and also giving them more freedom under the terms of legislation. (While the transformation as a whole is regulated by the above-mentioned Transformation Law in a rather detailed and complicated manner according to which the shares of the newly set up company are distributed between the state and the company itself, the partial transformation was, before the legislation on the protection of assets entrusted to state-owned enterprises, not regulated except for the general provisions of company law.) The newly set up company is under the exclusive control of the enterprise which, of course, continues to exist.

Until recent legislation the total or partial transformation of SOE's depended entirely on the decision of the SOE's themselves. In all these cases it was the SOE that "privatized" itself by selling state-owned assets to companies where there are several shareholders, private or other, including, in most cases, foreigners as well. This is what is called spontaneous or decentralized privatization or a "quiet ownership reform" which started about a year ago and which has gained remarkable momentum due to a number of economic and political factors. (One of these factors is the fear of central, government devised and implemented privatization measures.)

This spontaneous or "self-privatization" has some considerable drawbacks and involves serious risks such as undervaluation of assets or other unfavorable conditions for the legal owner, i.e., the state. There are also some political risks involved with respect to the negative reaction of the public opinion and of the political parties provoked by some dubious transactions.

On the other hand, in the light of the special circumstances presently existing in Hungary, such as the high degree of already achieved decentralization of state ownership that can be termed as a sort of semi-privatization and also the very high proportion of the nominal state ownership in the national wealth (about 90%), this peculiar form of privatization cannot be entirely dispensed with. Despite all the handicaps and risks involved, the spontaneous privatization has generated positive developments as well. It is instrumental in the separation of ownership and management (although in a contradictory and sometimes distorted manner), in breaking up and in decentralizing the closed and outdated structure of big monopolistic or oligopolistic enterprises and it therefore contributes to the increase in the number of economic actors and accordingly encourages competition and market mechanisms.

At the same time, spontaneous privatization is closely linked to foreign investment as in most cases there is a foreign equity participation in the company established by the enterprise. Partial transformation and setting up companies with foreign participation ("joint ventures") are, therefore, very much the same things. It is a well-known fact that foreign investment, and all that involves in terms of capital, technology, know-how, experience, marketing, etc., is a vital factor of the renewal and modernization of the Hungarian economy and also of the full integration of the national economy in the world economy.

As regards the evaluation of the present privatization process as well as the ways and means to be applied in privatizing SOE's there are—in present Hungary—two diametrically opposing views. One is the "liberal" approach which says that spontaneous privatization is, despite all the contradictions, distortions and possible abuses, fine. It must not be curbed; quite on the contrary, it has to be encouraged. In this philosophy, the changing of the ownership system has to rely primarily on spontaneous, organic evolution, on the self-generated forces of society. The state is the worst possible owner, second to none in inefficiency and anything is better than a revival of state intervention in the economy, a rebureaucratization of semi-privatized SOE's, be it in the guise of privatization. Spontaneous privatization of SOE's has, therefore, to be the basic form of changing the ownership system in Hungary, even if there is a price to be paid, inter alia, in terms of a lack of budgetary revenue. (In case of partial transformation of a SOE into a company no proceeds go to the state at all.) The essential thing is that the property will be operated in a more efficient manner and this is the basic macroeconomic purpose of the exercise.

The opposing approach—again with some simplification—advocates a global and immediate "re-nationalization" of self-governing ("self-owning") SOE's in order to de-nationalize them within the framework of a government-led privatization. In this view a consequent and successful privatization policy cannot be designed and implemented but by the state or government. Spontaneous or decentralized privatization, although ultimately contributing to the change of the ownership system, has serious harmful effects (undervaluation of national assets, disappearing of state property, abuses of all kinds, etc.) that endanger the credibility and efficiency of the whole privatization process partly because of the adverse political consequences that it brings about. Budgetary revenues are virtually missing and this is such a luxury that the Hungarian economy, especially in the present state of its indebtedness, simply cannot afford.

There are valid points and mistakes in both approaches. The self-governing (self-owning) enterprise is indeed a theoretically unworkable concept. However, it would probably be a dangerous exercise to abolish this enterprise form immediately and at one stroke. Such a radical measure may damage the economy and it would risk entailing unforeseeable economic consequences. Even if there is sufficient political consensus and determination to take such an action, the question may be rightly asked, who would run those enterprises, indeed the economy in the meantime, that is, until the time all these enterprises can be effectively privatized. (Full-scale privatization needs—and this is virtually not disputed—a relatively long period, the length of which cannot be easily predicted.)

In view of the present circumstances as well as of the long-term objectives, a realistic and successful privatization policy has to be built upon both the spontaneous and on the government-led privatization.

The legislation adopted at the end of January, 1990, and entered into force on March 1, 1990, reflected this compromise approach.

The law on the State Property Agency (Act VII of 1990) and the law on the protection of national property entrusted to enterprises (Act VIII of 1990) are inspired by the following fundamental considerations:

- to bring the spontaneous privatization under a degree of national control in order to prevent or at least to reduce abuses and losses resulting therefrom and at the same time to protect the actors of the spontaneous privatization against subsequent accusations;
- to create the institutional framework for a well-designed and properly coordinated privatization policy in order to speed up the changing of the whole ownership system;

- to concentrate and to strengthen the state powers and to improve the legal conditions for a government-led privatization policy.

To achieve the above objectives the following main provisions were included in the two legislatory texts:

- Since March 1, 1990, it is the State Property Agency that has the authority to corporatize state-administered SOE's, i.e., to convert them into joint stock or limited liability companies. (State-administered enterprises constitute only around 25 percent of all SOE's but represent almost 50 percent of their production.) Previously, the authority to transform state-administered enterprises belonged to the so-called "founding organization" which was either the branch ministry or the local council.
- The Board of Directors of the SPA has the right—on the recommendation of the Prime Minister or the Managing Director of the SPA—to "re-classify" self-governing enterprises into the group of state-administered ones, i.e., to take them under state administration in order to convert them into companies. Simultaneously with or subsequently to this conversion the new entity having corporate structure and owned by the state can be partially or totally privatized by the SPA.
- In respect of the partial transformation of SOE's which is carried out essentially by transferring the assets of the enterprise to newly set up "secondary" companies the SPA has important control rights. These include the compulsory valuation of the assets transferred to companies as in kind contributions, sold or leased. All transactions above a certain value have to be either notified to the agency or published, inviting the public for competitive biddings. In other words, notification would have to be made only in case the enterprise does not want to publish the transaction and does not want to invite competition. The SPA has the possibility either to ask for additional valuation or to prescribe competitive biddings, or, in exceptional cases, to veto the transaction.
- The transformation as a whole of self-governing enterprises decided by the enterprise has to be notified to the SPA which has a right of veto over the transaction. (The condition of exercise of the veto right in respect of total, as well as of partial transformation, is that the transaction would damage the national economy or it would seriously prejudice the public interest. The enterprise has the right to contest the SPA's decision vetoing the transaction before the court.)

The above rights give the SPA relatively wide powers to design and implement a coherent privatization policy. The state-administered enterprises can be corporatized without difficulty and they can be sold by applying the various internationally known privatization techniques. (The actual privatization operations can themselves be privatized by using the services of a wide range of contractors and consultants relying upon their knowledge and expertise.) Self-governing enterprises can be taken under state-administration and thereafter the procedure can be the same as in the case of those which are presently state-administered. The most difficult and politically most sensitive decision is the reclassification which may also be considered as a kind of, albeit provisional, "renationalization" of the self-governing SOE's. This is, however, pending future legislation, the main legal means of widening the scope of government-led privatization where the most efficient techniques can be used and where the proceeds from the sales go to the SPA. This income can be used either for the settlement of the state debts or for being reconverted in the economy. (Self-governing enterprises can be directly corporatized as well under the terms of the Transformation Law which, as mentioned above, provides for a very complicated scheme for the distribution of shares in the new company as well as of the proceeds; as a result of these provisions only a limited part of the shares resp. of the proceeds belongs to the state. These provisions can, however, be departed from by common agreement of the Agency and the enterprise.)

(In the control area, the SPA acquired very important intervention rights to safeguard the transparency, the efficiency and the cleanness of the spontaneous privatization, i.e. the self-selling of the SOE's. The right of veto gives the SPA a strong bargaining position to negotiate with the self-governing enterprise and to make reasonable recommendations. At the same time, it is vitally important that the control remains sufficiently flexible so that the progress of privatization and the influx of foreign capital and technology are not hampered. The essential purpose of the control is to ensure a preventive effect against possible abuses or negligence and not to hinder reasonable transactions promoting the changing of the ownership system. Another important function of the control is to provide protection of the actors of the transactions—management and foreign investors alike—against subsequent reproaches and accusations. The control also enhances the legal security of the buyer/investor in view of the fact that the owner, after having the possibility of reviewing the transaction, has given his approval to it. (The clearance is granted simply by silence; if the SPA does not react to the notification within 30 days the transaction is deemed to be approved of.)

The SPA has to carry out its activity in conformity with the Asset Policy Guidelines adopted by the Parliament. The Guidelines can be considered as the basic framework of the privatization program for a given period. They set the criteria for the selection of state administered SOE's to be corporatized and privatized as well as for the selection of self-governing enterprises to be reclassified, corporatized and privatized. The Guidelines also establish the basic objectives and techniques of privatization, the procedures to follow, and the criteria of contracting out. The conditions and expectations relating to the selling of state property to foreigners (technological progress, prospective markets, reduction of state debts) are also specified in the Guidelines.

The role of foreign direct investments is fundamental in respect of both the spontaneous and the government-led privatization. The FDI and privatization are, indeed, interdependent to the effect that on the one hand, privatization of the Hungarian economy is impossible without a major contribution of foreign capital resources while, on the other hand, the qualitative increase of foreign direct investments in Hungary is dependent upon the establishment of a market economy environment where the role of private ownership is predominant. At the same time, FDI is an indispensable prerequisite not only of a successful privatization policy but also of the modernization and restructuring of the industry and the re-integration of the national economy in the world economy. These are the main reasons why foreign investments have been encouraged and attracted by a very liberal legislation as well as by a wide range of incentives for a number of years. Privatization opens new possibilities for foreign investors, for commercial partners and for financial institutions alike. Commercial partners are active mainly in the field of spontaneous privatization involving, in most cases, the sale of physical assets and establishing companies with foreign participation while merchant and investment banks will have to play a major role in the field of government-led privatization primarily involving the sale of securities. (A new law on the establishment of Stock Exchange and on Securities was also adopted and entered into force on February 1, 1990.)

The legislation adopted early this year is certainly not the final word in creating the necessary institutional legal and financial conditions for the privatization of the state-owned enterprises. These have only been the indispensable steps for the launching of the historic operation, the successful performance of which requires many further legislative and other measures. There are, inter alia, as follows:

1. The issue of the self-governing enterprise, i.e., the problem posed by the delegation of ownership rights to the enterprise councils and the difficulties resulting therefrom will have to be resolved by the strengthening of ownership controls and by the progressive removal of the self-governing enterprise as a corporate form having neither corporate structure, nor real and external owners. Corporatization will have to be promoted and enforced in a more direct, more simple, and more efficient manner.

2. The development of financial institutions (investment banks, funds, foundations, etc.) indispensable for the successful implementation of any privatization policy will have to be encouraged by all possible means. These institutions would be instrumental not only in selling state property at the best possible conditions and on a competitive basis, but also in channeling and attracting private savings of the population to be mobilized for privatization.

3. The accumulation of presently scarce private savings and their direct or indirect investment in presently state-owned shares will also have to be encouraged by all sorts of incentives, such as tax allowances, credit facilities, etc.

4. To increase financial resources for privatization special attention has to be paid to employee ownership arrangements. A Hungarian ESOP scheme has to be elaborated which would facilitate the purchasing of stocks by the employees. This approach is warmly supported by many of the political parties and it could enhance employee and management motivation which is badly needed to increase the efficiency of the Hungarian industry. The Hungarian adaptation of the ESOP would be based upon corporate tax allowances regarding the dividend due to the employees as well as on credit facilities offered by commercial banks to the stock purchasers and refinanced by the note bank from the proceeds of privatization.

5. In specific sectors such as the retail trade, restaurants and services special, sector-specific legal methods should be applied in order to eliminate state ownership from an economic sector where at that time nationalization had the most absurd consequences. This sector-specific method would consist in the mandatory privatization, i.e., selling to the general public of not the enterprises themselves, but their "units" (shops, restaurants, etc.) many of which already operate on a contractual (lease or other) basis and are, indeed, semi-privatized.

It is evident that the success of the Hungarian privatization policy depends on a large number of interconnected factors all being related to the establishment of a workable market economy (capital market, competitiveness of products, liberalization of imports, convertibility of currency, etc.) as well as a genuine political democracy. Privatization is therefore a means and a goal at the same time. Its successful accomplishment would ensure that this time we do not miss the chance of history.

Poland

OUTLINE OF ECONOMIC PROGRAM[4]

I. The Starting Point

1. The Polish economy requires fundamental system changes. Their objective is to set up a market system akin to the one found in the industrially developed countries. This will have to be achieved quickly, through radical actions, so that the transitional stage, so hard on the society, be cut as short as possible. Selection of this way is also dictated by the bad experience with surface-only reforms of the eighties. The causes behind the acute floundering of the reform are imbedded deeply in the economic system applied so far. Without their fundamental change we will continue to sink in an atmosphere of general incapacity and a permanent crisis situation. No expedient measures can change this situation.

2. We are embarking on the reshaping effort under extremely adverse conditions. The economy is in ever more tenuous disequilibrium, on the verge of financial collapse of the state. The ecological disaster, the housing crisis, the foreign debt burden, emigration to earn money by the most active part of the young generation—these have been swelling for years.

In recent months additional crisis symptoms surfaced or mounted in force: rapid price climb linked with wage explosion, the flight from the zloty, growing deficit of the state budget, and also a drop in output.

3. Only a courageous breakthrough to match the historic challenge faced by Poland will allow the country to extricate itself from a civilizational collapse, to build an order corresponding with social expectations. The Government has decided to effect a system breakthrough, and the ensuing program expresses this determination.

---

[4]Submitted by the Ministry of Finance and approved by the Council of Ministers at its meeting on October 9, 1989.

II. General Premises Underlying the Program

1. The Government economic program calls for two types of action. First, stabilizing the economy, and in particular bringing inflation in hand, and second, transforming the economic system.

2. The program is to be implemented in two phases. In the first stage, which is to last no longer than to the beginnings of 1990, actions will be taken to slow down the rate of price increases, stem the flight away from the zloty and curb the budget deficit (see III, points 1-9).

This phase also covers designing the proposed changes in the economic system and taking appropriate organizational and legislative action.

3. The phase of the substantive changes will begin not later than in early 1990.

It will imply the application of a set of radical anti-inflation measures which, carried out into effect consistently, will allow for decisively reducing the growth rate of prices and to recapture market balance (see II, point 12). The earlier conceived, fundamental system changes will also be carried out during this phase.

4. One should note that effective implementation of the economic stabilization program is the necessary prerequisite for success in pursuing the system changes, as such changes cannot be carried out effectively to the accompaniment of rampant inflation. Furthermore, only with implementation of the described stabilization measures, combined with system changes, can one expect real foreign assistance.

III. Stabilizing the Economy

1. The aim of phase one in the Stabilization, to last not longer than to the turn of 1989/1990, is to prevent further acceleration of the inflation rate and, inasmuch as possible, to slow it down, also to reduce the budget deficit to below its October 1989 level and to arrest the flight away from the zloty.

2. In order to check further acceleration of the inflation rate, the following main steps will be taken in this phase:
- monopolistic practices in the area of prices will be counteracted and monopolistic structures dismantled; the Government has already tabled with the Sejm a revision of cooperative law; a draft of a new anti-monopoly law is also ready;
- an active policy of keeping reserve commodity stocks to allow for market intervention;
- discontinuation of production in selected plants marked by extremely high use of raw materials and energy per unit of output or representing a menace to the environment (such as obsolete coke oven batteries, old steel furnaces, lines for production of cement in so-called wet technology). This will enable the use of the freed raw materials and energy in more efficient enterprises;

- modification of the wage indexation rules and bolstering the fiscal mechanism of counteracting the inflationary climb of wages;
- introduction of attractive forms of long-term saving; by adjusting the interest rate to inflation levels, as well as extending the possibilities for investing money in bonds; this has to be accompanied, for financial balance, by higher interest on credits;
- stemming the excessive investment demand, particularly by suspending certain centrally-sponsored investment projects, particularly in the fuel and energy field, and desisting from central financing of some investment tasks;
- starting to divest certain elements of state assets;
- a stricter financial, including credit, policy vis-a-vis enterprises.

3. The guiding objective behind the revision of the wage indexation law presented to the Sejm (parliament) is to disallow a yet more rapid climb of prices and total destabilization of the consumer goods market.

The main change comes down to accepting the rule of so-called compensatory indexation. This means that the indexed increase in wages will accrue only to those enterprises which have not already paid out wage hikes compensating the defined percentage of price changes. As a follow-up to this move, appropriate tax sanctions will be applied and exacted with respect to those enterprises which step beyond the indexation structure.

4. Still in 1989 certain material components of state assets will be sold, and above all:
- housing;
- land and building lots;
- small plants, service and trade outlets;
- shares of the State Treasury in existing companies;
- productive assets from liquidated enterprises and suspended central investment projects, along with privatization of selected enterprises.

There will be absolute observance of the rule of public, auction form of sale.

5. Certain of the actions outlined under point 2 (such as stemming the investment demand, modification of indexation rules, sale of some state assets), will be at the same time instrumental to reducing the 1989 central budget deficit.

This aim will be further served by other measures, and in particular:
- reducing the subsidy to coal;
- reducing the number of subsidized foodstuffs and inputs for farm production;
- markedly cutting down the subsidy for social and political organizations; maintained will be only the subsidies connected with the tasks entrusted by the state, such as for instance the subsidies for the Polish Red Cross;
- suspending the central budget payments to local budgets for compensating the effects of increases in the cost of investment equipment and services;

- reducing the value, in real terms, of spending on public security and national defense;
- applying stricter fiscal discipline towards the enterprises which are late in meeting their liabilities to the budget; the practice of granting reliefs to specific enterprises (subject reliefs) will also be done away with;
- raising the turnover tax and, correspondingly, prices for certain consumer goods.

6. The Government will ask for a change of the system, spelled out in the law establishing the Coal Community, of subsidizing coal, tying the amount of subsidy for coal to the transaction (international) price. The subsidy for the last two months of 1989 will be set in such a way that it will be just slightly higher than what would be needed to just compensate the mining industry for the losses resulting from the fact that the officially-set price for coal is lower than the average cost of mining the coal.

Even taking such measures, the subsidies to coal would climb rapidly. Therefore, it becomes necessary to considerably increase the price of coal and, linked with that, the price of other fuels, electric energy and heating. This has to be accompanied by countermeasures to any overreaction of prices and wages to the increases in the price of fuel and energy. This is mainly the question of revising the system of allowances-in-kind for employees and preventing an increase of price levels in farm produce procurement above that warranted by the share of fuel in total costs of farm production. The excessive passing on of the effects of fuel and energy price hikes onto the prices of manufactured products will be counteracted by stricter fiscal and credit policy.

7. The Government will ask the National Bank of Poland to apply a stricter credit policy with respect to enterprises. In the fourth quarter of 1989 the interest rate on credits and deposits should be raised significantly, so as to reduce credit demand and offer greater inducements to save.

The Government will also apply to the NBP to take action to speed up banking operations, something that will help eliminate the liquidity bottlenecks in settlements between enterprises.

8. There will be a gradual shrinking of the scope of applying official prices and other administrative methods of price control. In particular, official prices will be lifted on bread, milk and skim cheese, a move accompanied by introduction of food coupons for the poorest people.

9. There will be a marked raising of the official exchange rate to the dollar, thanks to which the spread between this rate and the open market rate will be reduced. This in turn will facilitate the switchover to a uniform rate in the next phase (see IV point 9).

10. At the turn of 1989 and 1990, after completion of the necessary preparations and legislative efforts, the country will pass to the basic phase of the economic stabilization effort. That phase has the following interlinked objectives: stifling inflation and

balancing the state budget, eliminating the shortages in the economy, bolstering the zloty through, among other things, its convertibility.

11. After attaining these objectives, a set of measures, concentrated in time, will be applied, and notably:
- radical reduction in the scope of tax reliefs, including elimination of tax reliefs for exports. Export incentives will be provided through the right level uniform exchange rate;
- elimination of all, or practically all, subsidies to enterprise investment projects;
- reduction (in real terms) of budget spending on national defense, public security and state administration.
- a comprehensive reform of the system of settlements under the title of coal subsidies, and subsequently total elimination of these subsidies;
- adoption of the rule that budget deficit cannot be financed with interest-free NBP credit. The deficit can be covered only through treasury bills or credit taken outside the NBP on commercial terms. The Government shall also agree with the NBP strict observance of the rule of adjusting the volume of money supply according to requirements of the anti-inflation program, and methods of exacting stricter money-credit discipline, i.a. through introduction of a positive, real interest rate. The category of preferential credits will be eliminated. Subsidies for credit repayment will be offered directly to the credit takers taking up activity in areas of state preference;
- elimination, with the exception of cases dictated by anti-monopoly legislation, of administrative price controls;
- application of the sort of instruments to check the excessive rise in nominal wages and other incomes, which will allow for breaking the inflationary spiral.

12. Initially, following introduction of these measures, there cannot but follow a temporary rapid jump in prices and a drop in the statistical index of real wages. Some enterprises may also be forced to declare bankruptcy. It is also not possible to preclude a temporary decline in output in certain areas along with unemployment caused by letting go the employees from the liquidated plants. Following that, prices and incomes will begin to stabilize. Reduction of the inflow of money to the economy will become the barrier to price increases. Consistent implementation of the outlined anti-inflation program will cause that by the end of next year inflation will be reduced to a level not higher than 3-5 percent monthly. The market balance situation will also become perceptibly better. The first production effects of the demonopolization and privatization processes should also appear by then.

13. To alleviate the negative effects of the anti-inflation efforts, a social umbrella system will be applied (see V).

IV. System Changes

1. Parallel with efforts to counteract inflation and stabilize the economy, the Government shall take steps leading to fundamental altering of the economic system. This will consist of introducing the market economy institutions which have proven themselves in developed Western countries.

Instrumental to that will be:
- ownership changes, resulting in an ownership structure akin to that of industrially developed countries;
- greater autonomy of state enterprises;
- application of a full market mechanism, particularly the freedom of price-setting, elimination of rationing and mandatory intermediation;
- establishment of an environment conducive to domestic competition, through an anti-monopoly policy and full liberty in setting up new enterprises;
- opening the economy to the world by introduction of convertibility of the zloty, which will allow for increasing domestic competition and permit rational specialization;
- restructuring state financing, including a thorough reform of the taxation system;
- further reform of the banking system and the rules of money-credit policy;
- launching a capital market;
- establishment of a labor market.

Preparations for introduction of the outlined changes are being started already this year. The fundamental changes are to take place in the years 1990 and 1991.

2. Under a Resolution of the Council of Ministers, an office of the Plenipotentiary for ownership transformations has been created. That office will work out proposals for the required legislative changes and set up the organizational framework for the process of ownership transformations, as well as will supervise their progress.

Ownership transformations shall take place openly, according to rules accepted by Parliament. The basic rule will be the public sale, open to all citizens, and also the institutions devoted to efficiency of economic operations. Solutions will be applied to facilitate the purchase of stock by employees. In case of privatization of large enterprises, certain preferences will be offered for citizens purchasing small number of shares. There will also be a place for other efficient forms of ownership, including authentic cooperative ownership, employee partnerships and communal property.

Ownership transformations will be accompanied by demonopolization of the market and of production; there will be a possibility for change-over to autonomous operation by the organizational entities which are part of an enterprise and render specific services on its behalf (such as maintenance, transportation, carpentry services). This will be conducive to better use of the production capacities and formation of a market of production services.

3. Set out of state assets will be communal assets to be administered by local self-government agencies. Towns and communes will be empowered to conduct economic

activities, also to float community bonds. Communal unions could be formed for the conduct of economic activity going beyond the bounds of a single commune or town.

4. The Government shall apply for lifting the applicable constraints on the size of a private farm and shall review the other acts pertaining to trade in land, with a view to eliminating all the unnecessary barriers. At the same time facilities will be created, with the aim of encouraging investors (private and state) to increase outlays on the development of rural services and small scale food processing. Creation of new jobs in the agricultural services sector and in the industry linked to agriculture would help in changing the agrarian structure and in making better use of the potential of agriculture.

The Government shall also make efforts to secure World Bank credits for use in restructuring agriculture and the industry linked with agriculture.

5. The Government will apply for elimination of constraints on the freedom of: disposition of buildings and residential premises, building housing for sale, setting rents and charges according to market rules. Special measures will be applied to soften the shock for those social groups whose living standard would be particularly severely affected by the increase in rents and charges.

6. Draft bills to amend the laws on state enterprises and on self-management of state enterprises along with the follow-up regulations shall be tabled with Parliament still in 1989. The changes will entail increasing the scope of autonomy of state enterprises. Modifications will be made in the rules governing the financial management of state enterprises and other economic entities in which the State Treasury holds shares.

There will be stricter supervision over the operation of stock companies and their impact on operation of the mother companies, particularly on shaping the payroll. Such efforts, however, will not mechanically curb the development of go-between outfits in marketing, but are designed to prevent the use of dishonest competition methods.

7. The so-called price ceilings shall be eliminated at the latest in the beginning of 1990. Price controls shall be limited to exacting the provisions on counteracting monopolistic practices. Rationing and mandatory intermediation in trading production inputs will be eliminated. Arbitrary rationing shall be considered as violation of the anti-monopoly regulations.

Equal rights treatment of economic entities, and particularly a ban on awarding individual tax reliefs and exemptions and on offering supply guarantees will be instrumental to consolidating market relations.

8. In order to set up an environment conducive to competition in the economy, an active anti-monopoly policy will be pursued. The anti-monopoly agency will be set apart from the structure of the Ministry of Finance and will be given more extensive powers.

9. A uniform exchange rate and domestic convertibility of the zloty to convertible currencies will be introduced in the beginning of 1990.

Initially the applicable restrictions on transfer of currency abroad will continue in effect. Conditions for full external convertibility of the zloty will emerge only after stabilization of the economy, and particularly after bringing the balance of payments into equilibrium.

More extensive opportunities for foreign capital investment in Poland will also be instrumental to increasing competition. Foreign investors will be able to purchase stock in Polish enterprises and also set up wholly foreign-owned enterprises.

Transfers of currency representing the profit share will be governed by currency law and bilateral agreements on protection of investment.

10. A fundamental reform of the system of state finances will be launched. Its main elements will be:
- amendment of the Budget Act;
- reform of the taxation system;
- integration of the system of extra-budgetary funds with the state budget;
- adaptation of the rules governing the financial management of enterprises to market economy conditions;
- sprucing up the currency market.

11. The Government shall propose sweeping changes in the current budget law and other regulations governing budget management. These changes should come fully into force starting with 1991. Following are some of the proposed changes:
- the draft budget submitted to Parliament will specify only the revenues and expenditures of the central budget and the support subsidies for local budgets;
- adoption of the rule that a budget deficit cannot be financed with an interest-free NBP credit;
- rules for supporting local budgets out of the central budget shall be adjusted to the new model of local self-government; objective rules are to be applied in determining the amount of subsidy due to a specific local budget;
- tax collection rules will be modified so that an increase in income and turnover, representing the base for tax assessment, should result in immediate increase in the payments effected to the budget; more severe sanctions will be applied for late payment of liabilities to the budget.

12. A fully reformed tax system should apply, starting from 1991. The main elements of that system will be:
- an income tax on corporate entities, uniform for all economic entities;
- a value added tax (VAT), replacing the present turnover tax;
- a personal income tax, the basis for assessing which should cover practically all the incomes earned by any specific individual.

13. The taxation system applicable in 1990 will represent a transitional stage from the present to the target model. In this connection, the following assumptions are proposed:
- the number of turnover tax rates is to be further, and considerably, reduced;
- the scale of equalization tax will be designed in such a way that it will encompass a much broader group of taxpayers than has been the case so far, with moderate progression; the scope of equalization tax reliefs and exemptions will be radically curtailed;
- the farm tax rates will brought up to date.

14. The Government shall review the extra-budgetary funds. Support of these funds counted against enterprise costs will be eliminated (with the exception of the Social Insurance Fund, and the Culture Development Fund).

After analysis, proposals will be formulated concerning liquidation of some of the funds, particularly those for which a direct budget subsidy is the sole source of revenue.

Irrespective of the budget drawn up in the format spelled out by the present Budget Act, starting with 1990 the Government shall publish data pertaining to the financial system of the state in a format corresponding to IMF standards.

Jointly with the Central Statistical Office, the Government shall strive to streamline the system of operational financial and economic statistics, to secure for all economic entities possibly quick and full information concerning the financial situation.

15. Working in conjunction with the National Bank of Poland, the Government will strive to evolve market relations within the banking system, and particularly in the credit system. The government considers as the most important moves in this respect:
- introduction of a system of settlements preventing debtors from profiting on the difference between the interest rate on credits and the rate of inflation; this can be attained either by applying the rule of reassessing the value of liabilities (periodically raising the amount of liabilities corresponding to the rate of inflation) or by setting an interest rate which would be positive in real terms (higher than the rate of inflation); work on the conception of the rate has already been launched by a joint team of the Council of Ministers Office, the Ministry of Finance and the National Bank of Poland;
- elimination of the category of so-called preferential credits;
- simplification of the procedure for establishing new banks, including banks with foreign capital shares;
- application of more efficient banking techniques;
- introduction of the institution of promissory notes for reciprocal crediting of enterprises.

The Government shall strive to secure funds for advancing the technical aspects of banking (communications, computers, training) in the forms of credits extended by the World Bank and credits (or other financial facilities) placed at our disposal by the Governments of Western states.

16. A securities exchange shall be established at the latest by the close of 1990.

Getting a capital market on stream will be conducive to reallocation of productive resources to high return areas. Instrumental in this respect will be the change of the legislation governing bankruptcies. The amended rules should be secure:
- awarding each creditor whose claims have not been satisfied on time, the right to apply bankruptcy proceedings;
- shortening and streamlining the procedure connected with declaring bankruptcy.

17. Preparations will be undertaken still this year to shape a normal labor market. This will require updating the Labor Code, to make it easier for plant managements to adjust the structure and number of employees to real needs as well as to draft and apply the required social program (see V point 4).

V. Social Policy in the Light of Altering Economic System

1. Institutional changes in the economy and the process of economic stabilization will be matched by due alterations in social policy. On the one hand, new needs arise from the social consequences of short-term stabilization measures, and on the other hand, the new conditions of market economy will call for different mechanisms of securing the generally accepted social policy objectives.

2. In order to somewhat alleviate the hardships stemming from stabilization measures, a program of shielding the economically weakest groups will be applied.

The shielding efforts will consist of:
- safeguarding the level of food consumption by introducing coupons for staple foods (bread, milk) and extending the network of free (cheap) eateries;
- assisting in the form of partially reimbursing the higher cost of house rent and heating;
- maintaining the ratio between the average pension and the average wage at the 1988 level (assuming a temporary reduction of their spread), with quarterly revalorization ex ante, starting in 1990;
- reorganizing the system of social assistance by making use of and coordinating both state and social funds and personnel and stimulating non-budgetary sources of financing.

3. Introduction of a labor market will require legislative regulations securing a protective shield for dismissed employees, the funds for training and retraining, and also creating new jobs.

This system should encompass all the jobless, with special safeguards extended to those released from folding up and liquidating enterprises and those losing jobs due to staff reductions, in other words, those subject to so-called group dismissals. The expenses connected with operation of the unemployment security system will be covered from the Labor Fund, supported by payments from every enterprise. The system of labor exchanges will be reorganized by extending its functions (registration, administering welfare, etc.); an institution of employee insurance (including formation of new, specialized insurance agencies) will be developed.

4. Parallel with institutional changes, there will be a restructuring of social policy mechanisms on the basis of effectiveness criteria. The crux of these changes will be the curtailment of state welfare functions, particularly elimination of irrationality in spending funds and application of the rule of the dominant position of income from work in the family budgets of working people.

5. In the area of social services (health care, education, etc.), the rule of effectiveness will imply, among other things, rationalizing their financing while securing a basic standard for all citizens and creating a market of above standard level services, as well as binding the system of health care with the insurance system through the Health Insurance Fund.

As the economy stabilizes, opportunities will be created for supporting the social programs with funds of economic entities, by applying the right tax policy instruments. Mechanisms will be created to foster decentralization of social policy and employing for its purposes the funds of local self-governments, social associations and individual donations.

6. As of 1991, the system of social insurance will be comprehensively reformed. It calls for, among other things, safeguarding the value of benefits in real terms, linking their value more closely with the time and amount of paid insurance dues, along with gradual dispensing with the practice of awarding benefits according to income criteria.

VI. Foreign Support of the Program for Stabilization and System Changes

1. An indispensable condition for carrying through the stabilization program and the proper package of system changes is the close collaboration with our creditors and their understanding for our economic situation, as well as the cooperation and assistance of international financial institutions and governments. The breadth and structural nature of the present crisis combine for a situation where meeting of our international obligations is not possible without fundamental changes domestically. Efforts to secure domestic stabilization of the economy must be awarded a clear priority, also in the interest of the creditors. The Government shall strive for early conclusion of arrangements with the IMF and the World Bank and for agreeing with the various groups of creditors on terms of debt servicing in keeping with our payment capacities.

2. There will be parallel undertakings to facilitate the inflow of foreign capital to Poland and to offer more stable terms for investment, more advantageous than at present, yet without infringing on our interests. The rules governing the foreign trade operations of joint venture companies should be the same as those applicable to purely domestic entities. Advantageous terms for profit transfers and the tax policy should be the main elements determining the attractiveness of investing in Poland.

3. Implementation of the outlined stabilization program and progress in further system changes will require in particular:

- obtaining from the industrially developed countries possibly early credits to cover the necessary imports of industrial and farm production inputs and intervention imports of items vital for the society (medicines and such) in the fourth quarter of 1989;
- agreeing with the International Monetary Fund, as soon as possible, on an adjustment program linked with a parallel US $ 700 million standby credit facility;
- getting on stream still this year on the World Bank credits for financing the already agreed projects;
- procuring so-called SAL credits, offered by the World Bank as structural change support;
- securing financial assistance from the International Finance Corporation to support the privatization effort;
- procuring guarantees from the industrially developed countries for a US $1 billion stabilization loan to permit introducing a uniform exchange rate and stabilizing the domestic currency (domestic convertibility of the zloty);
- obtaining better terms for refinancing the payments obligations to the Paris Club. We shall apply for full rescheduling of the amortization and interest payment in 1989-1992. Irrespective of efforts to secure debt relief we shall strive to make the payments to be made after 1992 contingent on the inflow of new capital and the foreign trade results. Conclusion of an agreement with the Paris Club should make it possible to again benefit from government credit guarantees and also to offer facilities and guarantees for foreign investors intending to engage their funds in Poland;
- reducing the nominal value of the debt owed to commercial banks (the Brady Plan), reducing the cost of servicing this debt and obtaining access to new bank credits. In pursuing this objective we count on active support from the IMF. There are also plans to convert a portion of the guaranteed debt to equity in enterprises and in environmental projects.

The Polish Government shall also start negotiations to reduce the burden of servicing the debt owed to the Soviet Union.

4. Closer economic relations with the European Community will become a vital element bolstering implementation of the economic program. In future negotiations with the Community, Poland will strive to lower the barriers to trade and to the streams of financial resources from the EEC. Poland assigns a priority to liberalizing imports, financial flows, direct foreign investment, and in exchange intends to secure better access for Polish exports to the EEC.

5. Poland attaches great importance to economic relations with the CMEA. It will actively strive for fundamental restructuring of the cooperation mechanisms applicable with the CMEA countries.

It is above all the mechanism governing commodity trade between member states which is due for a change: The current centralized system of trade should be increasingly replaced with a much broader scope of independent decision-making on the enterprise level, applying economic criteria.

A greater role should be assigned to free currency settlements based on current international prices, with a possibility for applying, in the transitional stage, the compensation of balances in convertible currencies.

During this stage, trade protocols would continue to apply, though with the commodity lists reduced to just strategic products.

The proposed solutions could be applied on a wider scale starting in 1991, since until that time the five year agreements adopted with the CMEA framework will continue in force.

6. The program for stabilization and system changes has chances for success only when the radical and consistent efforts will be supported through actions of the international financial organizations and governments of countries declaring assistance. For that reason the Government intends to present this program to the International Monetary Fund. This will pave the way to the last phase of talks, which as their effect should lead to agreeing an adjustment program. We count on early conclusion of the work on this adjustment program and its acceptance by the IMF Board. Such an agreement will not only allow for credits from the IMF and the World Bank, but will also considerably bolster Poland's position in negotiations with other creditors and potential investors, those considering investing their capital in Poland.

VII. The Socio-Political Modalities Determining Success of This Program

1. The radical economic program of the Government and the matching program of social action will have a chance for success only if endorsed by the majority of the society.

The fundamental character of the changes proposed in the program, in essence representing a change of the economic constitution, calls for all-out support from all the meaningful political and social forces, from the trade unions, and from both houses of Parliament. Effective implementation of the program would be spurred by major streamlining of the legislative procedure, due to the need for haste in introducing the various solutions, and for securing their cohesion.

2. Implementation of the program for thorough restructuring of the economic system in a situation of a deep crisis cannot yield palpable improvement in the coming few months. In such a short time frame it will not be possible to stifle inflation or improve the supply situation.

Yet failure to decide on this program would mean hyperinflation, erosion of the zloty as a currency, finally absolute disintegration of the country's economic life. The only foreseeable consequence of such a situation would be the introduction of a war-type economy, with full rationing and ration coupons.

Given the declining output, such actions could not secure meeting the most elementary social needs. By the same token, the prospects for making another turn in the direction of a market economy would be put off to the distant future, and even then it would have to be tried in much more adverse conditions than at present.

3. The outlined program, which at its start spells sacrifices and hardships for the entire society, does open prospects for gradual improvement; after one year we may expect a slowing down of the rate of price growth, better supply of the market, more rational operation of enterprises and an increase of pay in real terms, for honest, well done work.

Furthermore, a determined effort to carry out the program of economic reconstruction will make it possible to tap considerable financial support from abroad; this is an indispensable element to assure the success of this program.

The switch to a market economy will force the resignation from energy and raw material-gobbling technologies, allowing for undertaking effective struggle against the threats to our ecological habitat. First of all, thanks to the change in the economic structure and its modernization, devastation of the environment will be reduced. Second, a state which no longer has to directly administer the economy can pursue a more effective ecological policy. Natural environment protection will constitute an integral element of the economic system, reflected, i.a. in regionally differentiated cost of using natural resources by economic entities.

PART FOUR

THE YUGOSLAV-TYPE ECONOMY

CHAPTER 17

BASIC INSTITUTIONS OF THE LABOR-MANAGED ECONOMY

The Development of the Labor-Managed Economy in Yugoslavia

In 1948, the Yugoslav economic system was a carbon copy of the Soviet-type economy. After breaking with the USSR in 1948, the Yugoslav ruling elite embarked on a series of institutional changes. The purposes of those changes were several: to maintain the political and economic monopoly of the ruling group, to preserve some essential characteristics of socialism, to open the economy to trade with the West, and to improve the production efficiency of the system.

The turning point in Yugoslavia's deviation from the Soviet-type economy was passage of the Law on Management of Enterprises by Workers' Collectives of 1950. This law stated some general principles about labor participation in management, established the workers' council as the highest governing body of the firm, and promised to transfer some property rights in the enterprise to its employees.

The Law on the Management of Capital Goods by Enterprises of 1951 clarified the issue of handling the firm's assets. The law gave the workers' council a sui generis property right over the firm's capital goods: the right of use. The firm was allowed to sell its assets to other firms and to change the composition of its assets. The right of use is, however, a narrower right than the right of ownership because the firm must maintain the book value of its assets (reevaluated periodically for the rate of inflation). This requirement is satisfied via obligatory depreciation allowances and the proceeds from the sale of capital goods.

The Law on Banks of 1961 started a long, and perhaps the most difficult, process in the development of the labor-managed economy: the search for a method of allocating investment funds in an environment in which the ruling group has the right of ownership in capital goods, while the working collective has the right to appropriate the flow of returns from those assets. The investment behavior of the labor-managed firm is then the most crucial issue in assessing the behavior of the labor-managed firm.

By the mid-1960s, the Yugoslav system of labor participation in the management of business firms quickly captured world-wide attention. Disappointed with the performance of the Soviet-type economy, the critics of a private-property, free-market economy saw the labor-managed economy as a long-sought socialist alternative to capitalism. The supporters of the Yugoslav experiment paid no attention to the possible and, as it turned out, predictable consequences of the fact that the labor-managed institutions in that country were not voluntary arrangements.

The Constitution of 1974 introduced a system of "contractual" planning into the labor-managed economy which is discussed later in this chapter.

The Law of Associated Labor of 1976 addressed the issue of the collective decision-making powers in the labor-managed firm. The law said that if and when the results of the collective labor of a group of employees within the firm (e.g., shipping and receiving in a manufacturing firm) could be established in terms of value, the group should become an independent decision maker (the basic organization of associated labor) within its enterprise. When the firm has more than one of those basic organizations, the firm's workers' council should consist of representatives from each unit. Moreover, according to this law, basic organizations that belong to the same firm must negotiate among themselves a contract that would specify their mutual rights and obligations. In an ingenious and ideologically satisfying way the law of associated labor diluted managers' decision-making powers.

Those five major legal acts defined de jure principles of the Yugoslav labor-managed economy, the only labor-managed economy that has ever been tried on such a large scale. These laws should be recognized for what they are: the legal framework for a type of institutional environment preferred by the ruling group. However, to understand the system it is necessary to distinguish between the ruling group's intentions and the subsequent laws and regulations (de facto changes) that transform intentions into reality. The divergence between intentions and reality is inevitable for two reasons. First, the basic principles of the labor-managed system have unintended and unexpected consequences that force the ruling group to modify the components of the system as time goes by. Second, the translation of major institutional structures into real life is in the hands of the nomenklatura, which has its own interpretations of the Politburo's intentions. We shall make references to those clarifying acts as necessary.

By the mid-1970s, the major institutional features of the labor-managed economy of Yugoslavia were: (i) state ownership of capital goods, (ii) the employees' ownership of the returns from capital goods, (iii) the employees' right to govern the labor-managed firm, including the right to hire and fire management, (iv) the substitution of bank credit for the system of administrative distribution of investable funds, and (v) the system of quasi-contracts between all economic agents, including government agencies.

Nomenklatura and the Labor-Managed Economy

The legal requirement that business organizations be labor-managed precludes the choice of other methods for organizing production. The labor-managed firm then depends on the political monopoly of the Politburo for protection against competition by other types of business firms. We know, from our analysis of the Soviet-type economy, that the political monopoly of the Politburo requires a strong and loyal nomenklatura. It follows that the Politburo, the nomenklatura, and the labor-managed firm need each other. The argument raised in the late 1980s that the labor-managed economy has failed because of the size of its bureaucracy completely misses this important point. As we shall see in chapter 19, a decline in the political power of the Yugoslav Politburo has, predictably, opened up the market for other types of business organizations.

The labor-managed economy in Yugoslavia has produced a number of system-specific bureaucracies. The primary purpose of those bureaucracies is to maintain and strengthen the labor-managed character of the system. This chapter reviews two such bureaucracies: the Agency for Social Bookkeeping and the system of "contractual" planning.

THE AGENCY FOR SOCIAL BOOKKEEPING

The Agency for Social Bookkeeping (ASB) is a government agency with branches in all regions of the country. In the late 1980s, the ASB had about 27,000 employees. The agency monitors the financial transactions of all business firms, agencies, institutions, banks, and other organizations that hold capital goods owned by the state. The ASB must approve each and every invoice and authorize each and every payment by labor-managed organizations. In other words, business firms and other organizations cannot transfer their funds from one account to another without prior clearance from the ASB. The agency handles over 2 million invoices each day for about 182,000 clients.

The agency also audits books and approves income statements for all organizations holding state-owned assets. In 1987, it discovered over 700,000 illegal payments and prosecuted about 27,500 persons.

The Agency for Social Bookkeeping is a major source of information on the state of the Yugoslav economy. It reduces the ruling group's costs of controlling the terms of contracts among enterprises and other legal entities, lowers the cost of monitoring the use of state-owned assets, and facilitates financial controls of business enterprises through its supervision of the banking system.

CONTRACTUAL PLANNING

All labor-managed organizations in Yugoslavia must join the appropriate trade association; this requirement lowers the ruling group's costs of monitoring a wide range of activities. Annually, trade associations, labor unions, local governments, and other social organizations in each and every region must negotiate a social contract. Social contracts address the issues that are of common interest for each region, primarily the distribution of incomes. The contract also includes the so-called self-managing communities of interest, which were created to address the provision of many services, such as education, retirement, health, and electric power.

Within the framework of the social contract for a region, the labor-managed firms and other organizations pursuing the same or similar lines of activity are linked together through self-management agreements. The purpose of those contractual agreements is to specify the pooling of resources for joint ventures, criteria for the distribution of income, local subsidies, pricing policies, and other issues of common interest. In other words, the employees of any labor-managed organization must adjust their preferences and aspirations with respect to the use of their earnings and other funds to the "common good" as defined by higher authorities.

Regional social contracts are then linked together by the social contract of a republic. By putting together social contracts for all republics, the overall social contract for the country as a whole is set.

It is important to note that with those contracts a new type of planning was created in Yugoslavia. Self-management agreements and social contracts are required by law; they are not voluntary agreements. Moreover, the ruling elite also sets, often informally through its bureaucracy, the basic terms for those agreements. And, if the parties were to fail to negotiate a contract, the leaders would give them one.

In order to examine the effects of contractual planning on incentives, let us consider the 1982 social contract for the city of Belgrade and compare it with the social contract for 1972. The social contract stipulates rules for the allocation of enterprises' net income between the wage fund and retained earnings (profit). The crucial variable is the ratio of net income or earnings (E) to adjusted labor (L); that is, E/L.

The term "adjusted labor" refers to a labor-force figure adjusted for differences in skill and education levels, which vary among firms. The approach used in Belgrade in 1972 and 1982 was to attach a coefficient to each level of skill and education. The adjusted labor force was then obtained for each firm by multiplying the number of employees in each category by the relevant coefficients and summing the products. The coefficients used in 1972 and 1982 were as follows: 1.00 for an unskilled worker; 1.20 for a semiskilled worker or a worker with less than a high school education; 2.20 for a highly qualified worker; 3.00 for a worker with a college education; 3.30 for a worker with a master's degree; and 3.80 for a worker with a doctorate.

After determining all the enterprises' labor-adjusted earnings, the E/L ratios are stated in terms of index numbers, with the average earnings per adjusted labor set equal to 100. The social contracts then stipulate the share of earnings that must be retained (R/E) at each different E/L ratio. Since the sum of earnings going to the wage fund (W/E) and earnings retained (R/E) must be 100, W/E is determinate. The product of the E/L and W/E ratios gives us the ratio of wages per adjusted labor (W/L) at each different E/L ratio. These ratios are presented in Table 17-1, which shows the allocation of net income or earnings in Belgrade enterprises under the social contracts in 1972 and 1982. For example, in 1982 if earnings per worker doubled from 100 to 200, the wage per worker would have increased from 78 to 108, or only by 38 percent. The fact that the state needs social contracts in order to increase the share of retained earnings is the best evidence that workers would prefer to allocate a larger share of the firm's earnings to the wage fund. Thus, social contracts for both years penalize workers in an efficient firm for their efforts toward still greater efficiency.

TABLE 17-1. SOCIAL CONTRACT FOR BELGRADE ENTERPRISES, 1972 AND 1982

Earnings per Adjusted Labor (E/L)	Allocation to Internal Funds (R/E)		Allocation to Wage Fund (W/E)		Allowable Wage per Worker (W/L)	
	1972	1982	1972	1982	1972	1982
260	53	57	47	43	122	112
250	52	55	48	45	120	112
240	51	54	49	46	118	110
230	49	52	51	48	117	110
220	48	50	52	50	114	110
210	45	48	55	52	115	109
200	44	46	56	54	112	108
190	43	43	57	57	108	108
180	42	40	58	60	104	108
170	41	37	59	63	100	107
160	40	33	60	67	96	107
150	38	29	62	71	93	104
140	37	28	63	72	88	101
130	35	27	65	73	84	95
120	33	25	67	75	80	90
110	30	24	70	76	77	84
100	27	22	73	78	73	78
90	23	20	78	80	69	72
80	19	15	81	85	65	68
70	13	11	87	89	61	62
60	5	5	95	95	57	57

Suggested Readings

Bajt, A. Samoupravni Oblik Drustvene Svojine, Zagreb: Globus, 1988.

Pejovich, S. The Market-Planned Economy of Yugoslavia, Minneapolis: University of Minnesota Press, 1966.

Sekulich, D. "Socio-Economic Relations and Development in the Self-Management System," Paper presented at the 17th Karl Brunner Symposium, Interlaken, 1990.

CHAPTER 18

THE BEHAVIOR OF THE LABOR-MANAGED FIRM

The analysis of the labor-managed firm in this chapter will address the following issues: (i) the right to govern the firm, (ii) the formation and allocation of total revenue of the firm, (iii) the effects of property rights on the firm's economic behavior, (iv) the role of bank credit, and (v) governmental controls.

The Governance of the Labor-Managed Firm

The right to govern the labor-managed firm in Yugoslavia is vested in its employees. The employees exercise the right of governing the firm in two ways: indirectly and directly. General meetings and referendums are two basic forms through which the employees exercise their right to govern the firm directly. Indirectly, the employees govern the firm through the workers' council. The right to govern the firm directly is usually reserved for some critical issues such as a request to fire the firm's director.

Depending on size of the firm, the workers' council might have up to 120 members. Members of the workers' council are elected by secret ballot from among the employees. While the rights and duties of members of the workers' council have frequently changed, they could be summarized as follows: members of the workers' council, including the chairman, continue to work at their regular jobs; they get neither offices nor extra compensation for being on the council nor staff support. They exercise their rights of governance only when the council is in session. Appointment on the council is for a two-year period for a maximum of two terms. The workers' council's right to govern the firm includes price-output decisions, wage determination, production planning, internal organization of the firm, disposition of the total revenue, final decisions concerning employment, and approval of income statements.

Since the workers' council is a rather huge body, it selects from among its members an executive board which includes the director of the firm. The members of the executive board are elected every year for a maximum of two terms. The duties of the executive board are to prepare proposals for the council, to monitor the execution of council decisions, to supervise promotions and training of workers, and to approve monthly operating plans.

The director of the firm is appointed (and fired) by the workers' council for a specific period of time and his contract can be renewed indefinitely. However, an appropriate political agency has to confirm the appointment. It means that the director occupies a middle ground between the firm's employees and the political leadership. On the one hand, his job security as well as his current income depend on his popularity with the workers' council and the financial performance of the firm. On the other hand, the director's long-term career is influenced by the degree to which his management of the firm contributes to the preferences of the political leadership.

The director has a unique position in the firm. The members of the council have neither the resources nor the skill necessary to engage in identifying and evaluating the set of opportunity choices which are available to the firm. It is a job for an expert, and the director is the council's expert. Thus, the director's presentation and evaluation of the available alternatives must have some considerable influence on the workers' council policy decisions.

The Total Revenue of the Yugoslav Firm

The formation and allocation of the firm's total revenue has changed a number of times between the 1950s and the 1980s. The basic trend has been to define and allocate total revenue as follows:

Total revenue consists of sales of goods and services and returns on external investments such as time deposits, credits to other organizations, and receipts from joint projects. The first deductions from the firm's total revenue are production expenses and depreciation. The second category is quite important in Yugoslavia because it affirms state ownership in capital goods. The firm must maintain the book value of its assets (which is periodically adjusted for the rate of inflation) by reinvesting legal depreciation allowances. Also, when the firm sells an asset to another firm, the proceeds must be reinvested. If the sales price is less than the asset's book value, the firm must make up the difference from its total revenue. At the same time, the firm is free to change the composition of its assets.

Dohodak is the amount of money left after production expenses and depreciation are subtracted from the firm's total revenue. Conceptually, dohodak is similar to value-added or net product. From dohodak, the firm pays taxes, insurance premiums, and other legal obligations that have averaged about 15 percent of dohodak. The firm also meets its contractual obligations from dohodak, such as interest payments and banking services, fees for (obligatory) membership in various trade and other associations, contributions for civil defense, and court costs, including damages. Those obligations vary from one firm to another, but a consensus among Yugoslav experts is that they take about 18-20 percent of dohodak.

The remainder is the firm's earnings. The employees have the right to appropriate the firm's earnings, and to allocate it between the following four funds: the wage fund, the investment fund, the collective consumption fund, and the reserve fund. The first two funds are the important ones.

The wage fund is for distribution among the employees. The firm pays taxes and social security contributions from the wage fund before the employees are paid. Those payments have averaged about 30 percent of the wage fund. The remainder is allocated among the employees in accordance with the firm's internal bylaws. A unique aspect of the labor-managed firm is that the employees are residual-takers. They receive no contractual wage like their counterparts in the West and the East. Their income comes from and, in effect, depends on the firm's earnings.

Allocations to the business fund serve two purposes. First, they are used to finance new investments. Second, they are used to repay loans (only the principal, because interest is a contractual payment that is paid from dohodak). Thus, there is a minimum amount of money that the workers' council must allocate to this fund. A small tax of up to 8 percent is paid on the allocation to the business fund.

The collective consumption fund is used to provide the workers with some specific consumption goods, such as subsidized apartments, child care centers, recreation halls, and low-cost vacations.

The reserve fund is used to cover the firm's operational losses. In addition, there is a minimum wage in Yugoslavia. It is equal to 55 percent of the average wage in the area during the preceding year. When the firm's earnings are not sufficient to pay this amount, the workers' council can use its reserve fund.

Economic Behavior of the Labor-Managed Firm

The most important property rights that influence decision making in the Yugoslav firm are: (i) The right to govern the firm is in the hands of its employees. (ii) The workers' council is the highest management organ in the firm. It makes output and employment decisions, wage determination, production planning, and disposition of total revenue. (iii) The employees own the firm's earnings, that is, they should be free to choose its allocation among the four different funds. The firm's earnings are equal to total revenue minus the cost of all inputs excluding labor costs. (iv) The employees have only the right of use of the means of production held by the firm. This right allows them to produce, buy, or sell capital goods. But the firm must maintain the book value of its assets via depreciation or other means (i.e., the firm must reinvest the proceeds from the sale of capital goods).

Given the institutional setting, employees have two major investment alternatives available for increasing their wealth: joint investment in the earning assets of the firm through retained earnings (nonowned assets) and individual investment in other assets (owned assets).

As for nonowned assets, workers may choose to accept a reduction in their current take-home pay and leave some of the profit with the firm for investment in earning assets. Their property rights to those new earning assets are limited to higher future wages and only for as long as they remain employed by the firm.

Owned assets are limited to savings, investment in human capital, and some limited types of physical assets, such as taxis, artisan shops, and jewelry stores. According to Professor Sekulich from the University of Zagreb, about 90 percent of all assets in

Yugoslavia are still state owned.[1] We shall assume that the rate of interest on savings accounts represents the rate of return available to the employees from taking the firm's earnings out as wages and investing it individually. Historically, the rate of interest in Yugoslavia has been determined administratively.[2]

To understand the investment behavior of the labor-managed firm requires a common denominator for comparing these two investment alternatives. Since the employees cannot withdraw their nonconsumed income once it is invested in nonowned assets, the two wealth-increasing alternatives are (1) an annuity for a fixed number of years with no return of capital and (2) a savings account. The employee's annuity from investing one dollar in owned assets is

$$y - \frac{i(1+i)^n}{(1+i)^n - 1}$$

where (i) is the rate of interest paid on savings accounts. One dollar invested in nonowned assets must yield at least the same annual return. It follows that the rate of return from investment in nonowned assets is

$$r - \frac{i(1+i)^n}{(1+i)^n - 1}$$

where (n) stands for the time horizon of the collective.

The rates of return that would make investment in nonowned capital goods as attractive to the employees as savings deposits at 5 percent are 23 percent, 19 percent, 13 percent, and 9 percent for time horizons of 5, 6, 10, and 15 years. This relationship is shown in figure 18-1. The rr curve shows the rate of return from nonowned assets that would make an average member of the collective indifferent between investment in

---

[1]D. Sekulich, "Reforms and Ownership," Danas, April 10, 1990, p. 26).

[2]The market rate of interest brings into equality the rates of return from capital goods, the community's valuation of future income relative to current consumption and the interest rate implicit in relative prices of capital goods. Therefore, it is not clear what a market rate of interest would mean in a labor-managed economy in which financial markets do not exist and the rate of interest implicit in relative prices of capital depends on the employees' time horizon.

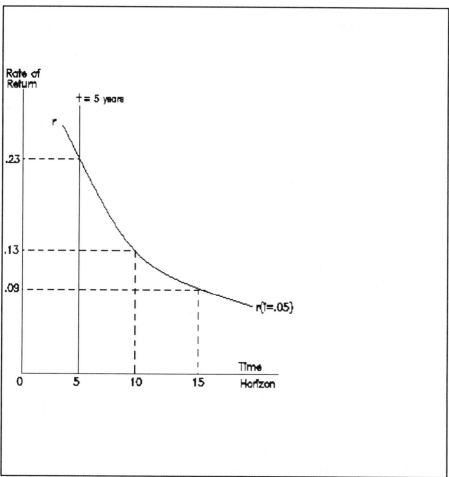

Figure 18-1.

nonowned and owned assets at a stipulated rate of interest (i) on savings for alternative time horizons of the collective. Since curves similar to rr can be established for any rate of interest (i), the rr curve makes it possible to compare all investment alternatives available to the employees.

The S_1S_1 curve in figure 18-2 represents the amount of income the employees are willing to divert from current consumption to accumulation of owned assets for the various rates of growth of wealth. Given the median (we can also assume that the employees have the same time horizon) length of employment expected by the employees of the firm (t_o), the S_2S_2 schedule can be easily calculated. It shows the amount of income the collective is willing to divert from current consumption for investment in nonowned assets. More specifically, the S_2S_2 curve is the S_1S_1 curve adjusted for the behavioral effects of a change in property rights from owned to nonowned (i.e., labor-managed) assets. The rate of return (r) on nonowned assets has to be greater than the corresponding rate of return (i) on owned assets to elicit any given volume of retained earnings from the collective.

Given the rate of interest (i_o), the employees have no incentives to make an allocation into the business fund unless the yield available from investment in nonowned assets is at least equal to the rate of return (r_o) in figure 18-2—where (r_o) is the rate of return on nonowned assets that is equivalent to the official rate of return (i_o) on owned assets.

The investment schedule II shows the expected increase in wealth per marginal unit of investment in capital goods; that is, the return that employees can expect from investment in nonowned assets. While the concept is analogous to the conventional marginal efficiency of investment function, the schedule reflects the opportunities the given firm possesses for the use of additional capital.

It is now possible to discuss the allocation decision of the collective between the wage fund and the business fund. If the employees are granted the right of ownership in the firm's earnings, the amount of income allocated to the business fund for investment in nonowned assets would be OB for the time horizon in figure 18-2. For a shorter time horizon the S_2S_2 schedule would be higher and the rate of allocation to the business fund lower, and vice versa. Thus, the median length of employment expected by employees of the labor-managed firm is an important variable. If workers are granted full ownership of capital goods acquired by the firm during the period of their employment, the S_1S_1 schedule would be the only relevant one, and the volume of saving would be OC. This case corresponds to a private property capitalist society.

A reduction in the rate of interest in figure 18-2 would leave the S_2S_2 curve above point A unchanged. Consequently, the firm's rate of investment would remain at OB. A fall in the rate of interest would have an effect on the firm's investment in capital goods only if its investment demand schedule happened to cut the S_2S_2 curve somewhere along its horizontal stretch. In that case, the collective's savings would be divided between investment in nonowned and owned assets.

Our analysis suggests three general conclusions: (1) The voluntary allocation of the labor-managed firm's earnings favors current consumption relative to what it would be in a private property, capitalist society; that is, a change in the structure of property rights affects the choices individuals make with respect to the allocation of resources between present and future consumption, other things being the same. (2) Investment projects with a relatively long-gestation period have to be externally financed in a labor-managed economy. At the same time, the absence of financial markets makes the evaluation of alternative projects difficult. (3) New workers could easily affect the planning horizon of a firm and place the welfare of the original group of workers in jeopardy. Moreover, all workers share in the firm's earnings, but the new employees have not participated in financing additional capital. Thus, the marginal product of labor must be in excess of the average product of labor if the increase in the labor force is to be acceptable to the original group. It follows that the high unemployment rate in Yugoslavia is generated by its institutional structure.

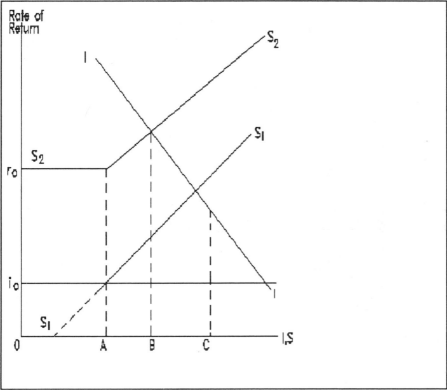

Figure 18-2.

The Role of Bank Credit

The labor-managed firm has two major sources of funds for investments in capital goods: retained earnings and bank credit. Since the prevailing property rights provide few incentives for the employees to sacrifice their current wages and make investments in nonowned assets, bank credit has become the most important source of financing investment projects in Yugoslavia.

Let us assume that the price of a bank loan is (i_3) in figure 18-3. Suppose the firm receives a loan of LL dollars. The employees' saving schedule would shift to the right by the amount of credit at every point on the horizontal scale. The resulting schedule cuts the firm's investment schedule at a lower point, showing that one effect of bank credit on a firm's investment is a higher rate of purchase of capital goods and a lower rate of return. However, the bank credit reduces the amount of retained earnings allocated to the business fund for investment in capital goods (BB_1 in figure 18-3). In fact, each additional dollar borrowed from the bank would increase the firm's investment

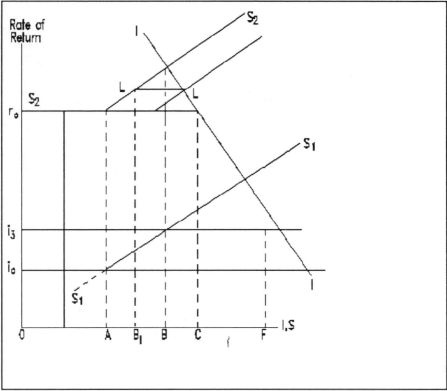

Figure 18-3.

by less than $1 because the employees would reduce the share of their income allocated to the business fund (that is, the allocation of earnings to the wage fund would increase). If the rate of return falls below (r_o) the collective would want to allocate the firm's entire profit to the wage fund.

Given the bank loan rate, the firm's demand for credit is OF in figure 18-3. Whether the firm can borrow the entire amount depends on the total supply of loanable funds and the investment schedule of other firms. In either case, however, the analysis suggests that the allocation to the business fund decreases with an increase in the amount of bank credit granted to the firm. Suppose the firm receives bank credit in excess of OC but less than OF. The firm would behave as if its demand for investment funds were insatiable, while at the same time, the employees would allocate the firm's entire profit to the wage fund. Indeed, that is exactly what happened in the late 1960s and the early 1970s. Incentives to maximize the firm's near-cash flow by allocating its earnings into the wage fund created strong inflationary pressures, a high unemployment rate, and liquidity problems in the labor-managed economy of Yugoslavia.

The Allocation of Earnings and the State

The behavior of the Yugoslav workers up to the 1970s was fully predictable and consistent with incentive structures of the labor-managed type economy. However, relative to the ruling elite's expectations, the behavior of the Yugoslav workers was disappointing. In order to "correct" inefficiencies, Yugoslav leaders chose to attenuate the employees' right of ownership in the firm's earnings. In the 1970s, the ruling elite introduced a number of legal and administrative constraints on the allocation of the firm's earnings between the wage fund and the business fund. The mechanism used by the state to attenuate the employees' right of ownership in the firm's earnings has already been explained in chapter 17. In this section, we shall only review some implications of the so-called self-management contracts.

The fact that the status quo could not be sustained suggests that the pure labor-managed firm is essentially an <u>unstable</u> construction. The Yugoslav ruling elite failed to anticipate the problems that emerged from it in the 1960s because it did not take into account the interdependence between property rights, incentives, and economic behavior. The ruling elite made the same mistake in the 1970s. Its decision to use a political process to control the firm's allocation of earnings between the wage fund and the business fund was bound to impose a very heavy toll in efficiency. First, social contracts had to be negotiated, interpreted, and enforced. It means that substantial resources had to be allocated for the creation of new bureaucracies. Second, an attempt to control the distribution of income via "contractual" agreements had to backfire as well. Since greater earnings by the firm yielded only modest gains to workers in the form of money wages, they had fewer incentives to seek the most productive uses for the firm's assets and more incentives to seek ways for substituting nonpecuniary income for pecuniary income. The result was a continuous increase in the cost of producing goods and services in Yugoslavia that led to a crisis of enormous proportions in the late 1980s.

Suggested Readings

Furubotn, E. "The Long-Run Analysis of the Labor-Managed Firm," <u>American Economic Review</u>, 66, 1976.

Furubotn, E. and Pejovich, S. "Property Rights and the Behavior of the Firm in a Socialist State: The Example of Yugoslavia," <u>Zeitschrift für Nationalokonomie</u>, 30, 1970.

Jensen, M. and Meckling, W. "Rights and Production Functions," <u>Journal of Business</u>, 52, 1979.

Ward, B. "The Firm in Illyria," <u>American Economic Review</u>, 48, 1958.

CHAPTER 19

FAILURE OF THE LABOR-MANAGED TYPE ECONOMY

The labor-managed economy of Yugoslavia—the only type of labor-managed economy that has been tried on a serious basis—has failed. It has produced a crisis of enormous proportions in Yugoslavia. By the end of December, 1989, the rate of inflation was about 60 percent per month, the value of the dollar rose from 4,500 dinars in December, 1988, to about 125,000 dinars in December, 1989. Unemployment in Yugoslavia is in two digits, while real personal incomes have been declining. Many Yugoslav firms are in the red and are being subsidized in order to protect the ruling elite from the political consequences of an even larger increase in unemployment. By most accounting standards in the West, a majority of Yugoslav banks are illiquid. Table 19-1 provides some key statistical data on the Yugoslav economy. Those data are quite revealing. Clearly, it is important to raise a question: what is wrong with the labor-managed economy?

One explanation for the economic crisis in Yugoslavia is that the government has pursued a wrong set of economic policies. For example, Branko Horvat, a Yugoslav economist, claimed in 1988 that he could formulate a set of policies that could turn the economy around. This type of attitude, the interventionist approach, seeks remedies for economic problems in the relation between policy instruments that are available to government and goals expressed by a social welfare function that is constructed by social engineers. It reflects a conviction that there must exist a set of discretionary economic policies that could set the economy right. The interventionist approach to economic problems depends critically on a set of assumptions, such as that politicians and their scientific advisors know the social welfare function, that they are unselfishly guided by it, and that they know the responses of individual citizens to their policies.

The fallacy of the interventionist approach to social issues arises from two conditions. First, policy makers could not possibly have full and reliable information about the economy's dynamic responses to their policies. Thus, the implementation of economic policies contributes, with a substantial probability, to a number of unanticipated and undesired consequences. Second, the interventionist economic policy implicitly assumes a public-interest theory of government, which is a remarkably questionable assumption.

The property rights analysis is another method of explaining current economic problems in Yugoslavia. In the context of this approach, economic analysis examines the effects of institutional arrangements on the economy. In the rest of this chapter we shall use the property rights approach to discuss the Yugoslav labor-managed economy.

TABLE 19-1. The Yugoslav economy in statistics

	1965	1975	1980	1984	1985	1986	1987	1988
Employment (in 000)	3,662	4,758	5,966	6,355	6,516	6,716	6,866	6,884
Unemployment (in 000)	267	584	833	1,013	1,064	1,084	1,087	1,173
Real incomes (1965=100)	100	153	151	123	125	138	129	119
Real GNP (1965=100)	100	176	231	238	239	248	245	241
Investment as % of GNP (1965=100)	30	32	32	21	21	20	20	20
Money Supply (000,000,000 dinars)			462	1,272	1,864	3,896	7,786	25,193
Cost of Living (1975=100)		100	230	926	1,601	3,028	6,670	29,651

Source: Statistički Godišnjak Jugoslavije, Belgrade: Statistički Zavod, 1989.

A Property Rights Analysis of the Labor-Managed Firm

We described the most important institutions of the labor-managed economy in chapter 17. It is through their own system of incentives and varying transaction costs that those institutions influence individual decision makers in ways that are both specific and predictable. The behavior of individual decision makers, in turn, determines economic outcomes. A property rights analysis of the labor-managed economy must then establish the effects of incentives and transaction costs on the social opportunity set.

TRANSACTION COSTS AND THE OPPORTUNITY SET

To recall our earlier discussion, the costs of transactions are the costs of all resources required to transfer property rights from one economic agent (individual) to another. They include the cost of making an exchange and the costs of protecting the institutional structure. Most importantly, transaction costs are not invariant with respect to various institutional structures.

The costs of transactions that are specific to the labor-managed economy of Yugoslavia arise from: the choice of organization, the labor-managed bureaucracy, and the location of decision making within the firm.

The Choice of Organization. In a free-market, private-property-rights economy, we observe a variety of organizational structures such as small proprietorship, multinationals, not-for-profit firms, and labor-managed firms. All those different types of firms have emerged through voluntary contractual negotiations and have survived competition from other types of firms in their respective lines of activity. In fact, capitalism generates a selection process among various types of firms that is consistent with economic efficiency. It is a survival requirement for the owner or owners of resources to seek the most efficient form of business organization in the owner's or owners' specific line of activity.

In Yugoslavia, the choice is mandated by law. The labor-managed firm has not emerged voluntarily in Yugoslavia; it has not survived by demonstrating its superiority over competing types of firms. The very fact that the ruling group had to mandate the labor-managed firm and protect it from competition means that the transaction costs of maintaining and enforcing the prevailing institutional structure in Yugoslavia must be high.

The Bureaucracy. The ruling group's mandate that business organizations must be labor-managed precludes the choice of other institutional forms, while the state ownership of capital goods precludes the capitalization of the expected future benefits of a current decision into their present market value. It means that labor participation in management and state ownership create a divergence between the allocation and use of resources by the labor-managed economy and the valuation of resources by the individual persons in the society. Thus, it must be costly to monitor the labor-managed firm.

The institutional structure in Yugoslavia produces two kinds of governmental controls over business firms. Those controls could be called the system-specific controls and the political controls. The system-specific controls are those whose primary purpose is to maintain the labor-managed character of the system—for example, the Agency for Social Bookkeeping (see chapter 17). Political controls are rules, regulations, and behaviors whose primary objective is to preserve the ruling group's political monopoly within the framework of the labor-managed economy. Examples of political controls are social <u>contracts</u>, subsidies, and so-called informal controls by local party organizations.

Political and economic analysts who argue that a reduction in the size of the bureaucracy could improve the performance of the Yugoslav firm are missing an important point: the labor-managed firm needs the bureaucracy to protect it from competing institutional forms. According to <u>Danas</u>, an influential weekly magazine, the number of nonproductive employees in 1988 stood at about 40 percent of total employment in Yugoslavia.[1]

The Location of Decision Making in the Labor-Managed Firm. The following quote from McManus describes one of the most crucial issues in the labor-managed economy.

> On the Yangtze River in China, there is a section of fast water over which boats are pulled upstream by a team of coolies prodded by an overseer using a whip. On one such passage an American lady, horrified at the sight of the overseer whipping the men as they strained at their harness, demanded that something be done about the brutality. She was quickly informed by the captain that nothing could be done: "those men own the right to draw boats over this stretch of water and they have hired the overseer and given him his duties.[2]

The story makes an important point. Those who support the labor-managed firm have confused participatory democracy within the firm with the specialized knowledge required to run it. The right of all workers to participate in running the firm rules out the right of any individual to make key decisions. Thus, decision making in Yugoslavia is a time-consuming process carried out by resources that do not have the specialized knowledge required to identify and evaluate business decisions.

Moreover, the collective hires and fires the manager and approves the hiring and firing of workers. It means that the manager of a Yugoslav firm, who is supposedly hired because of his or her specialized knowledge of business, has strong incentives to

---

[1] <u>Danas</u>, February 14, 1989, p. 10.

[2] John McManus, "The Cost of Alternative Economic Organizations," <u>Canadian Journal of Economics</u>, 8:335 (Fall 1975).

substitute policies that are consistent with his or her perception of the collective's preference for those that would maximize the market value of the firm. The result is an increase in transaction costs and a contraction in the social-opportunity set. To make the labor-managed firm more efficient it would be necessary (i) to transfer to the manager a broad range of property rights, the most important being the right to hire and fire workers and the right to be independent from the collective's preference; and (ii) to design a new penalty-reward system for the manager that would give him or her incentives to seek and pursue policies that maximize market value. The problem is that if those changes in property rights were made, they would de facto, if not de jure, do away with labor participation in the management of business firms.

INCENTIVES AND THE SOCIAL-OPPORTUNITY SET

The prevailing incentives in Yugoslavia affect the social-opportunity set via the employment problem, the allocation of risk, the demand for investment, and the flow of innovation.

The Employment Problem. As we know, employees of the Yugoslav firm have the right to appropriate the residual, determine its allocation among the wage fund, the business fund, and other legal uses, decide on the distribution of the wage fund, and approve the firm's employment policy. With workers given such decision-making powers, Professor Ward demonstrated that the level of employment in a labor-managed firm is determined by the equality between the average product and the marginal product of labor. It is clearly a restrictive and inefficient solution to the problem of employment.[3] As it was pointed out in chapter 18, the employment policy of business enterprises in Yugoslavia is even more restrictive. Evidence supports this analysis.

The rate of unemployment in Yugoslavia is difficult to estimate for at least two reasons. First, most blue-collar workers react to unemployment by either staying in or returning to their villages. Second, more than 1 million Yugoslavs are working in the West. Leaving those two groups of workers out, total employment in the labor-managed sector increased by only 4.6 percent from 1980 to 1987, while the rate of unemployment increased from 12 percent to 14 percent. During the same period, total employment in the private sector of the economy increased by 39 percent.[4]

The Allocation of Risk. The nontransferability of the workers' right of ownership in the firm's earnings means that the labor-managed economy provides no room for specialization in risk bearing across individuals with different degrees of risk aversion. Moreover, the workers are forced in the aggregate to bear risks that are in fact insurable

---

[3]Benjamin Ward, "The Firm in Illyria: Market Syndicalism," <u>American Economic Review</u>, 48:566-89 (Sept. 1958).

[4]<u>Statistički Godišnjak</u> (Belgrade: Statistički Zavod, 1989).

by diversification. Thus, the labor-managed economy does not provide incentives for risk takers and risk averters to engage in transactions that move resources to more highly valued uses.

Investment Decisions. As we know from chapter 18, the employee of a labor-managed firm has the right of ownership in the firm's earnings but not in its assets. When workers leave the firm, they lose all their claims to the future returns from investment decisions that were made during their tenure. Thus the employees have incentives to choose investment alternatives that promise to maximize cash flow during their expected employment with the firm. Moreover, the collective has strong incentives to seek long-term loans for either short-lived investments or for investments that promise a larger cash flow in the initial period following investment. In general, the labor-managed firm creates incentives for the collective to choose investments that shift the flow of income forward and postpone costs—to be borne by the next generation of workers.

Incentives to Innovate. Given the prevailing property rights in the labor-managed sector of the Yugoslav economy, the pool of those who have the right to innovate is restricted to the working collective. The term "working collective" is important here. Individual employees can neither acquire productive assets nor determine their uses. Only the working collective as a whole can, through its workers' council. An employee who perceives an opportunity to innovate must sell his or her idea to the workers' council, a group of people who have diverse attitudes toward risk, limited business experience, inadequate understanding of production techniques and market processes, and different time horizons. This process impedes the flow of innovation.

Moreover, the prevailing property rights in the labor-managed economy preclude the capitalization of the future benefits of successful innovations into their present value. The absence of the right to capture the future consequences of current innovation in one lump sum means that the collective has incentives to seek primarily those innovations that increase the near-cash flow.

In conclusion, the property rights analysis indicates that the labor-managed economy creates some positive transaction costs and negative incentives that are specific to its institutional structure. They contribute to a contraction in the social-opportunity set. Lack of incentives to innovate also limits the expansion of the social-opportunity set in response to new technical opportunities.

The labor-managed economy is not a viable institutional arrangement. Recent economic reforms in Yugoslavia support this conclusion. The package attempts to save the basic outline of the labor-managed economy while making institutional changes in the direction of a private-property, free-market economy. The former is essential for preserving the ruling group's political power. The latter is necessary for making the system work.

Suggested Readings

The best source of statistical information is Statistički Godišnjak Jugoslavije published by the Statistical Institute in Belgrade in most languages.
The best source of current events in Yugoslavia is Politika, a major daily newspaper in Yugoslavia which is published weekly in English.

APPENDIX

ECONOMIC REFORMS IN YUGOSLAVIA

While most East European countries are searching for a set of institutions to replace their Soviet-type economies, the Yugoslav government is looking for ways to modify the labor-managed economy. The key provisions of economic reforms in Yugoslavia are the convertibility of the dinar, restrictive monetary and fiscal policies, and the right of private ownership. The latter is envisioned as a competing alternative to the labor-managed firm. Ante Markovich, the president of the Federal Executive Council, outlined the program of economic reforms on December 18, 1989. Reprinted below are excerpts from his statement that deal with the most important provisions of the proposed economic reforms.

The basic characteristics of the model for the recovery of the economy and of the financial system, with both immediate and long-term effects are the following:
- convertibility of the dinar in current transactions with foreign countries, with the citizens having the right to freely exchange dinars for foreign currency at the official rate;
- the dinar rate of exchange will be pegged to the German mark and will not be changed until June 30, 1990;
- a tight monetary policy;
- a balanced budget with its own real revenue;
- the free formation of the interest rate, with an appropriate role for the National Bank discount rate;
- the free formation of prices, except in infrastructural and utility services, the exception for the latter being in force until June 30, 1990;
- until June 30, 1990, personal incomes will be formed on the basis of advance payments paid out (until December 15, 1989) for November, indexed according to the changing exchange rate for the German mark relative to the convertible dinar.
- the dinar will be denominated from the current 10,000 to 1 convertible dinar, or 7 convertible dinars for 1 German mark, i.e., 12 convertible dinars for 1 U.S. dollar.

Thus, the basis of the model are three levers: dinar convertibility, and, on that basis, the designed disinflation strategy as well as corresponding fiscal and monetary policies.

These will be accompanied by corresponding supporting policies in the areas of foreign economic relations, prices and personal incomes as well as by a corresponding policy of interest rates, which will be freely formed. Appropriate social and development policies will also be designed to ease the disinflation burden and initiate the process of economic restructuring and a new development cycle.

There exists no better market-based way of ushering in a new economic system than the convertibility of the national currency. Thanks to, primarily, the stock of foreign exchange reserves and to the economic-systemic prerequisites that we have created, dinar convertibility shall be employed as a means for achieving stable economic flows and sustainable development, and not as an end unto itself. Convertibility is in fact a measure of ability, an indicator of efficiency and productivity, and the factor required to deal with the absence of a genuine national market unlinked and unintegrated with the world market. It is a barrier to voluntarism and calls for discipline on the part of all factors in charge of making economic policy decisions as well as for rational behavior on the part of every economic agent.

A move towards convertibility shall create conditions for firmer links with the world, promote greater foreign capital inflow, and substantially bolster the confidence of our foreign partners and financial circles in our resolve to ensure a sound economy through the implementation of the economic reform.

In our internal relations dinar convertibility would constitute a key parameter determining and influencing the quantitative expression of all other measures and the behavior of economic policy makers at all levels and the adoption of decisions by economic and other factors.

The monetary policy cannot successfully carry out its functions and tasks in preserving the convertibility and stability of the dinar and curtailing inflation, as primary objectives, if the federal budget and fiscal policy do not take over from it all those operations which the National Bank of Yugoslavia performed so far—and which are not within its competencies. Monetization of these operations with primary money issue would cause major monetary and inflationary effects. Therefore, it is particularly important to consolidate the federal budget and secure funds from real sources for covering all its projected expenditures so as to make it solvent and capable of servicing on time all its dues.

The federal budget proposal for 1990 represents a further and decisive step in that direction. Namely, in addition to financing the classical functions of the federation on the basis of the existing constitutional and legal responsibilities, and interventions in the economy, the federal budget for next year contains some additional obligations and burdens. These are liabilities of the federation on account of foreign exchange deposits and other exchange rate differentials, i.e. public debt servicing; taking over of partial subsidizing of interest rates on credits which agriculture uses from the selective program; funds for the rehabilitation of commercial banks, as well as funds for financing a part of social adjustment programs. These additional liabilities and burden cumulatively amount to 12.8 billion in convertible dinars.

Commodity and services prices will continue to be freely formed, with the exception of electricity, coal for thermal power plants, the oil industry, railway traffic, PTT services, ferrous and non-ferrous metallurgy, prices of medicaments and utilities for which the upper limit will be fixed in the next six months—till the end of the first half of 1990. After that period prices for these services will be revised upward to take into account the average increase of industrial producer prices.

The Law on Social Capital is among the system related laws which we think should be adopted without delay. In keeping with the latest scientific views and international experience, this bill proposes arrangements for a fuller operation of the capital market and addresses the issue of the selling and buying social capital. No restructuring of our economy and operation of the integral market shall be possible unless we adopt such provisions. The bill proposes that it be clearly stipulated that employees participate in management on the basis of their current labor and on the basis of the share of social capital in the total capital. Workers may decide to put up social capital for sale, and it can be purchased by all domestic and foreign legal and physical persons. Proceeds from the sale of social capital would be allocated to development funds to be set up as public enterprises by Republics, i.e. Provinces and other interested founders.

In evaluating proposed reforms in Yugoslavia we should adopt the same attitude as in evaluating reforms in the Soviet Union and other East European countries: wait and see what is actually going to happen. In the case of Yugoslavia, the following events reveal the ruling elite's attitude toward private-property rights:

1. A Yugoslav can have a private taxi business. However, the car he uses in his business is not treated as a capital good (e.g., for depreciation and other tax purposes).

2. A party leader in a small Yugoslav city recently argued that private ownership must not be given the same legal, financial, and administrative "rights" as state ownership. "Otherwise," he said, "private owners of business firms could get economically so powerful they could threaten our jobs." He was unusually sincere. What you hear from the nomenklatura in Eastern Europe is a façade of words about the "undesirable" consequences of private ownership with respect to inflation, unemployment, income inequalities, and the fate of socialism.

3. Writing in Danas, an influential weekly, Professor Sekulich drew an important distinction between the law on private ownership and its application in Yugoslavia. He said that working collectives are selling shares in their enterprises only to other labor-managed firms. This only works to propagate the so-called social ownership (i.e., state ownership). The proceeds from selling shares go to a special state investment fund (a predictable consequence of state ownership). Those funds are then used for investments in additional

state-owned assets. According to Sekulich, the public sector owns about 90 percent of capital goods in Yugoslavia.[5]

---

[5]D. Sekulich, <u>Danas</u>, April 10, 1990, p. 26.

Index of Names

Page numbers in boldface type indicate that the name appears in a bibliography listing.